# Handbook of good business practice

A corporate code of conduct is an essential asset in today's business practice. Using his study of 125 of Britain's best-managed firms, Walter W. Manley II argues for the establishment of such codes and sets out, clearly and practically, how to go about developing and implementing corporate codes of conduct to deal with the critical, legal, social and ethical issues which arise in everyday business practice.

Dealing with every aspect of business from recruitment policy to marketing and customer relations, and with both internal and external company relations, the *Handbook* is a complete guide to good business practice. Based on important research carried out by Professor Manley at Cambridge University's Management Studies Department, in which Britain's most successful businesses were surveyed, the *Handbook* presents a thorough analysis of the business conduct practices of these businesses, and how their codes of conduct have contributed to their success. It also contains excerpts from policy statements and interviews with top executives, giving precise examples of how codes of conduct are put to good effect.

Educated at Harvard and Duke Universities, **Walter W. Manley II** is Professor of Business Administration at Florida State University, and has been involved in the development of an ethics centre at the Cambridge Federation of Theological Colleges. He has been a visiting scholar on six faculties at Oxford and Cambridge, is a partner in Florida's oldest firm, is a successful businessman in the US, and is the author of three books addressing the critical legal, social and ethical issues which business firms should address in the 1990s.

# Handbook of good business practice

Walter W. Manley II

London and New York

First published 1992
by Routledge
11 New Fetter Lane, London EC4P 4EE

Simultaneously published in the USA and Canada
by Routledge
a division of Routledge, Chapman and Hall, Inc.
29 West 35th Street, New York, NY 10001

Typeset by LaserScript, Mitcham, Surrey
Printed and bound in Great Britain by
Mackays of Chatham, PLC, Chatham, Kent

*British Library Cataloguing in Publication Data*
A catalogue record for this book is available from the British Library.


ISBN 0–415–06232–2

*Library of Congress Cataloging in Publication Data*

A catalogue record for this book is available from the Library of Congress.

ISBN 0-415-06232-2

To students, colleagues, and friends at Florida State University, Duke University, Ridley Hall College and the Cambridge Federation of Theological Colleges, and Cambridge and Oxford Universities.

# Contents

# Foreword

Walter W. Manley II is a successful professor, business executive, and lawyer. Holding degrees in business administration and law from Harvard and Duke, respectively, Professor Manley has authored two other books which address critical legal and ethical issues in business: *Executive's Handbook of Model Business Conduct Codes* (Prentice Hall: Englewood Cliffs, New Jersey 1991) and *Critical Issues in Business Conduct: Legal, Ethical, and Social Challenges for the 1990s* (Greenwood-Quorum: Westport, CT. 1990). His books are based on consultation and research with top executives of 401 leading American and British companies.

President of Exeter Leadership Training Institute in Tallahassee, Florida, and Professor of Business Administration at Florida State University, Mr Manley recently served as a Visiting Professor at Cambridge's Ridley Hall College and the Cambridge Federation of Theological Colleges, and as Visiting Scholar on six Cambridge and Oxford faculties. Professor Manley is one of the most outstanding teachers at Florida State University; nearly one-half of his students, in confidential course evaluations, have noted him as the 'finest teacher' they have encountered in their educational experience.

He is currently writing the authorized history of the Supreme Court of Florida, serves as President of the Florida Endowment Foundation for Vocational Rehabilitation, is a member of the Board of Visitors at Duke University, writes a business ethics column which is circulated amongst Knight Ridden newspapers, and is a partner in MacFarlane Ferguson, Florida's oldest law firm.

# Acknowledgements

For over four years I have conducted research regarding business firms' responses to critical legal, ethical, social, and business conduct issues. The material in this book is based on a two year project with 170 executives of 125 United Kingdom and 20 multi-national firms. In the process, I have read over 2,000 pages of codes of conduct and similar policy documents, and have compiled over 900 pages of interviews and correspondence. I appreciate their assistance and permission to publish in this book the most useful excerpts of such codes and company policy documents.

Ridley Hall College, Cambridge University, and Oxford University provided visiting memberships on six of their faculties and an opportunity to conduct the lengthy consultations and research with participating United Kingdom firms. I particularly wish to thank Ridley Hall Principal, Hugo de Waal and Dr Richard Higginson, and Professor Stephen Watson, Professor Malcolm Warner, and Lecturer Andy Cosh of Cambridge University for their thoughtfulness.

My research assistant Erik Korzilius provided significant insight and organizational talent and deserves my sincere thanks. Darlene Sterling conscientiously typed the manuscript and Stephen Peake, a doctoral student at Cambridge University, provided valuable assistance in England.

Finally, Rosemary Nixon and Francesca Weaver of Routledge were always supportive and cheerful.

Walter W. Manley II
Cambridge University
Cambridge, England

# Chapter 1

# Business codes and company image

If there has been a loss of public confidence in British companies in 1991, misconduct is likely the reason. Recent scandals involving National Westminster Bank, Aish and Company, and a number of other British companies have focused attention on British business conduct. Predictably, public opinion reflects this loss of confidence: only 17 per cent of respondents in a 1988 Market Research Society random opinion sample rated the standards of honesty of British business executives as 'high'. Increasingly, the British public expects higher standards of conduct and ethical behaviour from the business sector.

The challenge to British, and to all advanced nations' business firms is to offer products and services of high quality and variety, to fashion them for consumers, and to compete in a complex global market. These requirements for success go far beyond the traditional concept of a manufacturing concern. Now, managers and employees must think in abstract terms, and effectively and frequently interact with customers, suppliers, and fellow employees.

In addition, in the shift in Britain from a manufacturing to a service economy, sound personal relationships, and hence proper conduct and high standards of ethical behaviour, are critically important as never before. This change coincides with a change from line relationships to a team approach. Moreover, surveys of university students indicate that the reputation of a firm for proper conduct and ethics is an important consideration in choosing an employer.

There is no doubt that organizational changes are needed to unite company behaviour with good intentions. One effective way a company can address these concerns of corporate culture and conduct is by creating and implementing a code of conduct. As Prime Minister Asquith learned in 1909, when the House of Lords rejected the Liberal budget, traditionally a prerogative of the House of Commons, it is often necessary to supplement unwritten customs with written regulations and procedures. In that instance, the supplement was crafted in the form of the Parliament Act of 1911.

This chapter details the substantial benefits which accrue to a firm which has a comprehensive, enforced code. Corporate codes of conduct are business conduct guidelines that, at a minimum, companies utilize to navigate the conduct of the firm and its employees in their business activities. As every experienced manager knows, a company's culture can destroy the best-intentioned, necessary initiatives. A code of conduct, properly created and implemented, can change a company's culture for the better, and provide many other benefits, as well.

In 1976, the multi-national firm, IBM proclaimed: 'We believe that every company should have such a code of conduct . . . that clearly spells out the legal and ethical obligations of corporate leadership.' IBM asserted that having and enforcing a rigorous code of conduct or ethics 'is the best way to assure the survival of business tomorrow' and '[i]ndeed, it may be the only way'.

A decade and a half later, many well-managed British companies and multi-national firms doing business in Britain understand fully, as did IBM in 1976, why codes of conduct or ethics, and value statements, which promote proper conduct and ethical practices, not just the notion of morality, are critical assets for success in the 1990s. Certainly, one of the reasons for this appreciation of codes is the number of studies which indicate that companies with codes, and a strong conviction to pursue proper conduct, are highly profitable concerns which have reputations for seizing new opportunities to increase market shares.

Moreover, as this chapter indicates, there are numerous, substantial benefits beyond greater income for business firms which establish codes of conduct with ethics sections. Consider the case of Peugeot Talbot. The demographics of the company work force in 1987 demonstrated a significant polarity: double-shifting and a two-fold increase in the size of the company created as many employees who were 25 years old and less of those 45 years old and over. 'It was therefore a critical necessity to let the newcomers know and remind the longer-service employees what kind of a company we were – so we needed and, subsequently created, a company charter', advises M. A. B. Judge, the company's Director, Personnel and Industrial Relations.

A precedent for such code creation can be traced to *The Theory of Moral Sentiments*, whose author, Adam Smith, the eighteenth-century guardian saint of classical economic theory, underscored the beneficial impact of ethical values in restraining the reckless pursuit of profits. In *Management*, moreover, Peter Drucker attacks the lack of significance of business morality without concomitant action as follows: 'Morality does not mean preachments,' but, rather, 'morality, to have any meaning at all, must be a principle of action. It must not be exhortation, sermon, or good intentions. It must be practice . . . .' In this regard, the promulgation and observance of a code of conduct with an ethics section can comprise that desired action.

Further, in the thoughtful estimation of a former chairman of a multi-national firm doing business in Britain, 'not being able to discern right conduct from wrong' is tantamount to the 'plea of insanity' in a criminal action. Executives and employees, alike, despite their different hierarchical levels, appreciate the many benefits of codes. At the very minimum, codes provide guidelines and rules for correct, as opposed to improper, conduct.

A firm's code of conduct often is the 'embodiment of the spirit of the firm', and an 'important, success factor', as are Hewlett Packard's standards of conduct codifying the 'HP Way,' a philosophy which has guided that successful firm for 50 years, according to that company's Director of Personnel. One chairman of a health products company believes the firm's code is the 'glue' and 'unifying force of our corporation'. Similarly, the chairman of a banking concern considers that organization's code of behaviour a critical ingredient in its mission to strive for excellence in every regard. In addition, the top executive officer of another company credits that firm's code as 'often referred to, and, at least at the top, company decisions are made after careful consideration of core value implications'. Because a strong sense of right and wrong doesn't merely appear, every generation of management can keep that distinction alive and flourishing by creating and modifying a code of conduct.

Often, as a result of adherence to standards in the firm's code, employees do inform a superior, or another party, often an outsider, of the unwanted or illegal behaviour. Until recently, exposing substantial improprieties, commonly called whistle blowing, resulted in many firms', British and multi-national alike, imposing severe penalties, including dismissal, on the whistle blower. Historically, such punishment provided an employee with strong disincentives to act correctly by disclosing misconduct. Unfortunately, too often, firms or managers determined it was preferable to punish the messenger instead of addressing the illegal, unethical, or unwanted conduct.

Nonetheless, without a check on unacceptable behaviour, a firm's efficiency, reputation, and employee morale suffer. Absent effective channels available for an employee's speaking out on matters of conscience, the sanctions for disclosure may preempt the firm's addressing the matter of conscience prior to the ensuing public embarrassment. The subject of whistle blowing is often that of corruption, a defective product, or pollution – early warning signals which any firm's top management desperately needs.

Many British companies are making whistle blowing to entities outside the firm unnecessary by adopting corporate codes of conduct to provide guidance to their employees' experiencing such dilemmas. More than that, however, firms are implementing codes to capture a host of other benefits. From simple employee guidance to improved client relationships, firms are implementing codes of conduct as a necessity to ensure successful operations in an increasingly competitive environment.

Furthermore, the arguments of a popular management commentator, Peter Drucker, as noted, support the need for proper conduct 'with action'. Drucker faults the notion of business ethics, without application in practice, as creating self-righteous moralists of those practitioners who focus almost exclusively on the conduct to be condemned. There is no doubt that many firms agree with Drucker's contention and, hence, have created comprehensive codes of conduct. Through these codes, firms realize that, in Drucker's terms, honesty and integrity are absolute requirements of a successful manager.

There are numerous ways in which codes, when effectively implemented, are critical factors in the success of firms utilizing them. While the reasoning most often proffered for code development is that codes guide employee behaviour, the codifying of ethical and business conduct guidelines provides firms with numerous benefits, and communicates, by the mere act of codification, that ethics, proper conduct, and the code policies are important, and comprise the aggregate precepts of the firm.

There is a wide consensus, too, that a company can respond to internal, as well as external, constraint mechanisms to increase its integration of ethical and proper conduct principles with the firm's operation. For example, Johnson & Johnson demonstrated in the Tylenol poisoning circumstance that self-regulation can be strikingly effective. Another matter is certain: since each company's situation, problems, and culture are unique, every firm should design a code tailored to its individuality.

## DRAFTING A CODE

Drafting a code of conduct is not a gimmick. Rather, it is a time-consuming process, especially if attempted without reference to procedures and lessons learned by other successful companies.

This book provides those invaluable experience methods, guidelines, and references, including a substantial number of excerpts from codes or policy documents of successful firms, which afford a more facile, concise, and simplified way to create and implement an effective, comprehensive code of business conduct.

One hundred and twenty-five well-managed British companies and twenty multi-national firms conducting business in Britain, each with its own code of conduct or ethics, or similar policy document (such as a values statement), have participated and consulted in the author's two-year study of the creation, implementation, and substantial benefits of such policy documents. More than 170 business leaders were consulted and over 2,000 pages of codes and similar policy documents were reviewed for the examples used in this book. Over 900 pages of interviews, transcripts, and correspondence were generated – and this book is based on the factual evidence, experience, and beliefs of the participating firms' top managers. Focus was directed on realistic and practical initiatives by a wide range of companies. These corporations report that they realized numerous benefits by designing, developing, implementing and maintaining corporate codes of conduct. While ethics sections, values and missions statements, and guidelines for business conduct comprise a complete code of conduct, any one of these policy documents provides benefits, although not to the degree of a comprehensive code of conduct.

## EIGHTEEN PRIMARY BENEFITS OF A CODE OF CONDUCT

This two-year interaction with top executives of 145 British and multi-national companies has identified eighteen major benefits a code of conduct provides a business firm.

1 *Providing guidance to and inculcating the company's values and cultural substance and style in managers and employees.* A code provides 'guidance to managers and employees in disseminating to or acquainting employees with Touche Ross' traditional values and culture', asserts Managing Director, M. J. Blackburn. Further, notes ICL Director of Human Resource Development, Steve Williams, the 'principal benefit was to define our cultural beliefs and encourage managers to work to achieve them'.

Because managing directors' duties have expanded in a fissionable manner in the last three decades, they are no longer as effective, due to time constraints, in establishing, by word and deed, the firm's ethical tenor and values supporting proper conduct. Moreover, the activities of firms are often complex; it is impossible effectively to control or manage the dispersed and larger business firms of the 1990s without written guidelines. Further, many firms inevitably expand geographically and/or grow in size far beyond the dimensions where founders, executives, or managers can effectively verbally transmit their firm's values and ethical procedures.

A firm's code is the 'embodiment of the spirit of the firm and an important success factor', relates a Hewlett Packard executive. Geoffrey Dale, Cadbury Schweppes Group Human Resources Director, confirms this organizational necessity: 'In a company which has a long history (over 200 years) but which has grown rapidly in the last five years with a number of strategic acquisitions and is now a truly international business, there is a need to define the identity and values of the group in terms relevant to the future rather than as a mere reflection of our past.' A code 'provides an important statement of company values which becomes more important as we grow rapidly and become a multi-cultural organization', Dale continues.

It is critically important that firms' values are inculcated in employees, especially managers. Integrity is one of the key characteristics which employees expect of their organization's leaders. One way executives demonstrate this quality is to define and institutionalize the high standards of the organization. Codes of conduct envelop and restate those values of integrity and honesty.

Moreover, the chairman of another company notes the facility with which employees can comprehend and form allegiance to the values expressed in a code: 'While a lot of people do not understand numbers, everyone can understand and commit themselves to values.'

Another aspect of inculcating values relates to a succession in senior management. K. T. Derr, Chairman of Chevron, attests to one primary benefit of a code: '[A] change of executive officers can create an environment of uncertainty for employees . . . stockholders and customers . . . [however, we experienced] a smooth transaction, which can be attributed, in part, to the strong presence of our code of business conduct.'

Generally, employees wish their company to communicate explicit ground rules so they know what is expected of them. The company's sharing of values and principles with employees also demonstrates respect for those employees. 'Periodic distribution and acknowledgement of our business conduct policy serves to remind our employees of our commitment to values which support high standards of ethical and proper business conduct', under-scores the chief executive of another company. Last, a code serves as a means of reinforcing the behaviour of those who are sympathetic to the company values expressed in the code.

2  *Sharpening and defining the company's policies and unifying the workforce.* In 1991, many commentators assert ethical or values training is not sufficiently administrated in British churches and schools. This fact almost certainly is a result of the collapse of hierarchies of family, church, and school in Britain over the last three decades. Consequently, many employees are in dire need of ethical guidelines, and the code's enforcement mechanism provides a social cohesiveness which reinforces ethical behaviour. Peter Bijur, Chairman of Texaco Ltd, emphatically notes that a code 'defines the company's policy in areas of ethical and business conduct concerns'.

Codes of conduct, by establishing a common language, attitude, and consensus regarding ethics, proper conduct, and honesty, operate to support and guide the employees so they may follow the course of action desired by the firm's top executives. In addition, a code, as Digital Equipment Vice President, Corporate Relations, Albert Mullin recognizes, serves 'as the basis for certain decisions and actions of the [c]ompany'.

Further, a code which is at the leading edge of managers' thinking alerts them to potential difficulties, and empowers them to create a culture where values and ethical and proper business conduct are important considerations.

The substantial majority of ethical and business conduct issues are com-monplace, not extraordinary. Consequently, codes can clearly delineate the company's policy and response to the most common problems. Normally, these problem areas are apparent and there is widespread consensus regarding the company's response, thereby allowing the code to be helpful. In this process, codes reduce overtly unethical or improper practices, while providing a sense of direction to the executives and staff.

Further, the act of promulgating a new code or modifying an existing code enables a firm to formalize its defined goals and policies, or re-define them. One such goal, for example, relates to guidance in the formation of com-mercial relationships. Codes of conduct are designed to provide a model such that those affected by them have ethical and proper conduct guidelines by which to gauge their actions. For instance, codes define corporate positions on difficult issues such as employee substance abuse and conflict of interest. 'The code's value as a symbol is even more important . . . to remind our employees that we care about right and wrong', relates the chairman of one company.

Conduct based solely on maximization of profit, without regard to ethical dimensions, can prompt ruinous results for the enterprise. Unfortunately, employees make difficult ethical and business conduct decisions frequently without the benefit of proper guidance. Although the motives of such employees may be well-intentioned, adverse consequences for the employee and his firm, nonetheless, often ensue from injudicious decisions. 'The firm's environment improves when it adopts a code which clearly communicates where the company stands on ethical and business conduct issues and what is expected from the employees', advises one top executive.

3 *Codes provide overall strategic direction.* British companies employ thousands of employees to plan and carry out business strategies. A code helps them choose the proper course as they consider the day-to-day and longer-term decisions. A policy document of this sort 'provides overall strategic direction', advises Tony Withey, Remploy Chief Executive. Firms must fill this potential void with guidelines, or suffer the vagaries of each employee's reliance on his or another's arbitrary standards.

Occasionally, a group of executives promulgates an improper act even though no one individual would, alone, have chosen that course. 'It's no coincidence that our company's Statement of Values is consistent with our corporate vision and strategic plan – all three focus on our customer and the superior service we must provide if we are to differentiate ourselves from our competitors', reflects the chairman of a bank holding company.

Another senior manager describes how that company utilized a code to change the firm's culture as a strategic planning objective: 'Our company was suffering from stagnation, reduced profitability, and lack of competivity . . . we found that a common denominator of successful companies was a more enlightened management style built around employee involvement and participation . . . in mid-1985 we embarked upon a group-wide program to shift our culture from an autocratic, top–down style to one which was more participative in nature.' To assist this change of strategic direction, the company created a code of values which has nurtured a recognition of the critical importance of long-term orientation.

Firms use codes to resolve strategic dilemmas employees face when the proper interests of the company may conflict with the ethical beliefs of the individual. Other firms use codes to mollify the risks of substantial conflicts of interest which are strategic, as well as operational, concerns. Furthermore, in situations where significant conflicts of interest arise, the company can apply the code as a starting point for business conduct resolution.

4 *Contributing instruction in interactions with pressure groups from outside the company.* A thorough and proper business conduct policy-base, embodied in a code of conduct, assists managers in dealing with and lessening any baleful effects of scrutiny by outside interest groups, television media, and the press. For a company which demands and rewards appropriate business conduct, such scrutiny is more annoying than embarrassing. B.B.A. Group's statement of philosophy 'provides managers with direction in dealing with outside interest groups', counsels Dr John White, Company

Managing Director. In today's climate of public scrutiny, British companies can expect intense public examination of their activities. By institutionalizing and monitoring its business conduct through a code, a firm better prepares itself for the inevitable close attention of outside groups.

Clearly, firms enact codes of conduct to contend with and effectively reduce the pressures exerted by outside groups. By naturally offering established, proper behaviour as a rejoinder to the searching scrutiny of outside pressure groups, firms can divert company managers' and employees' attention and energy to their natural focus: internal business relationships and interaction with direct purchasers of the company's products and services.

5 *Signalling expectations of proper conduct to suppliers and customers.* By encouraging a high standard of conduct in its employees through its code, a firm signals suppliers and other entities with which it interacts, that it categorically rejects illegal or improper business activity. A code 'assists managers in communicating the company's expectations to suppliers, agents, and customers', advises London Buses Managing Director, C. Hodson. Similarly, another company created a code 'because we have many people who deal with external vendors and we believe it was important to set the relationship straight from the first day of our relationship so that vendors would not embarrass themselves by doing things that were against our policies and employees would know how to act in all circumstances', a senior executive of a computer software firm acknowledges.

When a third party suggests any act of questionable propriety, a manager or employee can refer to the code to deflect any pursuit of that requested activity.

6 *Delineating rights and duties of the company, managers, and employees.* The process of creating and implementing a code especially hones management's realization of its responsibilities, and, therefore, imbues that leadership group with a proactive attitude to meet those obligations. One substantial benefit of the Bank of England code, asserts D. A. Sharp, Head of Personnel, is 'its clear outline of the responsibilities and privileges of the organisation and those who work there'. Moreover, by accurately defining and disseminating a written policy explaining those rights and responsibilities, a company creates a climate where all persons are respected and knowledgeable members of the team.

7 *Effectively responding to government pressures and rules.* Self-regulation is an effective counter-measure to demands for greater external regulation, notes James Alexander, Burmah Director of Corporate Affairs & Management Resources. Firms have developed and implemented codes of conduct to combat the long litany of British government regulation. Codes assist companies in assuring their policies and practices accommodate regulatory requirements. Moreover, firms have also contended with cycles of regulators' stricter interpretation of laws, and the increasing severity of penalties for transgression.

British government-run enterprises have had a sorry history of failure. Self-regulation preempts increased government interference, thereby removing barriers to the generation of wealth and the efficient provision of products and services.

8 *Enhancing the company's public image and confidence.* Public confidence in business firms, and response to community needs are a foundation of any private enterprise system. A code communicates to consumers and the public that a company stands for ethical principles. Maintaining high standards through a policy document 'improves the company's business reputation', advises Rolls Royce Director of Personnel, D'A. Payne. While a good reputation takes time to be developed, it may take even longer to rehabilitate a damaged one. Most consumers don't wish to interact with a firm which doesn't adhere to a high level of ethical conduct. Without public confidence, a firm has a miserable, and probably short, future.

9 *Preempting legal proceedings.* A code helps a firm avoid lawsuits because it deters questionable activities from which legal suits emanate.

10 *Improving bottom-line results.* Studies in America indicate firms with high ethical standards have outperformed broad market indicators. For example, the Ethics Resource Center examined twenty-one American companies which maintain codes of conduct that delineate principles and standards. The results are instructive: if a person had invested $30,000 in the Dow Jones Industrial Average, it would be worth $134,000 three decades later; however, the return from investing a like sum in those twenty-one companies would be almost nine times greater. Other studies demonstrate a high correlation between firms which establish codes and a proper business conduct culture, and considerable long-term financial success.

A British company's ethical conduct reflects how it manages its business affairs, which, in turn, directly effects its financial performance. M. A. B. Judge, Peugeot Talbot Director of Personnel and Industrial Relations, believes a code 'improves a company's financial performance by enhancing efficiency through internal controls and productivity by clearly communicating standards of conduct'.

In addition, for many companies, a code's financial benefits are multifaceted. For instance, sales opportunities, as well as employee productivity, may increase. In any event, firms reap rewards from ethical behaviour by establishing a work environment in which the employee does not consider, for a moment, that he will benefit from unethical or questionable conduct. In addition, the code usually elicits a better performance from those it directly addresses; in this regard, performance is 'morality in action'.

Last, as the code normally aids the firm's financial performance, it thereby further insulates the firm against having to engage in questionable conduct to survive. The firm will be in a position where no single order or sale will determine its survival.

In today's fast-paced, high technology economy, competition, both foreign and domestic, has accelerated. Competitive forces have jeopardized the very existence of many British firms. Some firms have parlayed their codes into sources of competitive advantage. Increasing competition in the global marketplace has complicated business activities and forced firms to improve efficiency. One electronics retailer relies on its internal control system to improve its competitive position. A top executive describes the reason: 'We feel that our written code of ethics is the basis for our entire control system; strong controls lead to efficiency and effectiveness and result in the achievement of corporate goals and better bottom-line results.'

Further, codes of conduct provide guidelines to individuals in the conduct of their business affairs, thereby reducing uncertainty and anxiety. With such guidelines firmly in place, employees are reluctant to undertake unethical or questionable activities for fear of sanction. Codes and their underlying values clearly improve efficiency by reducing the need for more extensive managerial overview of employee conduct.

11  *Enhancing employees' self-images and recruiting.* Employees naturally take pride in a company that communicates highly ethical values and beliefs, especially when an effort is made to mould the corporate culture to reflect high-minded values. Ian Bell, Managing Director of Town & Country, confirms this code benefit: 'Enhancement of morale, pride, and loyalty and recruitment.' In fact, employees have a more profound sense of empowerment and confidence in knowing actions they take consistent with code values are protected, and that deviating behaviour is penalized. Further, with a code as a ubiquitous standard, employees are more confident of their ability to make proper decisions.

One benefit of improved morale is the reinforced and amplified collective-belief in the legitimacy of the firm's purpose. The by-product of that commonly held purpose is a heightened sense of loyalty. Employees naturally desire their work to be meaningful and their conduct appropriate. By working for an organization with a code which reinforces a person's sense that he is a member of an upstanding firm, that employee naturally experiences a heightened self-esteem.

Pride in employment, and an increased sense of loyalty improve productivity because the employee is pleased to be an efficient part of a successful team organization. Further, through the implementation of its code of conduct, a firm is able to improve the moral character of the organization. The resulting public image of the firm attracts like-minded individuals whose employment the principled firm has a better opportunity to maintain.

Since unethical employees rarely wish to be part of an environment in which misconduct is penalized, the presence of a code actually screens unethical employees. Employees not judged to have strong ethical and moral character probably won't rise by promotion in firms with well-developed codes of conduct and enforcement mechanisms.

12 *Promoting excellence.* 'A code of ethics or conduct promotes the inheritance of company culture and helps satisfy management's responsibility to nurture a climate of integrity and excellence', asserts Ranald Noel-Paton, Group Managing Director of John Menzies.

An ethical environment is created and maintained by individuals in the organization; a business firm's conscience exists only as a result of action by individuals to establish standards of behaviour. Management has a duty to provide an atmosphere of integrity; enhanced performance and achievement are the natural offspring. In any firm, no matter how well managed, an improved environment is an invaluable asset, yielding tangible and intangible rewards.

The code can also preserve a cultural inheritance passed from older to newer employees, or pave the way for substantial changes in the firm's culture. For instance, the Xerox code owes its philosophical underpinning to Joe Wilson, the founder of modern-day Xerox, for 'he set the tone . . . he defined our values', stresses John McGinty, Vice President of Management Control, Evaluation, and Corporate Audit. Similarly, Digital Equipment Vice President, Corporate Relations Albert Mullin believes the firm's code 'provides clarity, consistency, and continuity of the company culture'. Also, high standards of conduct and honesty are essential characteristics of effective leaders, whether managing directors or line managers. Few modern organizations place people in leadership positions who are known to be unethical or underhanded.

Further, without codes in force, firms may have a more difficult time consistently communicating with and directing employees. Achieving the company's goals and objectives without a guiding force is nearly impossible; codes provide those necessary, conspicuous guidelines. Codes provide a vehicle around which management, leadership, and goals coalesce. Moreover, when it implements and enforces a comprehensive code, the firm strengthens the position of the key code administrators, such as internal and external auditors and legal counsel, who cannot function effectively without the respect of managers and employees.

13 *Realizing company objectives.* A company, through its code, can clearly establish the firm's objectives. 'Our group statement has enabled AMEC to clearly enunciate company goals and thereby assist in their realization', notes Georgina Lloyd Drummond, Head of Strategy. By incorporating proper business conduct principles in a company's strategies, a company can facilitate growth with integrity. Ethical guidelines methodically remind the decision-maker of his basic goals, those of his colleagues and, most importantly, the objectives of the company. Explicitly expressed aims expedite normal business activities.

Success can be fully appreciated when it is measured against prior performance. Codes of conduct provide good benchmarks for performance-measurement.

14 *Responding to stockholders' concerns.* M & G's business philosophy 'helps satisfy the needs of stockholders who place high priority on proper conduct', relates Finance Director, A. P. Shearer. Highly principled stockholders of British firms are becoming a more powerful, vocal force. A code, with specific guidelines, provides assurance to investors that the firm is doing everything it can do to assure proper conduct.

15 *Strengthening the British free-enterprise system.* Compliance with the Ciba-Geigy code, in the estimation of Company Secretary, I. E. F. Stewart, 'demonstrates adherence to social norms which provide the foundation for Britain's enterprise system'.

Britain continues to endorse the market system as the best means of communicating consumer needs and delivering desired goods and services. This communication and delivery process normally serves the welfare of society. Society, through its elected representatives, grants liberties of existence and operation to those institutions which generally conform to society's norms, which are often expressed as legal statutes. As codes formalize accepted values, they promote harmony between those societal norms and those business activities which comply with the code values.

16 *Nurturing a business environment of open communication.* A code 'enhances frequent, honest, open communication', relates Wagon Finance Chairman and Chief Executive, D. B. Jones. A British company's success in the 1990s is based on fast information transmittal among all levels; the vital element of this information-sharing is effective communication. This critical element of free, open communication is especially important in the knowledge-based climate of the 1990s, and, also, for organizations which operate in several settings, whether domestic or foreign. Open, honest, direct communication, encouraged by codes, bridges areas where information gaps or breakdowns might otherwise exist.

17 *Integrating the cultures of acquired or merged companies.* A code can 'facilitate the integration of acquired or merged firms and of dispersed arms of a firm', advises C. S. Cockraft, Company Secretary for Halifax. Firms merging or joining through acquisition in the hope of improving operational efficiency frequently encounter difficulty in integrating their cultures, or in transferring the culture or values of the acquiring firm to the acquired firm. Successful integration or transfer requires the goals and planning of the firms become unified.

Once employees are informed about the surviving or parent firm's ethical and business conduct guidelines, the new employees are, at once, integrated into that company. In addition, this operational and cultural fusion is uniquely important because growth in an organization's size diminishes the sense of individual responsibility. Codes can effectively set and enforce standards as no single individual can.

18 *Deterring improper requests of employees by supervisors, and vice versa.* 'A code effectively impedes managers' and employees' requiring improper

actions from each other', notes P. J. K. Ferguson, British Steel Director of Personnel. A code clearly communicates that no one at any level in the organization has authority to require or request an improper act.

The next several chapters detail how a business firm can prepare a code of conduct.

# Chapter 2

# Creating the code

Bill Hewlett, co-founder of Hewlett Packard, describes the 'HP Way' as follows: 'I feel the HP Way is the policies and actions that flow from the belief that men and women want to do a good job, a creative job, and that if they are provided the proper environment they will do so.' Moreover, an article appearing in *Peat, Marwick, Mitchell and Company World* concludes that business firms are entirely capable of effective self-regulation but that transforming negative public opinion toward business morality to a positive one depends on whether the business sector can 'provide assurance of [the] dedication to protecting the public interest'.

In fact, codes of conduct or similar policy documents can create a proper environment and culture and restore public trust through enhanced accountability.

A firm's code of conduct , if properly formulated and implemented, can assist every employee in resolving a moral dilemma or in answering a business conduct question, and ensure that no career disadvantage will ensue from raising such questions or declining to engage in questionable conduct.

Without generally agreed-upon values and guidelines, a company's manager's or employee's choice of action, when confronting a business conduct or ethical issue, is based almost solely on the values of that individual. A code of conduct is an excellent means of providing guidelines and procedures to deter improper acts.

While the Code of Hammurabi was among the first of history's codes of conduct, the parent of the modern business codes of conduct or ethics is the code developed by the barristers of Medieval England.[1] The modern corporate code of conduct provides ethical and moral guidelines which a firm can utilize to guide the conduct of the firm and its employees in their strategic and daily business activities.

In addition, many codes are much more than standards; they act to weave the firm's activities to the social fabric of the community in which the firm operates. As a member of society, the firm can integrate itself with the community and profit by the process, because customers trust business and build confidence in firms through direct or indirect interactions. A code also shapes the conduct of the firm and of all employees so the firm can realize many of the advantages discussed in the prior chapter. Moreover, the guidelines categorized in a code of conduct define not only the firm's responsibilities toward employees, but also the duties owed the firm by its workforce.

For many business leaders and entrepreneurs, codes of conduct define the very essence of the business firm, and give birth to desirable cultures. Consequently, the way in which a firm creates its code reflects a process of a firm's self-probing and examining of its internal and external environments to discover its mission. In fact, 'one of the major benefits of establishing a code of conduct is the process of discovery and harmonisation of interests that occurs in the participation of different managers in the formation of the code'.[2] In the process, a firm's executives can rediscover the firm's key success factors, and integrate needed changes in the organization's environment – which are critical necessities for competing in the 1990s.

Reflecting these sentiments, Crawford Beveridge, Vice President of Corporate Resources for Sun Microsystems, reveals that Sun conducted a corporate culture survey of all the firm's managers and supervisors 'to describe what they believed were the important values in Sun's environment'. In addition, the firm conducted employee focus groups and sponsored retreats for managers to generate the body of the code of conduct. In this manner, the firm identified and reinforced in its organization those critical success factors which improve its capacity to compete in a rapidly changing environment.

The next chapter discusses the initiation and oversight of a code's creation.

# Chapter 3

# Initiating and overseeing the code's creation

Top level managers' commitment to the firm's code or values statement is a critical element for its successful implementation. Moreover, one top senior executive of a banking firm notes that the commitment of a company's employees using a 'top–down bottom–up approach' is helpful in creating a code of conduct that will be accepted by all employees. In that company's case, all employees participated, in one manner or another, in the initiation and implementation of the code. In most cases, however, a specific person or group, acting at the direction of the board of directors or top executives, serves as the catalyst for code development.

## MANAGING DIRECTORS, CHAIRMEN, AND CHIEF EXECUTIVES

The managing director, chairman, or chief executive of a company frequently initiates and oversees the creation of a firm's code of conduct, and his key role signals the entire company that code creation and implementation are serious matters. It is apparent that top executives are devoting more of their time to public issues affecting their companies. Consequently, their interest in developing codes or values statements is not surprising.

When the catalytic agent is the managing director, chairman, or chief executive, or another top-level executive, the code developer can meaningfully evaluate the company's operating principles to create effective and realistic guides for future business actions. For example, one chief executive developed the items he believed should be incorporated in his company's statement of values and beliefs by writing down on an index card those key words and phrases each day. By combining those abstract concepts (such as 'work ethic', 'competitive zeal', 'company loyalty', 'sense of belonging', and 'risk taking') with suggestions from other executive and top managers, that chief executive's corporate staff were able to draft the values and beliefs statement.

Moreover, one chairman recalls his creation of the firm's corporate code of conduct: 'The values of quality and of serving customers and people were established by me as chief executive, and I believe these values must be established at the very highest level of the company.' Codes must, by nature, reflect values and a long-term commitment, and the chief executive must strongly believe in them.

In some instances, a firm's chairman, who often has more time than the managing director or chief executive for philosophical and long-range reflection, has initiated the code formulation process.

Another chairman believes certain principles of business strategy and ethical conduct are 'important to the success of the Company', and these beliefs were the catalyst for the code's creation. In another case, the managing director and board of directors contemporaneously served as catalysts for creating the company's code.

Often, managing directors and chairmen have acted as vanguards for change because initiating or enlarging a code strengthens their control of the business conduct of the firm and its employees. A third chairman reflects on this often solitary process of stamping a personal imprimatur on the company as follows: 'I deem it important to develop the statement of values in order to identify clearly the limits of behaviour for any person within the company and to provide a set of overriding guidelines by which all problems could be considered, evaluated and decided.'

## BOARD OF DIRECTORS

The board of directors also provides leadership in identifying the need for a code and guiding its development. The board may designate a committee, composed of some of its members, or assign a company's audit committee responsibility to create a code.

At times, a board of directors assigns the audit committee responsibility for testing the appropriateness of various business conduct policies. Although one company commissioned its executive committee to formulate business conduct policies, that process of creation and implementation was 'monitored by the Board of Directors of the Company acting primarily through an audit committee which shares the values of the company and provides a very useful sounding board', according to one general counsel. At Boots, a sub-committee of the board of directors drafted the social responsibilities statement.

Furthermore, top management often dispenses responsibility for the promulgation of its company code among various entities within and without the firm, such as legal or personnel departments, task forces, employee groups, and outside consultants.

## CORPORATE LEGAL DEPARTMENT AND COMPANY SECRETARY

A number of firms indicate that the desire for development of codes of conduct stemmed from fears of legal liability. Given the fissionable expansion of legal liability over the last two decades, such fears are understandable. Often, the legal department incorporates regulatory requirements in the code to increase its relevance and effectiveness. At times, the company secretary takes part in actually drafting the document with the assistance of a chief legal officer. At Halifax, for instance, the group secretary drafted the guidelines on personal and corporate conduct in consultation with senior managers and directors.

## PERSONNEL AND HUMAN RESOURCES DEPARTMENTS

As managers of personnel, human resources directors have frequently assumed primary responsibility for developing sections of codes, especially those concerning employee rights and conduct. These executives are especially sensitive to the essential need for codes of conduct and similar policy documents, in part, to improve employee morale. The Bank of England Board of Directors provided the initiative for drafting its ethical business guidelines statement, and, together with the human resources department, promulgated that document.

## COMMUNICATIONS DEPARTMENTS AND CORPORATE TASK FORCES

The communications department is often well positioned to initiate the process of code creation. After receiving helpful information and language from the various functional departments, the communications department can create a code in much the same way as it does any general policy of the firm, and can shape that code so it is easily understood, with emphasis on feedback and interpretative mechanisms.

Moreover, a company task force, often composed of persons of various functions and rank (including board members, top executives, managers, and employees) can create a comprehensive code which addresses issues of importance to all segments of the company.

Furthermore, such a task group, since it represents numerous segments of the company, imbues a code with company-wide respect because of the group's consensus approach. It is important that the code or values statement be understood, accepted, and supported by the highest and lowest authorities in any company. By combining the initiatives and talents of the managing director, his deputy, the chairman or a member of the board of directors, the company secretary, heads of personnel and communications, and the legal department, a task force can have the backing of various pockets of authority and can create an effective, credible code. The Dixons' approach is not uncommon. According to R. E. Andrews, Group Personnel Director, 'The Human Resources Department created its code of staff rules and the document was edited by the Chairman, Managing Director, and Legal Department.'

Of course, the combinations of key groups and persons as code creators vary according to the company. Bradford & Bingley's managing director, corporate legal department, and communications department played key roles in creating that company's code. John Bibby's task force consisted of the legal department and the communications department. Meyer's managing director, chairman, human resources department, corporate development department, and communications department provided essential inputs for the creation of the firm's business aims statement.

Motorola assembled a task force composed of the chairman of the board, general counsel, and the chief financial officer. The group had as its primary task 'to edit and submit to the board of directors a completed version of the code of conduct'.

## EMPLOYEES

In a number of companies, employees played a key role in code creation by providing initial input, or by critiquing the first draft of the code. Such participation by employees in the drafting process enhances the likelihood of the firm's employees accepting and adhering to the code's provisions.

As more diverse individuals participate in the promulgation, the resulting code is more of a living document, truly representative of the entire firm. With employees' heightened sense of values through such contribution, overall employee morale often improves. The commitment of employees confirms the legitimacy of a code; firms with employees as participants report less resistance to the code's implementation. Norwich Winterhur and NPI solicited substantial employee involvement in the drafting processes of their policy documents.

## CONSULTANTS

Although many companies are reluctant to allow a consultant to assist in the creation of codes because of the latter's 'outsider' status, some companies have assigned valuable roles to independent consultants, and benefited in the process. When one engineering company assembled its code sections, it employed input from organizational development consultants. These consultants encouraged discussions among all employees to define freely the firm's culture and value system. At the conclusion of such discussions, the consultants summarized and distilled the comments. The employees' comments eventually shaped the firm's statement of guiding principles.

As had Leeds, Legal & General employed a consultant in creating its code. M. J. Essex, Education Relations Manager for Legal & General, explains how that company's code was created: 'Initially, the project started as a joint exercise between a consultant from the United States and myself, and then became a management development exercise for a team of three senior managers from different parts of the business with the consultant and me. In the course of this project we decided that working with "ethics" was essentially a long-term, business culture activity, and that we should view public statements as part of that process. Consequently, we decided that the first publication should concentrate on internal behaviour, and that it should be regularly reviewed.' This task force deemed the development of a code of internal behaviour as the first step towards expansion into more public and corporate areas.

Numerous groups, then, have had direct involvement in the formation of firms' codes of conduct. Although not all firms share the same experiences, clearly, top management initiates the code creation process most frequently, followed in descending order by legal counsel, boards of directors, founders or their lineal descendants, and consultants.

## TOP–DOWN, BOTTOM–UP, AND COMBINATION APPROACHES

The top–down approach, the bottom–up approach, and a combination of these two procedures comprise the primary means of integrating business conduct values and ethical concerns into a company's culture.

The top–down approach often involves the board of directors or managing director establishing values and goals, senior management overseeing an education and training programme for employees, and a director or top executive being assigned responsibility for assuring employees' compliance with the code or policy document.

The bottom–up approach normally includes middle managers' input and feedback from employees, and those managers channelling that information to senior executives. This method incorporates employee participation in creating the code, and employee discussion of values, business conduct, and ethical issues.

While these two distinct approaches to creating a code or values statement and inculcating those standards in the corporate environment have often been successful, a combination of both processes serves as the most powerful means to establish and maintain a viable, credible code of conduct. Generally, the greater the number of people involved, the more the company demonstrates respect for its employees and the more profound the common commitment.

The following chapter addresses the sources of values for incorporation in the code of conduct.

# Chapter 4

# Sources of values for the code

A company which develops a code or similar policy documents must also generate the values, guidelines, and principles which provide substance to those documents. Companies have utilized numerous sources, for example: prior codes or values statements, policy memoranda and procedures, and current legal guidelines. Some companies have examined codes developed by other firms for use in the development of their own codes. Other sources of values include those of the firm's founder, its chairman and board of directors, managing director, other executive managers, and employees.

## EXISTING CODES

Because they wish to rely on codes of conduct to guide the ethical conduct of their employees, firms often use an existing, familiar code of conduct, or ethics or values statement, as a source of values for a new, all-encompassing document. Existing codes such as those of the ICC and British Institute of Management provide fertile sources of values and guidelines. One top executive reveals the development of his company's code values: 'In the course of many discussions leading to the publishing of the code, the chairman and his colleagues studied many companies' approaches to the subject to corporate responsibility, including Johnson & Johnson's Credo.'

While companies utilize other respected firms' codes of conduct as sources of values to consider for their own codes, to expedite the process and refrain from 'reinventing the wheel', they also have analysed the various policies already in existence within these firms, and, in this way, have created a one-volume, firm-wide policy. 'The Town & Country Corporate Objectives had as a primary source of its values a prior, existing company document', notes Ian Bell, the firm's Managing Director. A company can amalgamate internal policies from various subsidiaries and divisions within the firm, in addition to other materials, for use in drafting a comprehensive, company-wide code. Sources of this nature included 'a number of statements proposed for different purposes' at M & G; the 'old code' at Burmah; the 'company strategy and experiences' at J. Bibby; 'a prior existing company document augmented by the company's understood values' at NPI; and 'a prior existing firm document' at Touche Ross. Firms using familiar and established written policies and statements of values as baselines are better able to create an ethical or proper conduct bridge between older and present practices. Such bridge-building firms maintain a sense of continuity regarding operational practices.

## BELIEFS OF TOP EXECUTIVES AND DIRECTORS, TRADITIONS, AND UNWRITTEN RULES

The 'collective experience of directors' at Yorkshire Building Society; the 'beliefs of the senior management group who drafted the ICL obligations of a manager statement'; 'Brainstorming' at Meyer; 'think tank and board discussions' at Remploy; 'discussion among company executives' at The Leeds, and 'consultation with people reflecting a wide range of age and seniority at Shell' are various methods used to integrate the beliefs of senior managers in a code or policy statement. These executives take the ethical and philosophical aspects of their firms seriously, and their experience and beliefs are important sources of values and guidelines.

A company can also draw upon its traditions and unwritten rules as sources for values. The firm's culture and those values characterizing it serve in many instances as the basis for the development of a code of conduct. One chairman reveals that 'basic values were always within the company but had never been articulated in quite the fashion which we have done over the past six years through development of our code'. Examining these values inherent in the firm's culture exposes the primary goals of the firm, and its critical operating principles to managers, as well as employees.

The development of a code of conduct often validates the firm's culture. Close examination of those values also reinforces appreciation of the firm's success factors. Development of a code often is the catalyst for a long-overdue self-diagnosis. At Peugeot Talbot, according to M. A. B. Judge, Director of Personnel and Industrial Relations, 'The Company Charter and Procedures was a natural and logical outcome of the way in which senior directors had encouraged the development of a management style over 7 or 8 years'. Moreover, the Prudential Code of Conduct and Mission Statement 'encapsulated a system of values and a culture that had developed over 140 years'. Tesco's Company Secretary, R. S. Ager, refers to 'perceived corporate values' already in existence as a primary source of the values incorporated in that firm's code. John Menzies made use of its traditions and various papers and discussions to flesh out those values which form the core of its corporate principles statement.

The process of developing a consensus as to values can lead to delays. True consensus takes time, but is essential to develop agreement within senior managers. Without a consensus developed in at least a quasi-democratic manner, the resulting code lacks credibility and is less likely to be effectively implemented.

Last, a number of companies, such as Ciba-Geigy, Kingfisher, Richard

Costain, and Smiths Industries, used existing laws and guidelines as sources of values and guidelines. There are many laws which govern corporate behaviour of individuals as corporate managers and employees which form the basis for code policies. It is important that every company abides by the spirit, not merely the letter, of the law in developing its code values. For the firm to respect the spirit of the law, the employees must first have a firm grasp of the statutory directions; a code provides this understanding.

Using applications of existing legal rules and standards as important sources of the firm's code values increases the likelihood of the firm and its employees earning the respect and trust of customers, and especially of regulators.

With the increasing number of statutes, regulations, and government studies specifically addressing the conduct of firms, it is not surprising that companies have resorted to creating codes of conduct using the letter and spirit of the law as guideposts.

## OTHER CODES OF CONDUCT AS PROTOTYPES OR SOURCES OF VALUES

An examination of existing codes of other companies provides a ready inventory of examples and comparative methods to identify critical issues and values. While this process provides pointers, it is important that the final draft of the code or values statement reflects that particular firm's, not another's, values and principles. Further, a divested company often relies on its former parent's code of conduct as a source of values for its own code.

Companies searching for sources of values or content from other organizations' codes benefit by contemporaneously reflecting on their own company values and policies. In this way, before directing its attention to other firms' more current or well-developed codes, the company can identify and preserve its own traditions, values, and policies in the code development process. A living document developed in a top–down, bottom–up fashion requires deliberation – which takes time. In the end, only code provisions which reflect the true character of a firm's operations are credible. One top executive of a communications company confirms this maxim: 'Although we used our old code and reviewed 50 other codes, the final code is modeled specifically to our own unique requirements.'

## THE COMPANY FOUNDER, EMPLOYEES, AND CONSTITUENTS AS SOURCES OF VALUES FOR CODE DEVELOPMENT

In addition to laws and other company codes, firms employ a variety of other, less obvious sources for ideas in formulating their codes of conduct. Often, when a firm seeks other sources of values, it settles on the moral and ethical philosophy of its top executive. For example, the Taylor Woodrow Group's team code was drafted by Lord Taylor of Hadfield, who founded the company in 1921. The 'ethics of the document has been carried on and the content altered accordingly over the years by the chairman of the group', notes Public Relations Officer, Victoria Woods. Ernest Bader, the founder of Scott Bader, was the driving force in that company's code creation. Bader drew upon the philosophies of Lord Sorenson, Fred Blum, and Ghandi.

One chief executive describes his experience in providing such values as 'an intense soul-searching by me, reviewing events in my personal and business life that turned out to be positive, and events that turned out to be negative'. Albert Mullin, Vice President of Corporate Relations for Digital Equipment, reveals the positive, long-term impact of having top corporate officers participate in the code creation process. He notes that 'in many ways the Digital Equipment statement of corporate philosophy is an amalgam of our founder's personal philosophy and that of the original senior managers and officers who helped found and advance the firm over 31 years'.

A by-product of incorporating the top executive's belief system in a firm's code is that such codification extends that executive's influence into every employee's work ethic. Marks & Spencer developed its statement of purpose based on the instincts of its powerful leader. That statement incorporates values and strategy consistent with Marcus Sieff's emphasis on the importance of good human relations. 'The origins of values on the code of conduct came from the leadership of the company's founder, Paul Galvin and his son, the present Chairman, Robert Galvin; and for more than 60 years, the influence of these two men has shown the way to uncompromising integrity', writes Motorola Senior Vice President and General Counsel, Richard Weise. Weise further underscores the benefits of having executive management's input in the code by relating that 'the language of our code of conduct has evolved from the combined experience of our senior management and their sense of need for guidance to our employees'.

A firm can also garner values important for the firm's success from employees by means of interviews, questionnaires, and focus groups. The director of human resources for a pharmaceuticals firm indicates the company's use of employee input, and the resultant 'finding indicated that our employees had a very clear idea of the core values of the company – even though they weren't emblazoned on our wall, or our note pads, or on other items'.

Other sources of values of company codes of conduct are the opinions and standards of the constituents of the code. Individuals who benefit from codes of conduct include employees, customers, suppliers, and others who interact with the company. Another company's director of human resources recognizes that customer interests and 'commonly held public standards of morality and ethics' comprise rewarding sources of the values in that company's code. Commonly accepted and admired standards of ethics coalesce from considerations of equity, rights, honesty, integrity, and truthfulness, and the exercise of corporate power.

The next chapter addresses drafting structure, format, and contents of a code of conduct.

# Chapter 5

# Developing the structure, format, and contents of a code

After a firm has identified important sources of values and determined the values it wishes to incorporate in its code, the company can proceed to the development of a code draft. The actual drafting of a code is a dynamic process often requiring the skills and talents of many individuals throughout the organization. Experiences vary in the way the code, after the key organizational values have been developed, is finally drafted.

First, a company can use the content of existing policy guidelines, administrative letters, or notices as a model for the code. TSB Trust, W. H. Smith, Dixons, George Wimpey, and London Buses formed new policy statements from prior company memoranda and policies. 'Shell', notes its Head of Communications B. K. Elms, 'revised its established statement by consolidating a range of views concerning structure and form within the Public Affairs Coordination; the contents were discussed extensively with our head coordinator and endorsed by the Chairman of the Committee of Managing Directors.'

Second, a company can develop the structure and the contents of a code without any written precedent at all. AMEC, BBA, Cadbury Schweppes, Ciba-Geigy, Granada, and Trusthouse Forte composed documents with no prior code or statement of values as a guide to content or format.

Third, a company can draft its code from focus group discussions. Norwich Union, Rolls Royce, Save & Prosper, Yorkshire Bank, and ICL utilized ideas from group discussions to develop formats and contents for codes or policy statements. R. E. Townsend, Group Corporate Secretary for Norwich Winterhur, relates the benefit of group discussions: 'We have learned that the exercise is more effective and efficient if there is widespread participation in the drafting stage. Early on, it was very much a "top–down" exercise with the CEO initiating much of the input and, thus, identification with, and commitment to, the finished product, and, thus, its practical application was limited.'

Last, collaborative efforts in promulgating a code are often utilized and they are often complex and lengthy undertakings, as several companies confirm. 'The Legal & General Code went through many drafts and changes of structure', confirms an education relations manager. One executive of a soft drink manufacturer relates that company's experience: 'In writing the code, senior management distributed drafts to many employees, gathering their ideas and questions in the process while the general counsel and senior legal counsellors, as well as the company's internal audit staff, worked closely together in drafting a code which would work and be understood by all employees.' The firm's final draft included input from many layers of managers and employees and bridged several disciplines.

Soliciting input from such a wide array of groups and individuals increases the likelihood that the code will be relevant and sufficiently comprehensive to generate acceptance. One top manager at an energy supplier 'interviewed a number of executives in legal, purchasing, human resources, accounting, and operations departments, before drafting the code which was then circulated among the top executives for comments before the CEO received and approved the final draft – I wrote it but the collaborative input was priceless'.

Moreover, a director at an engineering company recounts the variety of individuals who drafted that firm's code. 'The code is a product of a collective effort by a broad range of management and staff in various disciplines at both the corporate headquarters and operating companies and was drafted by our corporate business practices committee and reflects the input of the chairman of the board and other senior management personnel who are members of that committee.' The draft was then reviewed by corporate and operating company functional managers at all levels with their relevant suggestions about format and content integrated in the published code.

## PERIODIC REVISIONS TO MAINTAIN CURRENCY

A review and modification process assures that its code of conduct effectively serves the firm's purpose during the entire period of usage. Static codes provide the firm's leadership with a deleterious and false sense of security. A firm which revises its code, when appropriate, signals to the constituent groups addressed by the code that the code is responsive to changes in the values of the firm and to the environment in which the company operates.

## ISSUES IN THE CODE'S STRUCTURE, FORMAT, AND APPROACH

Many important issues arise in preparing, adopting, and promulgating a code including: the structure of the code; types of authority expressed; constituency relationships; use of objectives; operational relevance; legal matters; affirmative vs. negative tone; style of presentation; regulation or disclosure; audience level; implementation approaches; and code content and substance. It is helpful to review these issues and various companies' experiences in addressing them as follows.

## Text presentation

A company can present the text of its code in a number of ways. Typically, the perspective of the individual who drafts the code determines the content. For example, a human resources director may structure the code as a personnel guidance manual, while a public relations officer may fashion the contents as a document which may be widely distributed and cited publicly.

## Principles supporting the code

A code or similar policy statement is normally supported by principles or tenets which legitimize the document's policies. A philosophical buttress appears in the form that 'acting properly or ethically is correct in itself', and language in a code which reflects this philosophical tenet is similar to one of Trusthouse Forte's philosophies: 'To act with integrity at all times and to maintain a proper sense of responsibility toward the public.'

A second type of tenet which is commonly used is one which is legal–political in tone – and which refers to a social compact between the company and the public. This social compact as a basis for the code's existence is reflected in the following value: 'Our company will be a good citizen by conscientiously striving to assure legal and ethical company activities.'

British Telecom, Sainsbury's, and ICL rely heavily on statements of principles, philosophy, and values. Shell's code proclaims a 'constructive interest in societal matters which may not be directly related to business', and that the company will pursue 'all reasonable measures to ensure that our manufacturing operations and our products have no adverse effects on the environment'.

## Constituencies addressed by the code

Another issue which a company should consider in drafting its code or policy statement is the constituency or constituencies the policy document will address. Almost all policy documents speak to employees about their rights and responsibilities.

Typical codes which specifically communicate to multiple-constituencies are those of Boots, Coats Viyella, Shell, and Ciba-Geigy. Constituencies often addressed include customers, consumers, suppliers, governments, competitors, local communities, shareholders, and employees' families. For example, the Trusthouse Forte statement of philosophy delineates a number of groups to whom it recognizes a corporate responsibility: shareholders, customers, employees, and the public.

A firm's code is more complete when it selects the constituents it wishes to address and communicates a clear, steadfast message to them. Ciba-Geigy's code, for instance, projects a promise to consumers: 'We will supply products of high quality and at prices which are set, with due regard to all the circumstances, at levels which are competitive.'

### Code objectives

Companies draft codes or policy statements to achieve certain objectives. For instance, providing guidelines for employee actions in work-related activity is a typical goal. Firms which have such documents detailing rules and regulations with precise advice include Petrofina, British Gas, and Mobil Holdings. Another objective lies in addressing broader societal needs or external groups such as governments or consumers. A corporate-identity code may blend the internal focus of an employee-guidelines code and that of the outward-looking language of a code which addresses external groups.

Every code should have as its objectives the elimination of practices detrimental to the company's best interest, the establishment of procedures to resolve employees' business conduct or ethical dilemmas, and the implementation of a process which deters and disciplines violators. For example, Esso UK's code supports ethical practice: 'We will support, and we expect our managers to support, an employee who passes an opportunity or advantage which can only be secured at the sacrifice of principle.' Other meaningful code objectives are providing rewards for creative work; rewarding individual initiative and development; providing incentive for serving the community; encouraging leadership development; and promoting improved work quality.

### Making the code's objectives consistent with primary company functions

The drafters should also consider the best means of tying the code's values and objectives to operations. The code should be operationally relevant – so, combining theories or values in the code with the company's everyday functions has high priority in the drafting process. A top executive of a banking concern agrees: 'In the development of our company's code, we paid particular attention to combining the theories in the code with everyday functions – this practical focus is one of the code's most valuable characteristics.'

A company can link purpose to operations in a variety of ways including: relating the code to employee policy manuals, and connecting code statements to the company's internal planning process.

A second means of linking purpose to operations through code form exists when a firm connects its code statements to its internal planning process. For example, one company has developed a single, integrated statement of purpose to consider financial goals in the broader context of other corporate objectives, to superintend the development of operational programmes and strategies, and to provide a basis for communicating detailed positions to internal and external constituent groups.

Coupling the firm's values, purpose, and objectives expressed in the code to the planning process increases the likelihood of these values being important considerations when executives promulgate planning decisions. For example, planning processes which mandate the ethical evaluation of the firm's strategies and major business recommendations successfully integrate the code values and the planning process. Many companies include a wide range of societal objectives as strategic planning goals. Using this approach, management planners consider a plethora of trends, including those of a social, political, and economic nature. Planners have increasingly fused the concerns of the community and the public with the planning process, an emphasis requiring a broad corporate overview and a wide range of firm-performance expectations. Companies often consider additional constituencies beyond shareholders because confidence in the business enterprise relies upon the public's acceptance of the firm's activities.[1]

### Legal and non-legal issues

The drafters should also determine to what extent legal and non-legal issues are discussed. It is appropriate to include germane explanations of statutes and regulations which directly impact business conduct. For example, British Gas' policy document condemns gifts: 'It is a criminal offence to accept or solicit any gift or consideration from anyone as an inducement or reward for showing favour in connection with the company's business.'

Laws and regulations establish meaningful guidelines. Yet, in many areas, a firm may wish to require behaviour which surpasses the minimum legal standards. In any case, it is important to express clearly the rationales which support the code's legal and non-legal principles.

### Choosing an affirmative, prohibitive, or hybrid tone for the code

Drafters should also determine the extent to which a code's tone should be affirmative, prohibitive, or a hybrid of the first two types. The initial tendency, a natural one, is for the concerned firm to construct a negative code which proscribes every imaginable inappropriate or undesirable act.

According to Harvard Business School Dean Robert Austin, negative codes containing a great number of restrictions pose a number of problems:[2]

1 Prohibitive codes, generally compendia of 'thou shalt not', and often imposed from the top of the organization, inspire little support or respect.
2 The negative code presents interpretative problems because the manager often has a conflict of interest in the mere determination that the code governs specific conduct.
3 Completely prohibitive codes either involve overkill or cultivate loopholes.
4 As any statute or regulation, a negative provision depends for its effectiveness on the attitudes of the regulators who enforce it or the respect the regulated direct to it – both of which vary significantly depending on the parties' perception of importance and the advantages or risks involved in not adhering to the prohibitions.

A manager or employee who must decide if a prohibitive code provision applies to conduct he wishes to pursue faces a severe conflict of interest: if he decides that a particular code provision is inapplicable, he may on that occasion choose a more profitable, though questionable, course of action. As no system, not even one as extensive as the United Kingdom's array of laws and regulations, can proscribe all inappropriate actions, the prohibitive or negative code offers loopholes to those conditioned to take desired action if no code provision specifically prohibits that action. Because a negative code of this sort is no better than the actor's conscience, the preferable code is an affirmative one which incorporates 'the primary code of honour'.

A code based upon affirmative or positive principles is essentially founded on what Harvard Professor Lon Fuller characterized as the 'morality of aspiration . . . [which] is the morality of the Good Life, of excellence, of the fullest realization of human powers'. In this sense, such a code, in Fuller's estimation, is similar to the notions of Plato and Aristotle where there exists 'the conception of proper and fitting conduct such as beseems a human being functioning at his best'.

Moreover, the firm's statement of philosophy, a usual and natural element of positive or affirmative codes, permits the firm 'to state in general terms its basic ethical beliefs, rationales, and commitments; and provides broad principles that give guidance to employees confronted with situations not covered by rules'.[3]

Generally, affirmative codes are more persuasive and less indoctrinating than negative documents. Such codes invoke greater loyalty from employees who consider acquiescence to positive, affirmative statements to be inherently good. Since managers and employees frequently face business conduct and ethical dilemmas, a code should necessarily include expressions of affirmative goals, not just negative prohibitions which a manager or employee can disregard or circumvent.

Dean Austin has proposed guidelines for an affirmative code as follows:

1  The manager (and employee) asserts that he will place the firm's interest first.
2  He affirms that he will place his duty to society above his duty to the firm.
3  He avers that he has an affirmative duty to reveal to those in authority in the firm the entire facts of any situation where his private interests conflict with those of the company, or where the interests of the firm conflict with those of society.
4  He ratifies, when all persons in the organization adhere to the principles posited herein, that the 'profit motive is the best incentive for the development of a sound, expanding, and dynamic economy'.

While the purely affirmative code, which expresses a desired course in positive goals, offers a lucid, concise statement of general concepts and also addresses conflicts of interest through disclosure, not merely penalty, such a code has its deficiencies as well. Specifically, an affirmative code often assumes the firm's managers and employees possess a reservoir of legal and business knowledge by which to translate the code's general provisions into specific standards of conduct. In addition, the code may presume the manager or employee will not experience any preliminary conflict of interest in this translation-to-action process of determining whether certain conduct is permitted.

The foregoing deficiencies of prohibitive and affirmative codes suggest that a combination of the beneficial aspects of each in one code is preferable – the general statement can be supplemented by more specific provisions for guidance in certain areas and assistance to employees who obviously need to translate general statements into desired conduct. For example, the American Institute of Certified Public Accountants (AICPA) has pursued this compound approach in developing standards of conduct for its membership: the Institute's 'Concepts of Professional Ethics' comprises the affirmative guidelines while the detailed 'Rules of Conduct' embodies the minimum levels of expected conduct as well as a set of prohibitions and sanctions.

'It is counterproductive to dictate black and white rules in most cases; guidelines are much more effective in inspiring appropriate conduct', asserts a director of a banking concern. Likewise, another company considered this same issue when it created its code, which is an outgrowth of the firm's conflict of interest policy. That firm reduced the number of substantial proscriptions inherent in negative codes. According to its general counsel, the company's code 'emphasizes good behaviour, limits prohibitions to significant legal and ethical issues, and provides a formal mechanism for reviewing questionable situations'. Likewise, the Powell Duffryn statement concerning personnel, notes Chairman R. D. C. Hubbard, has an affirmative tone, as indicated in one particular section: 'It is the policy of the group to ensure equality of employment opportunity having regard to available skills and to provide suitable training courses and career development opportunities so as to enhance job satisfaction and to foster employees' commitment to their employing companies.' The better designed codes contain a combination of guidelines, rules, and sanctions.

### Writing styles

The writing style appearing in a code may range from conversational to formal. Any reasonable style will suffice provided it is lucid in presentation and thorough in explanation. If the code employs a legal style, it should avoid long sentences interrupted by phrases or clauses. 'One of the significant success factors of our company's code is its crisp, straight-forward language', asserts one company director.

The more comprehensible codes reflect the style of clearly expressed business correspondence, the important elements of which are organized and substantive content and attractive design. Another company's director, the author of that firm's code, relates that 'the code's success is at least partially attributable to the elimination of legal jargon, and the use of plain language in a concise document – in our review of some other firms' codes it is obvious a few firms rely too heavily on their legal departments to write codes'.

Moreover, a code's exterior format can vary from attractive covers to printed loose-leaf or stapled papers. The more pleasing the presentation, the more credibility employees and the public undoubtedly assign the code. Toward that end, codes with an attractive booklet and dignified layout and typography project an image of importance. It is appropriate, usually, to distinguish, by its presentation, the code from the firm's other written documents.

## Regulation and disclosure

Another preliminary issue the firm must address as it drafts a code is whether the provisions should regulate specific conflicts or activities, or whether they should require disclosure of such matters. Codes based on the 'regulation' approach prohibit specific activities which are detrimental to the company. 'Conduct disclosure', in business code vernacular, requires an employee to reveal matters actually or potentially adverse to the firm.

Several benefits accrue to a company using a disclosure policy. First, a disclosure-based code serves as a progression in the evolution of the code, from strict prohibition of activities to an attitude of trust that employees will disclose certain matters. The information pipeline of employee disclosure provides the firm's audit or ethics committee with more examples of questionable conduct so either can make a more informed judgement as to 'whether the activity should be accepted, informally censured, or formally restricted by a new law or code provision'.[4]

Second, a disclosure code is probably more flexible in its use by employees and application by the firm than a regulatory code that has broad proscriptions concerning a multitude of employee and firm activities. Managers require more flexibility than a litany of prohibitions provides.

Further, a disclosure code enables firms to create and preserve a specific and timely audit trail, since employees report activities on a periodic basis. Finally, such a code reduces conflicts of interest faced by a manager, because employees provide disclosure information about their own or others' questionable conduct to an unbiased superior other than the employee's, for the former's often more objective consideration. This procedure removes a time-consuming burden from the employee's immediate supervisor.

An electricity supplier's auditor underscores the importance of disclosure as an element in that company's code: 'Our disclosure feature is one of the linchpins of our code – periodically our managers and certain types of employees disclose their activities, primarily those in the areas of potential conflicts of interest and political positions – we really get a pulse-reading of the firm.'

Of course, some conduct is so undesirable or reprehensible that outright prohibition is the preferred response. Moreover, since disclosure alone is often insufficient to control questionable practice, every firm should include prohibitions in its code as well as disclosure with a system of review, judgement, and the imposition of sanctions.

### Determining the levels a code should address

Drafters should determine what levels a code should address. First, a code should contain a clear definition of the company's corporate mission and objectives. The statements should not be overly specific or tedious, but rather sufficiently unequivocal so the employees and managers clearly understand how to comply with the firm's expectations.

Moreover, codes should incorporate measures for properly handling constituency relations. 'Our goal is making certain that our conduct is above the minimum level required by law so that we are fair in our treatment of all constituency groups to the level addressed by the company' relates a human resources executive. Extensive sections discussing customer, suppliers, outside parties, and employees are essential elements, as well.

Furthermore, the code should identify and define specific policies and practices, such as those addressing workplace issues, conflict-of-interest, share-trading, and other legal regulations.

### Other important factors

Those charged with the drafting of a code profit by considering a number of other factors. First, the firm should examine its own product or product line, since that definition necessarily limits the code's scope. Second, the drafting committee should evaluate the general level of competitiveness in the firm's industry and the specific product groups. Codes that reduce organizational bureaucracy and expense are usually more beneficial than those which nurture the opposite.

Further, the firm should match its needs with the concerns of the external environment, including society. This approach is both externally and internally directed and moves the firm toward striking a balance necessary to properly address both facets of the business: its obligations to seek profits, on the one hand, and to act responsibly as a member of society, on the other.

### Striking a balance in the code's substance

Finally, the drafting committee should evaluate issues regarding the code's substance. Codes which are too brief often appear platitudinous and lacking in substance. The drafters should study the content or topics of codes from two perspectives: beneficial conduct on behalf of the firm and conduct detrimental to the firm. Areas which address conduct on behalf of the firm include: intercourse with the host governments, relations with customers and suppliers, employee relations, and dealings with competitors. Issues relating to conduct detrimental to the company include conflict of interest, use of company resources, and illegal activities.

## CODE INCLUSION OF SPECIFIC TOPICS

Every code should include a detailed summary of important laws and a compliance certificate by which every employee periodically signals his adherence to the code. Although the code should require conduct which goes beyond the letter of the law, a recapitulation of applicable statutes and regulations provides employees with essential information, a necessary prerequisite if firms are to avoid legal difficulties.

Firms wishing to address certain societal matters can state that commitment or compose a code section that reinforces and rewards employee behaviour beneficial to society. For example, Boots' code recites the establishment of the Boots Charitable Trust whose mission is to 'exercise an independent judgement in supporting a large number of charities in a wide range of activities'. Moreover, Esso UK's code recounts its commitment to making contributions in the 'field of education, welfare, and the arts'.

A comprehensive code addresses many other topics and issues including the following: employee conduct; environmental affairs; commitment to staff training and development; product safety; employee health screening; security of company records and proprietary information; shareholder interests; workplace health and safety; responsibility to society; political interests; relations with local government; interactions with customers, contractors, and suppliers; innovation and technological progress; employee relations; dealings with competitors; intercourse with UK and foreign governments; acceptance of gifts by staff; civic and community affairs; trade union relations; the integrity of books and records; insider dealing; and confidentiality.

The creation of a code is a complicated task that implies reliance upon numerous sources of information about values, preparation, and content. Firms can develop codes which specifically direct employees to conduct themselves in the highest ethical manner. In addition, firms can utilize their codes to create basic policy structures and patterns for behaviour in such a way as to elevate the firm's overall conscience regarding proper business conduct.[5] Codes are an important mechanism by which firms pursue excellence and obtain high standards of conduct. As employees read the code's text and consider its meanings they develop a sensitivity to the principles and values expressed in that code.

# Chapter 6

# A checklist for creating the code's final draft

After the drafter has addressed the various issues raised in prior chapters, he can complete a first draft of a new code or a revision of an existing code. Before completing the final draft, the drafter should read the following checklist and make modifications to his work-product as necessary. The following guidelines have been identified by the participating British and multi-national companies as key guidelines in designing and drafting a code of conduct or similar policy document.

1 *Apparent leadership of managing director or chairman in code development.* 'The managing director or chairman must be a leader in developing a code', advises BBA Group's Managing Director Dr John White. Likewise, the process of creating Prudential's code of conduct was led by its chief executive in conjunction with the board of directors. If properly endorsed and supported by top management, a code can be very helpful in 'the communication of traditional values and commitments and in the promotion of standards of integrity and excellence for the entire organization', advises the chief executive of an industrial products company.

Through the managing director's participation and leadership, a code gains legitimacy in the eyes of employees. As the head of operations, the managing director can ensure that the code does not include unrealistic standards, because such codes are unworkable and, eventually, rejected by employees. In carrying out this code-support function, the managing director should utilize all communication channels, formal and informal, to communicate that the code serves as an organizational ethic.

Moreover, the managing director's advocacy signals the development or preservation of an environment which values proper business conduct. As Dean Russell Palmer of the Wharton School asserts in a Touche Ross publication, 'The inescapable fact is that leaders set the moral and ethical tone for the organisations they run. If the chief executive tells lies – even small lies – his or her subordinates will perceive that lying is condoned behaviour . . . sooner or later the ethical values of top management will permeate the organisation, positively or negatively, as numerous case studies demonstrate.'

2 *Top management's timely identification of principal purposes of the code.* One critical guideline for code creation, notes Texaco Chairman Peter Bijur, is that 'the managing director or chairman, or those under his immediate direction, should identify the company's key objectives, which later serve as ground rules in the code's creation'.

Normally, a chief executive's beliefs as to what purposes a company policy document of this sort should serve have crystallized by the time the document's first draft is completed. In this way, every managing director can identify the code values as standards, not merely abstract verbiage, which he can defend and actively advance throughout the firm. In the opinion of one former chief executive, 'A chief executive must make his expectations explicit; in this way he can guide his people' in identifying ethical or other proper business objectives.

3 *Code draft written by a small group.* Certainly, it is important to seek input in creating a code from as many members of an organization as possible. Nonetheless, a large group's size is not conducive to decisive action. Touche Ross Managing Director Michael Blackburn agrees: 'The Statement of Intent was drafted by a small operating group of three to six people'. Representatives from the company's departments and power groups (for instance, human resources, finance, general management, marketing and sales, and board of directors) can draft a concise well-balanced and thorough document. Many companies, such as Tesco, Ciba-Geigy, Kingfisher, and British Steel, involve the legal staff in the drafting process. Another executive disagrees about involvement of legal staff: 'God, help us if the legal staff is involved!'

4 *An introduction in the code establishes a serious tone.* An imperative guideline in creating Town & Country's Statement of Corporate Objectives was the 'inclusion of a preamble', advises that company's Managing Director Ian Bell. An introduction should contain a short summary of the code's purpose, the need for the code, and of top executives' expectations of every employee's exemplary conduct consistent with code principles.

5 *Differentiating ethical and legal standards of conduct.* A code should be much more than a mere treatise on existing statutes. A critical success factor in Texaco Ltd's creation of an effective code, relates Chairman Peter Bijur, is that 'it clearly distinguishes ethical and legal requirements'. While there is a permanent connection between laws and ethics, the two are clearly not coterminous.

Moreover, in Harvard Professor Lon Fuller's estimation, 'The effective deterrents which shape the average man's conduct derive from a sense of right and wrong', not substantially by legal penalties.[1] Preferred ethical conduct normally exists at a level well above that minimum required by law.

Nonetheless, because morality cannot be assured or even determined by reference to an engineering model, in drafting a workable code the company must relate its code standards to contemporary concepts of morality.

6 *Requiring compliance with laws and professional standards.* According to Alan Smith, Secretary of Smiths Industries, 'the code should clearly require employees to comply with all relevant laws and professional standards.'

7 *Essential values defined and highlighted.* A must for a company's policy statement is that 'it should emphasize key values of the organization', counsels Ranald Noel-Paton, John Menzies Group Managing Director. These values, together with company objectives, general and specific priorities, and unambiguous guidelines, should be clearly described, nurtured, and communicated. 'Principles should have something enduring about them', relates B. K. Elms, Shell Head of Communications.

8 *Relevance, credibility, conciseness, and utility of the code policies.* The drafter should identify the most common concerns of the major external and internal constituencies, and relate these matters to actual code policies. This formulation process involves the drafting of 'sections which are comprehensive, concise, and inclusive', advises Remploy Chief Executive Tony Withey.

Further, to assure adequate coverage of the major concerns, the code should 'contain multiple, topical sections', according to R. E. Andrews, Dixons Group Personnel Director. Caution must be exercised by the drafter to reconcile the need for comprehensive and wide coverage, on the one hand, and utility and conciseness, on the other. Based on the Shell experience in drafting and revising a company policy statement, B. K. Elms, Head of Communications, offers this advice: 'The policy document should be as succinct as possible to avoid misinterpretation; Occam's razor should be used as freely as the pen!'

A more general code provides employees with guidelines, rather than a long litany of specific proscriptions, and thereby induces a specific, ethical manner. Requiring, as rule-based codes have a tendency to do, adherence to a large number of complicated rules is counter-productive – that type of code abandons its most important audience.

Finally, overly lengthy codes may have a chilling effect on employees' raising those critical questions which promote every firm's organizational health. If the code does not specifically proscribe the questionable activity, the employee may incorrectly assume the conduct in question is permissible.

9 *Inclusion of operating principles.* David Hanson, Director of Operations at Bradford & Bingley, has identified an important consideration for those who draft codes: 'Incorporate operating principles in the document'. Adherence to the policies of the code should assist the operations of the company. For instance, notes London Buses Managing Director C. Hodson, the 'most commonly arising conflicts of interest should be fully described'. By avoiding conflicts of interest, every employee eliminates a, not the barrier to smooth operations.

10 *Use of realistic examples and factual situations.* In order to explain more fully how employees should interpret a code's policies, the drafter should

provide illustrations of how policies and principles can be applied to specific situations. Ranald Noel-Paton, Group Managing Director of John Menzies, distinguishes the following as a critical drafting requirement: 'Specific examples and illustrations of the company document in action.'

11  *Expectation of proper behaviour in all situations and guidelines for employee conduct.* The drafter should incorporate a general principle that 'in all business dealings every employee should exercise upright behaviour', relates D'A. T. N. Payne, Director of Personnel at Rolls Royce. Such a declaration places all employees on notice that the mere absence of a definitive code principle directly proscribing specific conduct does not create a loophole or excuse for unethical or improper behaviour.

In addition, every code should include well-defined guidelines for employee conduct, notes D. M. Penton, George Wimpey Group Secretary. The code should unequivocally direct employees to conduct themselves in a manner consistent with code provisions. Helpful questions an employee should ask himself, when confronted with an ambiguous situation, appear in a later chapter.

12  *Inclusion of formalized mechanisms to resolve employee questions and problems.* Many ambiguous or potentially improper actions can be avoided if the employee has access to good advice within the organization. No policy, code, or values statement, no matter how lucid and thorough, completely eliminates circumstances in which the need for interpretation arises. In fact, one of the positive aspects of a policy document is that it compels employees to consider, to think. Consequently, as Dixons Group Personnel Director R. E. Andrews counsels, a critical need for a company is 'to exercise reasonable care and prudence by responding, through provisions in the policy document, to all likely questions posed by employees' and to provide 'details as to how an employee can resolve problems through defined, appropriate action steps'.

13  *Managing director's or chairman's careful review of draft.* Top executives of Bank of England, Beazer, Dowty, Granada, and Severn Trent have emphatically acknowledged the critical value of top-level participation in the drafting process. Texaco Ltd Chairman Peter Bijur stresses the necessity for the managing director's or chairman's 'careful and candid review of the proposed code draft'.

To most employees, the managing director's views represent the company's position. The more extensive his involvement in the drafting process, the greater the document's legitimacy. Furthermore, as the managing director invests his time in developing and supporting the code, his commitment to it should increase as well. Moreover, the corporate staff, correctly perceiving the code to be a work-product of the managing director or chairman, have a powerful incentive to communicate the code in an effective and professional manner, and, importantly, to effect its implementation.

14  *Circulation of draft for comment.* A company demonstrates respect for its employees when it solicits advice. Meyer, Norwich Union, Richard Costain,

Touche Ross, Burmah and Yorkshire Building Society solicited the viewpoints of senior management and other members of the organization. Because more views are requested and potential conflicts among various groups considered, the chance for a code's successful acceptance, implementation, and administration much more favourable.

15 *Comments by employees taken seriously.* Organizations with open lines of communication are generally more flexible and adapt better to the demands of a competitive market system. Hence, a company should not only solicit comments about its code, but should also make appropriate changes in that policy document to reflect a 'good listener' attitude. This approach, when sincerely implemented, builds a code's credibility.

# Chapter 7

# Implementing the code

British leaders and directors acknowledge that the business sector is indeed troubled by improper conduct and ethical problems. Many believe that companies actually strengthen their competitive position by sustaining high standards of business conduct and ethics. These leaders have identified two major threats to proper business conduct: first, the decay in cultural and social institutions, and, second, the pressure for short-term earnings.

These same British executives indicate that government intervention is the least effective way to promote proper conduct and ethical practice; instead they assert that companies should actively encourage proper behaviour by reinforcing good values which enhance the company's internal environment. Perhaps the most effective tool in this building and reinforcing of 'values' is the creation and implementation of a code of conduct. As the nineteenth-century American writer Ralph Waldo Emerson advised, 'Go put your creed into your deed, nor speak with double tongue'.

One way a firm can vigorously address the pressures on managers and employees to act improperly, after creating and adopting a comprehensive code or policy statement, is to institute vigorous implementation procedures which assure the code's continued application. In this way, firms provide organizational roadblocks to improper conduct, as well as education, training, and reinforcement for employees who have a dearth of values due to the decay of cultural and social institutions.

Even though a firm has created a code with clear purpose, comprehensive scope, and relevant topics, the actual effectiveness depends, as well, on constructing an implementation process that is vigorous and inexorable. A brilliant business leader, the former Chairman of General Electric Reginald Jones, emphasizes that 'it is essential . . . to have a system of teaching and enforcing codes of conduct'. The mere adoption of a comprehensive code does not ensure that employees will adhere to it. In fact, the implementation process is also necessary; and it must be dynamic – it never ends.

That implementation begins with the circulation of the code. The extent and the manner of that circulation establishes the nature of a code's acceptance. Employees are naturally sensitive to the ethical tone established by managing directors when new company policies, such as those contained in a code of conduct, are established.

## DISTRIBUTION OF COMPANY CODES

The manner and extent of a company's circulation of its code or similar policy statement signal the importance of that document. While some firms restrict circulation to top managers or boards of directors, others actively circulate the company policy document to all employees and interested groups. Some of the participating British and multi-national companies, such as Costain, limit distribution of their codes to top and middle managers, and a few, such as London Buses, also circulate their codes to top managers. However, the majority, including the BBA Group as related by Group Managing Director J. G. White, disseminate the code to every employee. Most codes and policy statements are available to outsiders upon request.

The distribution of a firm's code is one of the most vital activities a firm can undertake to successfully implement its code of conduct. When AT&T introduced its recently updated code of conduct, it followed a precise eight-page dissemination plan which specifically defined the recipients by job classification, the departments and managers who would distribute the code to those recipients, and a timetable for distribution to each recipient group. In most instances, the nature of the document or composition of the intended audience determined the scope of the document's dissemination. Dixons, Rolls Royce, Boots, and Tesco have disseminated their company documents to specified key groups or employees. At one multi-national firm, notes a director, 'we put codes into brochures which were mailed to all employees, and values plaques were posted in the business offices throughout the world'.

A wide distribution accompanied by a cover letter from the managing director or chairman is preferable since the company gives notice to everyone that the code is not frivolous and it provides all managers and employees with a frame of reference for their activities. If a company wishes to enlist its employees in a common cause, it should trust them with possession of its code of conduct. An employee can better help implement a document's policy directives when that employee feels individual responsibility or a stake in the success of that policy document. Consequently, relates Texaco Ltd Chairman Peter Bijur, 'Our values statement was reviewed as a part of our Total Quality Process training, attended by all company employees'. In another instance, the J. Bibby policy document is regularly distributed in the company's annual report and accounts, the annual employee report, and quarterly newsletter, notes the company's corporate finance director. In addition, there is a greater likelihood that extensive distribution increases every code's exposure and employees' familiarity with it. British Telecom's policy statement is highlighted in internal newspaper articles and reproduced on a pocket card. At Peugeot Talbot, managers display framed copies of the company charter and procedures.

Other firms stress the significance of the code by placing the employee's receipt signifying delivery in that employee's personnel file. Kimberly-Clark's code was distributed throughout its worldwide organization by line management. Similarly, John Menzies' Corporate Principles document is distributed through divisional managements.

Firms have disseminated their codes using several other techniques. Some companies post codes to all employees. Another frequently used method is placing the code in the company's policy and procedures manual. Other companies incorporate their codes of conduct in an employee information manual. Wimpey, relates Group Secretary D. M. Penton, 'circulates its statement of Corporate Purpose and Group Objectives to management, and incorporates it in the staff handbook'. Some British companies such as the Leeds, Prudential, AMEC, and M & G, prominently reprint group strategy statements, business philosophies, and codes of conduct in their annual reports and accounts. IBM, moreover, not only disseminates a code manual to all of its employees, but also makes a copy of its code available for review through computer systems for all employees who have dealings with outside parties.

In the process of dissemination, some firms translate their codes into many languages, because such copies provide better local access to the code.

## WHY THE MANNER IN WHICH A CODE IS COMMUNICATED IS IMPORTANT

The manner of communicating the importance of the firm's code of conduct to employees is critical to successful code implementation. Neglecting to communicate the essential need for the code often causes employees' failure to give the code credibility and proper attention. This failure often results in poor understanding, if only that, of the code.

Undoubtedly, the manner by which a firm communicates its code often colours the code's message. Consequently, many chairmen, managing directors, and chief executive officers communicate a code's importance through an individual cover letter or one incorporated in the code booklet to draw employees' attention to the seriousness of the document.

Clear, unhindered communication of this sort is a prerequisite of any effective organization because organizations are growing larger, are more complex, require greater efficiency and quality in producing goods and providing services, and wish to respond to employee demands for healthier organizational climates.[1]

Norwich Union General Manager and Secretary H. W. Utting notes a sure way to demonstrate the significance of a policy document: 'Copies were distributed to all managers and senior employees at meetings where the CEO explained the content'. Other companies, such as Bradford & Bingley, Burmah, Ciba-Geigy, Halifax, Smiths Industries, and TSB Trust, include a cover letter signed by the chairman or managing director pointing out why adherence to the company document is critically important.

An effective cover letter might indicate that the company prohibits any unethical or illegal action, that abiding by the code or similar document will prevent improper acts, that employees are trusted by the company to maintain the firm's high standards and values, and that the employee should ask himself the following questions if there is any doubt about the morality of the considered action:

1  Would I be willing to tell my family about the action I am contemplating?
2  Would I feel any misgiving if society knew of the action I am contemplating?

Any firm, regardless of size, requires an excellent level of communication performance, and, to establish and maintain such a level, the firm must provide a supportive climate, one which builds and maintains the individual's sense of worth. One of the keys to stimulate transmittal of information is trust, in which employees respond to the firm's managers confidently by performing at a high level.

When the organizational environment is trusting and supportive, informative processes are usually healthy for a number of reasons. Members of the organization have nothing to gain by miscommunicating deliberately. Moreover, openness nurtures candid expressions of ideas and feelings. Effective communication further enhances a trusting, supportive environment; however, when communication performance falters, the trusting environment may deteriorate.

Clearly, in suspicious, unsupportive environments, an employee often suppresses true feelings, and that employee's communication is characterized by a need to protect himself rather than by a desire to serve the best interests of the firm by adhering to code standards. While the leaders of an organization should bear these observations in mind as they communicate the imperative for a code of conduct, they should understand 'Needs of a moment prepare the individual for the perception of the next moment'.[2] As Demosthenes reflected, 'The easiest thing of all is to deceive one's self; for what a man wishes he generally believes to be true'.

One commentator maintains that employees receive meaning and enthusiasm by realizing value-related opportunities: a chance to be tested, to take part in a social experiment, to do something well, to accomplish a high-minded task, and to change the present for the better. Moreover, in a survey by a leading American journal of psychology, the top six respondent rankings of aspects of a job found 'most important' appear as follows: the chance to do something that makes a person feel good about himself; the chance to accomplish something worthwhile; the chance to learn something new; the opportunity to hone new skills; the degree of freedom in accomplishing a person's job; and the opportunity to do what a person does best.[3]

Consequently, in their communications about the code, the firm's leaders should integrate satisfying employees' needs with their accepting the importance of and becoming familiar with the code. People do not respond directly to reality, but, rather, to their perceptions of reality. Hence, the effective communicator who wishes to extol the benefits of code to a listening organization should communicate within the context of the employees' frames of reference.

Effective communication also includes images and word pictures, employing examples that people can readily understand, speaking or writing of traditional values, appealing to common beliefs, understanding the audience, repeating the message, being positive and hopeful, involving the audience in the undertaking, and expressing personal conviction.[4]

Chairmen and managing directors seize different media through which to translate their feelings of the code's importance. One chief executive introduced the company's code to employees through a videotape presentation. His message to the firm's employees was simple and direct: 'The document is important to employees and to the company'. Firms which actively seek to improve the environment for communication, lay the foundation for a thorough transmission of the importance of the code and of its attendant implementing procedures. In this regard, establishing a culture of open communication is complementary to effectively disseminating the code. For instance, Hewlett Packard has structured its office layout to facilitate easy-going communications among employees. With an environment functioning on a first-name basis, relaxed employees speak more freely about important topics, including applying the values and standards of the 'HP Way'.

Furthermore, the act of open communication concerning issues within a firm acts to reinforce itself. Sceptical employees witnessing the open, free dissemination of ideas and opinions become more trusting of any mechanism, including the code, in which values and standards are transmitted. Moreover, frequent conversation between peers or across executive levels within General Mills firmly impresses new employees that open communication is not only valued, but is an organizational norm. Toward this end, according to General Mills executives, by fostering and rewarding open communication[5] that company maintains a culture in which employees trust management directives, including any policies or codes.

The next chapter discusses how firms effectively respond to employee concerns and questions regarding the code, and relates how an 'open door' policy works.

# Chapter 8

# Responding to employee concerns and questions about the code: resolution and the open door policy

Even though a firm has widely disseminated its code or policy document and has thoroughly educated employees as to the meaning and procedures contained in such documents, employees inevitably encounter situations about which they must seek counsel, clarification, or interpretation to resolve. Often, these questions pertain to ethical or business conduct issues. At times, employees wish to raise concerns about the actions of other employees or the company's policies, usually when the firm is not meeting its standards or is violating policies established for the good of the firm.

Unfortunately, codes of conduct cannot provide complete or guaranteed means for employees to resolve all such dilemmas; however, the better-designed codes direct employees to resources within the firm from which employees may receive counsel and interpretation. Resolving such questions is in the best interest of every company. At one large chemical and plastics products company, according to a senior executive, 'We stress the point to all employees that raising questions does not present any problem – in fact we welcome them; however, not raising questions could bring serious repercussions'. 'Obviously, we sometimes don't live up to our expressed standards; we need employees to tell us', notes the managing director of another firm.

When firms close their ears to criticism or fail to respond to valid questions or concerns, they risk losing an opportunity to correct problems, learn from mistakes, and maintain the allegiance of their workforce. Worse, improper or unethical business conduct, when uncorrected, is often exposed publicly by high-minded employees. This exposure leads to loss of consumer confidence in the firm. And, most cases of product liability, from the Ford Pinto fuel tank to the McDonnell-Douglas DC-10 baggage-door, could have been avoided if the concerns of ethical employees had been heeded early in the product development.

Consultations with employees provide an opportunity for solving actual or potential problems. Lord Forte, Chairman of Trusthouse Forte, in referring to that company's written philosophy, writes in his autobiography, 'I would not claim that every single one of our employees is able to recite this [philosophy] by heart, but we do try to get the message over, down to the bottom rung. One of the main channels through which we accomplish this is our system of consultative committees, which exist in every one of our establishments. Each of our managers or manageresses is trained to chair a regular meeting with the staff, to listen to their suggestions as to how conditions can be improved, and to sort out any problems that have cropped up'. Similar forums for expression of views and complaints exist in other British firms.

A code should advise employees to seek advice in every ethically ambiguous situation. Several American studies indicate that, among managers, levels of 'moral reasoning and judgment are likely to be higher when managers get together and discuss ethical issues than when the choices are made in solitude'.[1] Dixons Group Personnel Director R. E. Andrews confirms this experience, as follows, 'People are more aware of ethical problems; they prefer to call me or the company secretary to discuss what should be done'. Andrews notes that colleagues want to discuss their actions now more than before.

Further, another survey indicates that 25 per cent of employees consult with their supervisors or managers when confronting dilemmas. The employee's spouse is the second most frequent choice for counselling, 24 per cent of the time.[2] When business executives ranked the sources from which they seek counsel, the favourite choice is 'spouse', 24.5 per cent of the time, followed closely by one's superior, 22.9 per cent, and that person's colleagues, 19.7 per cent.[3] More recently, when executives were asked to name the individual they trusted most when faced with an ethical or business conduct problem, 44 per cent indicated they turned to themselves, 29 per cent applied to their spouses, and 6 per cent called upon peers at work.[4]

Firms increasingly provide and communicate procedures by which employees can resolve dilemmas so that the firm can assure a consistent application of code and policy document principles in the resolution of those dilemmas. One way of assuring consistency is identifying persons and departments whose familiarity with the code or whose experience in addressing ethical dilemmas yields consistent responses to ethical and business conduct inquiries and dilemmas. McDonald's Restaurants' use of an ethics officer provides more consistent responses to complaints and to questions concerning that firm's code of ethics.

Participating firms have established numerous sources that employees with ethical or business conduct dilemmas and questions can call upon for resolution. These resources include the employee's supervisor, the human resource department, an ombudsman, an ethics or business conduct hotline, a business conduct committee or officer, the audit department, and the legal department. In the responding to complex ethical or business conduct dilemmas, some firms encourage an employee to consult higher levels of the firm, including the chairman of the board.

Under any procedure, it is critically important that the designated representative or procedure provide a prompt, consistent, and thorough response to the employee's question, or assistance in helping solve the employee's dilemma. In this manner, a firm demonstrates to its workforce a commitment to open discussion whenever concerns arise. Such an approach generates ethical credibility and cultivates a trusting environment.

Consistency in interpretation and advice is more often assured when careful attention to precedent is observed. An employee often turns to his supervisor or line manager when faced with an ethical or business conduct problem. Most firms invite employees to raise such questions with their supervisors. A few companies publicise the resources of the directors and other corporate officers which are available to any employee with an ethics or business conduct question. One transportation firm has established 'the supervisor as an employee's resource person for answering code questions or resolving a problem. However, that company's legal staff is available to resolve any question or problem, especially in the area of conflict of interest.' Moreover, Chevron has charged supervisors, along with human resource representatives, with responsibility to deal with employees' questions and dilemmas.

A banking concern, explains its director of human resources, advises an employee 'with an ethical issue to submit his request in writing, with supporting data, to his immediate department manager [and] the manager and group's managing director, following their approval, submit this request to the human resources director and corporate managing director'. The final response is communicated to the inquiring party in writing with a copy inserted in that person's personnel file.

Some firms have also established less formal procedures in which supervisors are still the pivot in the resolution process, as a company director for an electricity supplier describes. 'Ours is an informal process which uses the supervisor as the employee's first source for answers to ethics questions and we also make it easy for employees to find someone outside their organisation, usually in the human resources department, to talk to in case the ethics question concerns practices in that supervisor's part of the organisation.'

Further, most firms encourage new employees to direct questions to their supervisors regarding ethics or business conduct policies in order to enhance understanding and build employees' commitment to their codes. It is important that competent advice is provided; so an appropriate individual should field or screen questions and dilemmas. 'New employees', remarks an insurance firm's corporate secretary, 'are provided with a copy of the ethics policy and are encouraged to discuss any questions about the policy with their managers'. In the process of code interpretation, resolving dilemmas, or answering questions, that secretary is 'the traffic cop – in assuring that the proper person answers the employee's concerns'.

British firms report that the attitude, preparation, or training of the supervisor or line manager in responding constructively to employee concerns is as important as the structured procedure itself. Managers who are open and motivated to solve problems nurture an environment of trust and comity – one in which employees' concerns are addressed sincerely and effectively.

Employees also turn to the human resource departments within their firms for resolution of their concerns. A director of a pharmaceutical company affirms such a use of a personnel department: 'An employee has three sources by which to resolve a question: his supervisor, the human resources division representative, and the corporate general-counsel – when the employee feels uncomfortable discussing the matter with his supervisor, he usually seeks resolution with a human resources representative.' Similarly, 'Our personnel organization, the law department, and line managers responsible for our business are available to any Digital Equipment employee with an ethics or business conduct question', explains a DEC corporate relations officer. Another firm's legal counsel describes his firm's tri-functional process of question answering or interpretation: 'Simple questions and problems are normally handled by employee relations supervisors; more complicated problems are disposed of by the Employee Relations Staff; and I handle inquiries from all sources which are unresolved or unanswered at the other two levels'.

## THE OPEN DOOR POLICY FOR RESOLVING COMPLAINTS AND DILEMMAS

Many firms encourage employees to seek a resolution of their ethical or business conduct difficulties at successively higher levels of management. Such a process, often called the 'open door', allows any employee to offer criticisms or seek help or guidance from senior-level managers any time the need arises. Besides providing an effective resolution to business conduct issues and questions of ethics, an open door policy assures that a company is accountable to its employees. Firms with open door policies report a heightened awareness of ethical dilemmas and, by committing top executives' time and credibility to addressing them, a stronger resolve in seriously confronting questions of business conduct and ethics. Such open communication works only when it is free of reprisal to the communicator.

Whether standing alone or used in conjunction with a code of conduct or similar policy document, open door policies nurture a healthier, more ethical workplace.

Every organization needs to monitor its conduct in relation to its expressed ethical standards; toward this evaluation, employees are indispensable participants and their initiatives should be encouraged and protected. When an employee's concerns are accorded a fair hearing, moreover, there is less likelihood that he will resort to acts of corporate disobedience. Such open communication provides valuable feedback to top management and it empowers the workforce – both keys to success in the 1990s.

Open door procedures vary among companies. An electricity supplier, notes a senior auditor, provides a typical open door process: 'Any employee who needs interpretation of the code or to resolve a personally difficult situation regarding ethics or business conduct may resort to higher levels of management, if he is not satisfied with the results of discussion with his own supervisor'.

The Hewlett Packard procedure allows an employee to continue through successive management levels to resolve a dilemma until he is conversing with the chairman in his office. A sporting goods company, according to the managing director, encourages employees to proceed to the group's leadership or to surface a problem directly with the managing director.

IBM's open door policy is a flexible response system which is wholly integrated in the firm's culture. An IBM employee may select a supervisor, a manager, or an executive to consult, or he may leapfrog every level to the chairman. IBM's goal is to make certain that every employee's question is answered fully or his dilemma resolved – and the process continues until a resolution is reached. Similarly, a pharmaceutical company offers an array of resources for resolving questions, including: direct line management, legal counsel, employee relations assistance, and a problem solving process that allows that employee access to any manager, up to, and including, the chairman. McDonald's Restaurants combines an open door procedure with an ethics officer, ethics committee, and frequent discussion sessions about ethics.

Furthermore, an insurance brokerage company, notes a top executive, 'encourages employees to discuss ethical or business conduct questions with their immediate supervisor . . . [and a]t the same time it provides an alternate channel to our Legal or Human Resources Department on a confidential basis.'

Employee access to higher levels of management and a firm's by-pass system also allow employees to inform top management about suspected misconduct by supervisors, if those employees don't feel comfortable speaking with immediate supervisors.

# Chapter 9

# Using ethics officers, ombudsmen, and hotlines to assure consistency and confidentiality, and to make whistle blowing unnecessary

It is important that one person, or no more than a few who communicate frequently with employees concerning business conduct and ethical issues, provide code or policy document interpretation. Otherwise, there is a lack of consistency in the explanations to employees – a certain way to sentence the code to low credibility. One firm's corporate secretary has established a two-tier system: 'Although interpretation is my ultimate responsibility, our supervisors provide the first line of interpretation.' That corporate secretary's function is to assure consistency. Other British firms have designated legal counsellors and personnel officers as primary sources of consistent interpretation and practical advice.

Mindful of seeking dependable and uniform application of code policies, some firms have created committees or ombudsmen whom employees can call upon to resolve questions or report improper practices. At Unisys, an ombudsman functions as part of the law department, which advises the corporation on ethics matters; the ombudsman administers the company's hotline through which employees can maintain anonymity. An ombudsman acts as an independent channel for receiving and investigating employee concerns that cannot be readily resolved through normal processes.

Moreover, Unisys employees may use the ethics hotline to report confidentially and anonymously any possible violations of law or the code of conduct, as well as to seek advice. Further, employees may transmit information through the hotline by 'toll-free telephone, a specially designated post office box, and in person', according to information provided by Henry Ruth, Counsel to the Unisys Ethics Committee. The Unisys Ethics Committee, membership of which includes two executive vice presidents, the chief legal officer, and the general auditor, oversees all aspects of the ethics programme including interpretations of the code. Some British companies assure anonymity by raising employee concerns in newsletters, and through chaplains and stress counsellors who provide confidential advice.

A specifically constituted ethics or business conduct committee which is the final authority for responding to questions about ethics and for ensuring compliance with the firm's code offers several advantages: the committee, with its high profile, signals to the entire company that the code is very important; it can decide issues which are too controversial or major for top management to comfortably decide alone; it provides the chairman or managing director with a separate forum for discussion of ethical or business conduct issues; it can be a moral support for those who seek advice or report ethical concerns; it provides a fresh perspective, objectivity, and fairness, especially if some of its members are outsiders, and it reports directly to the board, thereby insulating itself from undue management coercion. In short, it advantageously appears as the 'Sword of Damocles' ready to arbitrate at short notice and used by management to promote adherence to the code or policy document.[1]

However, reliance on designated individuals, as in foregoing examples, does not absolve all members of the organization of a modicum of support for consistent application of code principles. Companies should emphasize that everyone in the company, not just the ombudsman or committee, has a responsibility to support and police proper business conduct and good ethical practices.

A British chemical company, as Unisys, has established a committee to provide a rapid-response mechanism for employee inquiries. That committee provides in-house interpretation of code policies, and advice to employees who, although encouraged to employ normal management channels, have the right of direct access to the committee. Another firm, engaged in production of paper products, has established a business conduct committee deliberately composed of members diversified in terms of experience, age, sex, race, and job function. That committee provides members' names, phone numbers, and short biographical profiles to employees.[2]

Another manufacturer has constituted an ethics committee appointed by the board of directors, which has established a subordinate business ethics review board to provide clarification and guidance to employees regarding business conduct and ethical issues in the application of the company's code. Employees may elect to circumvent normal management avenues to pose their questions directly to the review board.[3]

United Technologies and its British arm, asserts a top executive, has utilized a range of mechanisms which assure consistent and confidential resolutions of dilemmas: 'Employees are encouraged to pursue ethics or compliance questions through (a) their supervisors; (b) a confidential written communication system called "Dialog"; (c) a confidential "Hot Line" directly to the Corporate Ombudsman; and (d) contact with the unit and/or Corporate Compliance Officer'.

United Technologies' Dialog is a confidential communication process by which any employee may submit a comment, complaint, or question, and receive a reply letter prepared by the person most qualified to respond. The subject matter of Dialog is limited to an employee's concerns about practices which interfere with his job performance or suspected infringements of United Technologies' published policies. Upon receiving a letter of request or comment from the employee, the Dialog administrator sends the letter, after removing the employee's detachable name label, to the appropriate officer at the highest authority level who can effectively respond to the letter's contents. Often the respondent is a director, chief executive officer, or other top executive; the respondent must reply to the employee within ten working days.

Similarly, a manufacturer of automotive equipment maintains a toll-free hotline enabling employees to report anonymously any actual or suspected violation of the firm's code, seek advice in resolving dilemmas, or call upon others for code interpretations. Another company, moreover, has established hotlines in the groups, as well as the corporate headquarters, which employees may use confidentially, according to that company's chairman of the compliance board. In the case of an aeronautics company, employees abused the hotline by reporting matters that were not related to code violations, such as personnel disputes and union relations issues. That company solved the problem by instituting a separate hotline for reporting personnel and similar disputes – and educating employees to use the ethics hotline for code and ethics violations and questions.

Many firms refer employees to the audit department or central compliance department for advice. 'Any employee having an ethics or business conduct question has available the resources of the internal auditor, corporate counsel and corporate secretary', emphasizes the corporate secretary of a banking firm. Various combinations of resources are in place in other firms as exemplified by remarks by a manufacturing firm's general auditor: 'All employees are provided access to Auditing, Legal, and Human Resources Departments to answer any question regarding business conduct'. At 3M, employees may contact the auditing, corporate security, human resources, or legal departments depending on the subject for assistance in interpreting or applying business conduct and ethics policies.

Legal departments assume major roles in a number of British companies. For instance, in many companies an employee may seek advice from the company's legal counsellor when a line manager cannot adequately interpret the code of conduct or ethics to the employee's satisfaction. In another British firm, the legal staff has responsibility for educating employees regarding the code of conduct – and offering advice to employees who report misconduct or seek resolution of ethical or business conduct dilemmas. A consumer products company has placed legal counsellors in each group so that employees have a local source for consistent and fast resolution of questions and dilemmas. According to a legal counsellor of a soft drink manufacturer, all company employees are encouraged to seek advice from the general counsel for resolution of any matter involving the code, to seek approval of any future action causing uncertainty, and to alert the general counsel of any suspected wrongdoing.

Many firms, as the foregoing examples demonstrate, stress anonymity in resolving business conduct and ethical questions and dilemmas. Assuring anonymity encourages many employees, who would otherwise remain silent for fear of dismissal, to reveal their concerns. Top management can use such information as an early warning of improprieties, as well as a gauge of what employees are thinking. For example, the John Lewis Partnership has established a system in which thirty-two registrars provide confidential advice to employees, as well as a two-way information bridge between managers and employees. Registrars, accountable directly to the John Lewis chairman and securely independent of other managers, publish company newspapers in which employees raise issues of concern, and operate hotlines between visits to various company branches. Employees may visit registrars away from the formers' worksites. If an employee is dissatisfied with the written or published response, usually from a director or the chairman, he may seek redress through the company's independent ombudsman.

## EIGHT ELEMENTS OF CONSISTENTLY EFFECTIVE RESOLUTION PROGRAMMES

In summary, the most effective approach to responding to employee complaints, concerns, and questions comprises the following elements:

1 Establishing procedures which allow complaints, concerns, and questions to be manifested.
2 Preserving the anonymity of the inquiring employee.
3 Involving top management in the process.
4 Responding in a fast, thorough, and positive manner.
5 Allowing an appeal to higher or, in severe cases, to an outside authority.
6 Nurturing an open, trusting, and non-punitive environment for discussion.
7 Signalling by word and deed that assuring proper business conduct and ethics pervades all operations of the company.
8 Using feedback mechanisms to gauge the effectiveness of responses to employees' concerns.

No matter what procedures companies establish by which employees can receive advice or report questionable activities, it is essential that the business firm reinforces to all employees that those channels exist. 'Creating a climate that is supportive of employees' questioning proposed actions on ethical grounds is, I believe, the best guarantee a company can have against unethical behavior', asserts a former Control Data general legal counsel and top executive. When an issue is raised and discussed, it is unlikely that anyone in an organization committed to high standards of conduct will act foolishly. Towards this end a company must provide established channels of reporting, interpretation, and expression of concerns.

## WHISTLE BLOWING: STEPS TO MAKE IT UNNECESSARY

Historically, if an employee disagreed with his employer, the matter was either resolved quietly or the employee resigned. Some commentators have emphasized an employee's duty of undivided loyalty to his firm, reflected in the statement: 'We should want one sentiment to be dominant in all employees from top to bottom – namely a complete loyalty to the organizational purpose'. Yet, another sentiment respects an employee's freedom of expression: 'A system . . . that allowed private bureaucracies to throttle all internal discussion of their affairs would be seriously deficient'.

Most whistle blowing occurs because the business firm doesn't respond to an employee's complaint. For example, in 1986 a deputy constable's complaints to Scotland Yard's anti-corruption agency concerning the falsifying of certain clear-up statistics in the Kent Constabulary were disregarded until an article appeared in the *Daily Mail*. The typical whistle blower, often an 'ethical resister', is a dedicated, valuable member of the business organization. When companies fail to heed employees' criticism or expressions of conscience they often forfeit early warnings about product safety and quality, workplace health and safety, and illegal or unethical activities taking place in the company.

Employees' speaking out about matters of conscience is becoming commonplace. A company can take a number of positive steps to deal with complaints or statements that something is 'wrong' and, hence, avoid the damaging fallout, such as escalation into unwanted publicity and ignoring a chance to mend a problem, as follows:

1  A company should emphasize in its code and policy statements that every employee has a right to express his views.
2  Establishing an effective grievance procedure, such as an 'open door' policy and other speedy processes, demonstrates respect for employees and diffuses hostility.
3  A company should communicate and practise tolerance of dissent, and promote fundamental respect for the individual conscience. In this process, a company should heed, not ignore, the advice, criticisms, and individual consciences of its employees.
4  A company should nurture work environments which are ethical and value-laden, and encourage open communication.

The following chapter discusses effective education and training programmes regarding codes of conduct and similar policy documents.

# Chapter 10

# Education and training to improve understanding of the code of conduct

Following the code's creation, its successful implementation depends upon the firm's developing a congruence between that document's standards and the actual conduct of the employees of the firm. Codes of conduct or ethics (and value statements, too) require an intrinsic accountability. This responsibility can be reasonably assured when the firm thoroughly educates its managers and employees about the code's contents, and establishes an effective and fair enforcement mechanism to assure desired congruent behaviour. Such education programmes, affirms J. Bibby & Sons Corporate Finance Director A. S. Gresty, 'underscore the commitment of the company to its ethical principles'.

Codes which are neither explained to employees, nor enforced, suggest a mere window-dressing document. In fact, education and training about the meaning and application of the code develop a common language with respect to proper conduct and ethics for all employees in the firm. This common language can well fill the void, some commentators suggest, occasioned by the dearth of ethics and values training in schools, churches, and families. Many firms address the insufficiency of training through internal education programmes. The ICL statement of beliefs, 'Ten obligations of the ICL Manager', has been so intensively inculcated in the managers through training programmes that, according to Steve Williams, Director of Human Resources Development, it has 'genuinely become part of the way we do things around here'.

The imperative to educate is real, for without a common basis for understanding a code of conduct, compliance is nearly impossible. Certainly, the mere presence of a finished code or similar policy document is not sufficient, without an understanding of its contents, to ensure integrity and morality in business activities. After all, it is individuals within a company who determine, by their conduct and attitudes, whether that firm will meet or, indeed, compromise, the code's standards. In this regard, educating managers and employees in how to behave when faced with business conduct or ethical issues, as well as about the meaning of the words which comprise those company documents, becomes a critical need. In the words of Lord Forte, Chairman of Trusthouse Forte, 'Our people are integrated into the system from the top. Each senior executive has absorbed and applied the company's [written] philosophy and methods. They in turn educate the people below them so it goes right down the line.'

One way to improve the likelihood of compliance is for every company, as RTZ, to develop an ethics and proper business conduct educational and training programme as an integral part of new employee or management training. Cadbury Schweppes, for instance, uses its 'Character of the Company' in existing training development programmes. Wagon Finance, notes Chairman and Chief Executive D. B. Jones, 'developed an educational programme concerning proper business conduct as part of new employee and management training'.

Among other benefits, top managers regard the training of employees with respect to business conduct issues essential to success in dealing with real-life issues. One study of codes of conduct determined that most of the codes examined are ambiguous with respect to which audience they purportedly address, which, accordingly, encourages far too much variation in the interpretation of the codes.[1]

One method to reduce ambiguity in codes is to use training and education programmes to teach employees how to interpret codes for the firm's ethical benefit. Many firms go directly to the employees with such programmes; for instance, one company has conducted training programmes in over 800 locations. One top-level executive of an aeronautics company fully understands this challenge: 'A person's religion asks him to attend church every Sunday; ethics instruction has a "half-life" of one week – it is a perishable commodity – so we require bi-annual training; as a result, we trained 67,000 employees in ethics and proper business conduct last year'.

Firms which continually reinforce code and similar policy documents contents in employees are more successful in integrating desired conduct in their business operations. In any environment in which substantial pressures exist in the form of threats of lawsuits or government regulation, such frequent education generates substantial benefits.

## KEY ELEMENTS OF A SUCCESSFUL PROGRAMME

Successful training and educational programmes share common elements: a basic awareness programme which includes current materials, especially case studies; a curriculum dealing with business conduct and ethics; involving employees in discussions of actual problems experienced by them in the past; and the company's commitment to a comprehensive and continuing programme to create an ethical environment in the company. Texaco Ltd, relates Chairman Peter Bijur, utilized 'educational programmes that include interactive discussion formats, such as round table discussions after a presentation'.

The specific objectives of any training and educational process should include at least the following:[2]

1 Enabling managers and employees to recognize the ethical elements of a

business decision, and that many decisions at the managerial level, especially, involve such elements.

2 Providing them with means to address those, and any emerging, ethical issues.
3 Helping them understand that ethical situations are often ambiguous, not obvious.
4 Inculcating in them the reality that the courses of action they choose actually mould the firm's ethical environment.

Those conducting programmes should emphasize that some business conduct and ethical situations are not easily resolved. One difficulty in resolution occurs because those involved in an ethical dilemma leading to misconduct rationalize their unethical or improper behaviour by holding one or more of the following:[3]

1 A view that stretching the limits of legal and ethical boundaries reinforces the impression that the action in question is not really illegal or unethical.
2 A belief that an improper act is 'safe' because it will never be discovered.
3 A view that, if the improper action is in the best interest of the company, the individual is expected to engage in that activity.
4 A belief that, if the improper act benefits the company, the firm will protect the person who carries out that action.

Moreover, the firm should administer the education programme consistently to all managers and employees, and the chairman and managing director should make their commitments to the code clear and unquestionable. Town & Country Building Society's Managing Director Ian Bell relates that the company's 'Corporate objectives' were presented in a detailed manner 'at a series of road-shows throughout the UK by the Managing Director; all members of staff attended'. A then-chairman of a large industrial firm vigorously circulated this message: 'it is a primary responsibility of a business's management to instruct, motivate, and inspire employees to conduct themselves with honesty, probity, and fairness'.[4]

Another company requires attendance at biannual training sessions of every-one in the firm: the chairman and top executives attend five hours per year, a director attends four hours, and managers and hourly employees receive three and one hours of annual instruction, respectively. Similarly, a banking concern, relates its general legal counsel, 'emphasizes the importance of its code of conduct by directing the Human Resources Department to confer with every newly hired employee about the code and the company's expectations of that employee regarding the code'.

Other firms integrate the ongoing education in a personnel system in which knowledge of the code's or similar policy document's provisions is a required condition of employment; the code's contents and procedures are taught during orientation or subsequent management and personnel training. For example, every employee of Trusthouse Forte, upon his joining the company, is specifically directed to the 'Philosophy'.

Often, an understanding of the code is a requisite part of any employee-hiring or post-employment evaluation process. The Cadbury Schweppes 'Character of the Company' is employed in selection and recruitment of employees; thereby, at the earliest contact, the company affirms the importance of the document, notes Group Human Resources Director Geoffrey Dale.

Other effective training and educational measures include: assigning a personnel manager or staff librarian responsibility for maintaining an awareness of current books and articles on management conduct and ethics; securing such publications as company resources; circulating video tapes which discuss resolution of vignettes of ethical dilemmas; printing in the company newsletter or internal documents discussions of the code sections and their application to real-life situations; reprinting the company's standards of conduct in trade magazines; promoting professional and trade associations; recognition of proper and ethical leadership; and establishing a process by which employees can receive interpretation of the code.

## TWO TRAINING APPROACHES: 'TRICKLE DOWN' AND 'OUTSIDE–IN'

The most effective training sessions are those which are brief (two to four hours) and interactive – the group size should enhance every employee's opportunity to discuss his experiences concerning business conduct and ethical dilemmas. Remploy Chief Executive Tony Withey concurs that such interactions 'broaden and deepen employee awareness of our company's "Strategy Summary" directives'. Further, some firms believe that highly polished facilitation emphasizes the gravity of the subject matter.

Two training approaches are particularly effective: a system which appoints supervisors or managers as those responsible for the education of subordinates, as the 'trickle down' approach of Motorola; and the other, the 'outside–in' approach, which employs outside trainers or those trained by external consultants to direct the educational meetings.

Principal advantages of using a firm's own managers and supervisors, the 'trickle down' process, are those trainers' increased commitment to the success of the code and their existing credibility with employees. National Provident Institution's approach includes senior managers' meeting with groups of eight to ten employees. Such direct, highly individual contact is the norm at Tesco, as well.

The firm's providing training and support materials to these managers relieves their anxiety and demonstrates the firm's support of the code and of the managers who will be the first line (after the employee, himself, who has a responsibility to read the code) of educational trainers in the firm. Similarly, Hewlett Packard requires its general managers to become familiar with the 'Standards of Business Conduct' and be responsible for inculcating these standards in their subordinate employees. The HP managers have wide latitude to develop personalized programmes to educate their subordinates.

In a further variation, a banking concern conducted special meetings and training sessions for line managers and supervisors to prepare them to introduce and explain the code to employees in their respective departments and operations areas. As a result, every employee received a face-to-face briefing from his superior. Likewise, Colgate Palmolive designated line managers and department heads to discuss the company's code with employees and to solicit their comments. The human resources department prepared a comprehensive set of guidelines to assist managers and department heads in their discussions. Further, a large engineering company introduced its code at a two-day meeting of sixty top managers. Workshop sessions included smaller groups of these managers who discussed specific implications of the code principles in their functional or operational areas of responsibility. The sixty managers returned to their groups and educated their own employees regarding the code's meaning and implementation.

An effective 'trickle down' educational programme in use in one company assigns various responsibilities for training employees, agents, and consultants under his direction to each supervisor. Responsibilities include:

1 Ensuring that all employees participate in training and education regarding the firm's code.
2 Continually stressing to all employees in a direct, personal manner that their commitment to code principles is required.
3 Ensuring that the supervisor's department or group conducts all of its operations in accord with high standards of business ethics.
4 Maintaining an environment which encourages open, honest communication concerning the principles of the code, and assisting in the resolution of employee concerns related to the code or to business ethics in general.

The major advantage of the 'outside–in' approach is the assurance that the presentations at the educational sessions will be well rehearsed and professional, and the avoidance of any impression that 'more ethically perfect' managers and supervisors will sermonize to others regarding how to conduct their affairs ethically. Further, by the firm's carefully defining the scope of the training, and by familiarizing those outside trainers with the employees' work situations, the company can assist the trainers in effectively dealing with the employees' concerns in an operational context.[5]

A growing number of companies provide training sessions for employees to discuss the code's application to real-life situations. When standards are taught in a manner which integrates them with operations, the educational process is more pragmatic, and, hence, worthwhile. IBM has introduced specific sections in management development programmes which emphasize proper and ethical business conduct issues. Many companies, such as IBM, share a commitment to reinforce their codes' and similar policy statements' applications to company operations by whatever training and educational mechanisms are effective.

## DISCUSSION AND INSTRUCTION FORMATS

Furthermore, companies have concluded that training and education programmes which include discussion formats 'sensitize employees to ethical issues, broaden and deepen employee awareness of code directives, and underscore the commitment of the company to its ethical principles'.[6]

While many company programmes are limited to a thorough discussion of the code standards and principles, the more effective ones require the solving of hypothetical problems which have meaning to the participants. One example of such a workshop includes a five-hour programme with a brief introduction followed by a discussion of a hypothetical business conduct dilemma, together with a round table exchange of views about ethical or business conduct situations which the participants have encountered. Then, the session agenda proceeds to a discussion of a hypothetical case with a theme of individual and organizational responsibility to reach goals, and the attendant pressures involved. In the last session, the participants separate into groups to discuss business conduct and ethical issues which arise in connection with the firm's constituent groups, such as society, government, shareholders, employees, and customers.[7]

Texaco Ltd took such an approach, notes Chairman Peter Bijur: 'The communication of the Texaco "Vision and Values in the United Kingdom" included a series of training sessions during which all employees were given the opportunity of reviewing, debating, and considering the implication of the document as it affected their individual assignments'.

The successful use of cases and discussions is characterized by the following elements:[8] first, the hypothetical dilemmas discussed are those which confront mid-level managers, not merely managing directors or senior management; second, the case studies provide personal and career information about the characters in the hypothetical vignettes; third, participants receive detailed background information to appreciate more fully the context in which the hypothetical events occur; and, fourth, the participants' resolution of these hypothetical dilemmas requires the reconciliation of personal values with the firm's commitments to proper business conduct.

Further, the nature of the instructional techniques is important. Components of successful teaching include:[9]

1 The use of Socratic questioning in order to encourage the expression of views, and to focus on participants' processes of reasoning.
2 Employing a discussion process which avoids the appearance of the code as merely a set of rules dictated to employees by management, but which, instead, cultivates open, frank discussions.
3 Stressing that the programme is intended to help employees deal with ambiguous situations, and is not a result of the company's viewing its employees as unethical.
4 Drawing upon participants' real-life ethical dilemmas and forging resolutions to them.

5  Focusing on values and their application to ethical dilemmas.
6  Soliciting a variety of viewpoints.
7  Presenting a range of cases requiring easy, as well as difficult, choices.

The general context of the educational meeting should be: 'This code (or similar policy document) reflects our commitment to high standards of integrity throughout the company, and we seek your assistance in making the code as effective and useful as possible'. Moreover, the educational programme should serve as a method of integration and socialization for new employees. In these ways, firms effectively develop employees' acute awareness of ethical and proper business conduct, and emphasize those issues which are likely to occur in the individual firm's context of operation.

## ADVANTAGES OF CODE TRAINING AND EDUCATION

The training and education of employees with regard to codes of conduct and similar policy documents have several distinct advantages. First, rather than enacting a code and merely creating strict procedure to assure compliance, education is a persuasive, affirmative tool which convinces employees of the need for the code and the benefits it will bring to the firm if successfully implemented. Second, rather than merely providing information, education focuses on the critical problems and offers suggestions for reasonable responses to business conduct or ethical quandaries. Finally, the most significant benefit of education is that it raises the overall level of employee consciousness regarding ethics and proper business conduct.[10]

## DISCUSSION OF CODE VALUES AND PRINCIPLES

As noted, open and frank discussion of the meaning of code and values statement principles is important in training and educating managers and employees. Some commonly used principles and their interpretations include:

*Table 10.1*

| Principles, values, and beliefs | Possible areas of policies affected |
| --- | --- |
| 1  'We are committed to our customers'. | Providing value through high-quality products and services |
| | Efficient, courteous service and on-time delivery of products and services |
| | Listening to the needs of customers |
| | Fair pricing policies |
| 2  'We believe in the fundamental dignity of each individual'. | Respecting complaints and comments of employees, including dissidents |

|   |   | Providing assistance to employees suffering from alcohol or drug abuse |
|---|---|---|
|   |   | Maintaining safe and healthy working conditions |
|   |   | Affirmative action programmes for hiring |
|   |   | Using performance and contribution to the firm's progress as primary tools of evaluation |
| 3 | 'We believe in our responsibility to society'. | Responsible corporate citizenship through ethical conduct in every aspect of business |
|   |   | Programmes for charitable giving |
|   |   | Environmental protection policies |
|   |   | Allowing time for volunteer activities |
|   |   | Operating at a profit to provide stability to communities |
|   |   | Avoiding business which might be attained only by resort to questionable practices |
|   |   | Recruitment of persons of high moral character |
| 4 | 'We are committed to our suppliers'. | Emphasizing fair competition, responsibility and long-lasting relationships |
| 5 | 'We strive for excellence'. | Investment in state-of-the-art technology |
|   |   | Providing only high-quality services and products |
|   |   | Use of a merit system for promotions and salary increases |
| 6 | 'We are committed to our shareholders'. | Pursuit of growth and earnings targets |
|   |   | Increasing earnings per share |
|   |   | Exercising prudence in use of assets and resources |
|   |   | Conducting business in an ethical manner |
|   |   | Fair dividend policies |
| 7 | 'We believe in endless renewal'. | Providing training and education for the work force |
|   |   | Acquiring business in growth sectors and divesting declining operations |
|   |   | Revising code policies |
| 8 | 'We believe in responsible management.' | Listening responsibly to employee suggestions to make work more productive and meaningful |

Managers' having direct responsibility for the training and well-being of employees

Every manager's being aware of what is happening at his immediate level and several levels below

Maintaining effective communication at all levels to assist decision making

Respecting shareholders' proxy resolutions

Striving to maximize every employee's ability to work to his potential

Supporting managers and employees who use personal initiatives, within the parameters of the company's policies, to improve profits and quality

Considering implications of divestiture and redundancy for every affected employee

## PERSONNEL EVALUATION AND TOP MANAGEMENT SUPPORT

Without changes in incentive systems favourable to proper business conduct, training and educational programmes are not as effective as they could be. The ethical commitment of the firm is more pronounced to the same degree that it is integrated in the entire strategy and culture of the business. The AMEC 'Group Strategy Statement' is discussed in meetings as a 'framework for planning on company and sector levels', advises Georgina Lloyd Drummond, Head of Strategy. Moreover, Hewlett Packard's value system is 'strong because it is a part of every performance evaluation system, training programme, customer policy, employee relations policy, and virtually every person-to-person interaction which takes place within the company and between an HP employee and an outsider'.[11]

Furthermore, adherence to ICL's 'Ten Obligations of the ICL Manager', a statement of the company's attitudes and beliefs comprised an important element of a manager's annual appraisal for the three years after its development. ICL management believes that utilizing compliance as a standard was an effective way to secure the attention and loyalty of those the policy statement addressed. Moreover, a banking firm's 'education of employees concerning the code extends to the performance review, as well as new employee orientation and required workshop modules, where actual case examples were discussed', relates a top executive. Such interweaving and integration (training and education programmes, and every employee's reaffirmation of his adherence to code standards at his performance review) transmits a powerful incentive to conform to proper conduct and ethics.

Commitment by top management boosts employee adherence to codes of conduct and fosters a culture of integrity, candour, and ethical practice that most employees wholeheartedly endorse.[12] With the support of top management, ethics programmes avoid sinking into obscurity soon after commencement. At one company, for example, the chairman and president appeared in shirtsleeves at a conference, attended by fifty top-level marketing managers, and, after discussing the contents and importance of the code, expressed their support for education concerning the code. Video tapes of the meeting were distributed to legal counsellors in the various company groups for their training, and the education of subordinate managers and employees.

Every company should choose a means of effectively delivering the message that the code of conduct is a serious matter and has the active support of top executives, especially the chairman and the managing director. These executives establish the tone and drive that message all the way down the management line.

## MULTI-DIMENSIONAL APPROACHES TO CODE TRAINING AND EDUCATION IN SIX COMPANIES

Many companies employ a multi-dimensional approach to code training and education. For instance, Marks and Spencer Financial Services developed a business conduct educational programme as part of new employee training. That firm, relates Personnel Controller Margaret Hargreaves, also displayed its policy statement (of principles and mission) prominently on all departmental notice boards.

Unisys, according to information provided by Special Counsel Henry Ruth, to ensure its employees are familiar with its code of conduct, instituted a broad business conduct and ethics training programme in late 1987 under the super-vision of a full-time training director. The programme contains three elements:

1  25,000 employees participate in annual general-training sessions in which they review frequently occurring business conduct and ethical problems. The training comprises video programmes which include an admonition from the Unisys chairman, and senior management responses to vignettes of common business conduct and ethical problems.
2  10,000 employees involved in marketing, contracts, finance, procurement, quality assurance, engineering, and manufacturing receive in-depth training in their functional areas provided by in-house specialists in two-hour modules.
3  Managers involved in certain contracting activities attend special workshops.

One key to successful implementation of a code, as demonstrated by Unisys, is discussing the code with, and gaining the support of, line managers and other employees in operating areas. Without the active understanding and support of personnel in operations areas, the code implementation will likely fail. It is instructive to review the distinctive, multiple-approach code training and edu-cation systems in four other companies.

The head of human resources of a pharmaceutical products company des-cribed that firm's multi-faceted educational approach: 'The company conducts an orientation programme to educate new employees, an in-house video system to educate employees concerning code matters, lunch sessions where managers discuss code contents with employees, and an annual organization survey to measure the employees' comprehension of the major commitments required by our code'. In addition, almost every company publication periodically contains references to the code and to everyone's commitment to abiding by its contents.

Another multi-dimensional approach is exemplified by Motorola, which assigns its managers to educate its employees, notes the company's general legal counsel. The Motorola code of conduct is distributed to managers and supervisors with the imperative that they further educate each of their subordinates. Presentations are made to employees about the code of conduct at annual conferences of the divisions, groups, and sectors, or in connection with other, regular educational and training sessions. Also, video tapes made by the chairman and president, stressing compliance with the code, are required viewing. Motorola in-house publications regularly exhibit discussions of the code and relevant issues. Motorola law department and audit department members frequently speak about the code at meetings of company organizations and clubs.

A company engaged in supplying electricity also introduced its code using a multi-dimensional approach, which included a brochure, a training programme for managers, a video tape of the chairman's unequivocal support of the code, and a taped series of vignettes which dramatized business conduct and ethical issues. Thereafter, each company employee was invited to attend a meeting in which the video tape was viewed, the brochure distributed, and questions and comments answered. If any employee refrained from voluntarily signing a pledge to abide by the company's code, the company informed that recalcitrant employee that a memorandum would be placed in his personnel file indicating that the employee had received the material and an explanation of the code at the meeting, and that his declining to sign the pledge of commitment in no way relieved him of any responsibility to abide by the code's policies.

McDonnell Douglas[13] has also bundled numerous techniques for training and educating its employees. The company has designated all-day workshops for salaried employees. To realize the full educational potential of the workshops, the firm devised a video tape and workbook for participants. McDonnell Douglas moulded the topics and subject matter from a variety of sources, including several top managers, business conduct and ethics professors, and a review of current business conduct and ethics literature. The firm has extended its ethics and business conduct programme to all of its hourly workers as well, thereby increasing the number of employees exposed to the firm's code standards.

The benefits of McDonnell Douglas' programme were obvious soon after the training sessions began. Ethics and proper business conduct became an appropriate topic of conversation for the firm's employees. Furthermore, the strong endorsement of the firm's code by the chief executive officer in the seminar's video tape signalled to employees that top management remains committed to ethical and proper business conduct.

Following the training sessions, McDonnell Douglas employees identified a number of business conduct problems that otherwise would have remained undetected by top management. Employees' exposing ethical difficulties assisted the firm's top management by avoiding, or reducing, the firm's ethical conflicts.

## 'EVERYBODY DOES IT', AND OTHER RATIONALIZATIONS FOR UNETHICAL CONDUCT

A typical training session might begin with these comments, and proceed to a full exposition of the most common rationalizations for unethical conduct, and the questions every manager and employee should ask in an ambiguous situation.

'Guiness, Nat West, Aish and Company. Yeah, yeah, yeah'. A refrain from a new Elton John song?

'Oh, no'.

These terms and names conjure up British scandals involving bad ethics and, in some cases, law breaking. Clearly, someone's ethics light bulb did not illuminate values that could have prevented the improper conduct. While laws are often the lowest common denominators as guidelines for action, it is good ethical practice that provides the glue that holds society together.

Yet there are some who cynically justify or excuse any behaviour – they take a view that any person's or group's ethics are as good as another's. Of course, this value-neutral approach, in which good ethics are simply a matter of opinion, unwittingly supports the notion that the ethics of gangsters are as good as any other group's. After all, street gangs comprise a set of persons and should be able to establish their own ethical code – no matter how repugnant or harmful to law-abiding citizens.

What these value-neutral and 'tolerant' observers have obviously missed is a good history lesson: that there are indeed universal and timeless values fundamental to the ethical life.

Among these core values, as listed by a prominent ethics institute, are: integrity, honesty, promise-keeping, caring for others, fairness, responsible citizenship, fidelity, personal accountability, and pursuit of excellence. There are others, but these core values construct in most people, including managers and employees, the principles that provide an accurate guide to 'right' and 'wrong', or 'good' and 'bad' behaviour.

In fact, despite the business-bashing mind-set of many, public-opinion surveys and other research indicate that business executives actually apply higher standards when addressing ethical issues than do average citizens.

Why then do 'good' managers and employees make bad ethical decisions? It is apparent that four unfortunate rationalizations lead to much of the illegal and unethical conduct in organizations.

1  'I want to take this action so it can't "really" be unethical or illegal'. Many actions people wish to take are inconsistent with their ethical values.

Expediency over-rides core values, such as honesty and integrity, as when elected officials defend deception or hide outside gifts, when journalists justify outrageous invasions of privacy under the muddy conceit of the 'public's right to know', or when managers allow unsafe or defective products to be marketed.

Common statements supporting this rationalization of unethical conduct include: 'Everybody does it', 'It's not my responsibility', or 'Outsiders just don't understand'.

2 'The action is in my or the company's self-interest'. The concept that selfishness is an absolute ethical principle springs from many of the self-actualizing philosophies of the 1960s and 1970s that are actually disguises for the self-preoccupation and narcissism evident today in British and American society. Consequently, since the action is in the person's or firm's interest, the individual is expected to take it.

3 'No one will ever know'. What people don't know may hurt them, but that it won't harm the wrongdoer is the faulty logic underlying this rationalization. By utilizing this rationalization, the person is wagering that the improper conduct will never be publicised.

4 'The organization will protect me'. Because the improper act may temporarily help the business firm's performance, the manager or employee believes the firm will ignore it and protect the wrongdoer.

Yet, managers and employees who rationalize their unethical or illegal behaviour are simply living every day under Damocles' sword. Wrongdoing costs society, business firms, and the wrongdoers plenty: hundreds of millions of pounds every year as a result of white-collar crime and misconduct; hundreds of millions of pounds annually to comply with government regulation; profound damage to a firm's public image, with resulting, often catastrophic, effects on profitability; and terminated managers and employees.

So when a manager or employee faces decisions involving ethical or human fallout (and many everyday decisions involve these issues), he or she might avoid the roof's caving-in by answering the following questions before taking any action:

1 Am I justifying an action I want to take by resorting to the foregoing four, or similar, rationalizations?

2 Have I gathered all facts and considered the problem from every affected party's viewpoint?

3 What are the critical assumptions and values of all parties, including me?

4 What is the best course for maximizing benefit and minimizing cost or detriment to those affected.

5 Whose rights would my decision protect or injure?

6 What course of action best reflects honesty, integrity, and consistency?

After deciding upon a course of action, consider one final question:

7 Will this decision be valid beyond the immediate time frame, and could I disclose this action without misgivings to my boss, the head of the organization, my family, and society?

If a person is not satisfied with the answers to these questions, he or she should rethink the proposed decision.

The next chapter addresses how a company can change its culture and overcome resistance to change.

# Changing the company's culture for the better and overcoming resistance to change

A business firm's employees at times do not resist change and, often, even actively accept or create modifications of their organizational behaviour to successfully implement needed change, including that created by introduction of a code conduct. At one company, the well-communicated fact that the chairman published the code at the direction of the board of directors squelched any budding resistance to the code. At Kingfisher, the introduction of the policy document was simply 'uncontroversial'.

Perhaps the reason that some codes and similar policy documents are readily accepted is because they are codifications of missions, principles, and values that already existed in the firm's culture. Prudential employees offered no resistance 'because the Code of Conduct and Mission Statement represented a confirmation of largely existing values'. Likewise, according to B. K. Elms, Shell International Head of Communications, 'The Shell Statement of General Business Principles built on established attitudes, and generally, perhaps not entirely, matched employees' expectations'. Resistance was not manifested to the Bank of England's Ethical Business Guidelines or W. H. Smith's Business Conduct Policies because the former has been part of the bank's culture for a long time and because the latter was a distillation of previous policy documents.

At another firm, resistance was eliminated as a result of enthusiastic and strong commitment by top managers because the firm actually incorporated in its code the way it had operated intuitively. ICL, notes Director of Human Resource Development Steve Williams, overcame resistance through 'continued reinforcement' of the code's importance 'by underlying programmes especially our "investing in people" programme'.

Not all codes of conduct or ethics, values statements or similar policy documents are implemented smoothly, however, for human nature suggests that many employees often do not welcome change. At Peugeot Talbot some cynicism initially was evident at all levels, while Legal & General employees initially interpreted their code as emphasizing 'us and them' ethical standards.

In their infusion of codes, firms necessarily wish to modify the organization's design and dynamics without adversely affecting the firm's operations and performance, or damaging employee morale. Certainly, as predicted by futurists, change is a phenomenon that will more frequently occur in business and society. In the context of introducing new or revised codes of conduct, managers are actually attempting to influence members of their organizations to think and behave differently – whether carrying out tasks or relating to others in new ways. By implementing codes, firms signal employees that change, specifically a new pattern of behavioural responses and activities, is desirable.

## PRINCIPLES OF SUCCESSFUL CHANGE

One noted commentator concerning business organizations has determined that successful change, that which achieves the desired results, actually: is spread throughout the organization, while including and affecting many people; influences employees to behave more effectively in relating to others, and in solving problems; promotes positive modifications of line, as well as staff, attitudes; and results in enhanced performance of the organization.[1]

Other observers have similarly characterized effectively-managed change as existing when: the organization moves from the current to a desired future state of existence; the organization in fact functions in the new state as expected; the transition is without undue cost to the organization; and the transition is without undue sacrifice to individual members of the organization.[2]

## COMMON OBSTACLES TO CHANGE

The introduction and implementation of a code of conduct or similar policy document commonly present problems which the firm's leadership must address. One such obstacle, resistance to change, occurs primarily because employees desire a stable, safe environment and, consequently, wish to maintain that current environment until convinced that the proposed change will enhance their organizational comfort. At Legal & General, introduction of the code initially upset the employees' need for stability, control, and autonomy in their work environment. Any firm, in successfully introducing a new code of conduct, should directly address such concerns. One firm overcame resistance by communicating that the code was the best means of protecting employees in questionable and undefined situations. Save & Prosper employees welcomed the firm's new policy statement because it represented a clear, easily accessible, unambiguous statement of guiding principles.

Moreover, implementation of a new code or policy statement often creates uncertainty concerning existing authority relationships. As a result, managers and employees may perceive that they have less power in performing their traditional tasks, or may be confused because the normal functioning of the organization is disrupted. Dixons temporarily experienced such interference with existing systems of management control as a result of code implementation. In this regard, although another firm's code enhanced the working environment of the firm, initial resistance to the code occurred where some definitions were overly broad (and, therefore, unduly stringent), and where initial reporting requirements were too burdensome.

Every company should be sensitive to the timing of the introduction of new code procedures as well. One cause of resistance to the 'ICL Way' was the fact that employees were under great pressure from a heavy workload and viewed the new charter as a severe burden. Dixons staff felt a distinct 'sensory overload' of additional directives from corporate headquarters, relates Group Personnel Director R. E. Andrews. Although management patience and commitment can overcome such sincere or cynical attitudes, valuable time is lost due to such constraints.

Uncertainty as a consequence of change creates ambiguity which has a proclivity to increase the activities of individuals or coalitions competing for power. At one firm, resistance manifested itself in the form of operating groups' conducting operations contrary to firm-wide codes, and generally obstructing established centralized policy.

The individuals' or coalitions' negative activity may result, as well, from belief that change is inconsistent with their shared values or their particular images of the firm.[3] For instance, some Legal & General employees objected to 'statements of the obvious', while a few ICL employees resented the 'ICL Way' as an implied criticism of the way they had previously conducted their business affairs. Although code implementation may threaten certain reservoirs of authority or power, the active participation by all managers and key employees in creating or implementing the code eventually reduces the gravity of the threat.

## AVOIDING COMMON ERRORS AND ACTION STEPS TO MOTIVATE CHANGE

Every firm's successful implementation of its code depends to a significant degree on achieving desired changes by effectively addressing the problems raised in prior examples. In the process of responding to these obstacles, the firm's managers necessarily should avoid certain common errors:

1 Insensitivity to the manner in which change impacts the psychological contract of the employees.
2 Failure to periodically diagnose the current psychological contract with various employee groups, with the result being the manager's not realizing what employees expect to offer or receive from the firm.
3 Failure to adequately communicate and explain the change to the firm's employees, which results in employees' conjuring inaccurate conclusions regarding how the change affects their psychological contract.[4]

By keeping the goals and elements of successful change clearly in mind, and by avoiding the common errors in effecting change, the firm's managers should take a number of steps to motivate change, manage the transition, and shape the political dynamics of change.[5] Action steps to motivate change include, first, identifying and surfacing dissatisfaction with the current state, and 'unfreezing' people from their present inertia so that they will be receptive to change. In the end 'people want to conduct themselves in a manner that doesn't require them to compulsively remember what they said or to have to provide consistent alibis for inconsistent prior statements or actions', asserts one corporate counsel in explaining why that firm's employees have not resisted the code's introduction and implementation.

At Severn Trent, patience and profound understanding of these human dynamics associated with change were invaluable: 'Care and time', notes Corporate Secretary C. G. McMillan, were the foundation of successful implementation.

In the context of the new or the revised code's implementation, top management can disseminate data concerning some aspects of the firm's performance which are contrary to what are expected or needed to spur an acceptance of change. One firm explained the necessity for a code by communicating to employees 'that the code's promulgation is a function of growth – that with the code we could govern better and be more successful'. Correspondingly, another firm indicated a critical need to have a code that would assist the company's expansion into a new business area. Further, an external event which slowed entering a new geographic market served as the 'catalyst' for a banking firm's commitment to successful implementation of its code. Beazer employees realized that a formal policy statement of its mission could be a valuable foundation for future success and, consequently, were highly receptive, notes D. J. Heathcote, Group Legal Adviser.

Second, the firm should actively solicit employee input and involvement in changes prompted by a code or similar policy document because participation in the change reduces resistance. Participation also builds vested interests in promulgating the change itself. Requesting employees to assist in creating or implementing the code through work sessions, monitoring employee values through questionnaires, and effective educational programmes which encourage all employees' active involvement are valuable mechanisms to encourage widespread commitment to change. Feedback is very important: executives who do not listen to employees' reactions risk partial or an unsuccessful code implementation. At Legal & General, management developed a feedback mechanism that provided the transition managers with measures of effectiveness of that transition.

The one primary lesson another firm learned 'is to involve more employees in the communication of our ethics initiative'. Typically, the more employees and departments are consulted in creating and establishing a code or policy document, the more successful its acceptance. Legal & General, Remploy, and Inland Revenue were particularly mindful of building employee support through their active participation.

Third, a firm can overcome resistance by providing rewards for that behaviour required to effectively implement a code policy document. For example, employees who exhibit a company's values can be selected for special recognition, such as being publicized in company newsletters or publications. At

Remploy, according to CEO Tony Withey, 'Top management lessened resistance to change by constructing rewards for the desired behaviour in accepting change'. A company can successfully encourage implementation by a number of means: particularly cooperative managers and employees and their contributions can be praised in company bulletins, rewarded with gifts, and presented with awards at company outings.

Further, if a firm wishes to reward acceptance of and adherence to the code, it is appropriate to punish conflicting behaviour. As one British company's managing director observed, 'Those who interfered with or resisted the code's implementation were terminated; as a result our people take it seriously'.

In addition, firms which incorporate an employee's acceptance of, and adherence to, the code in his annual performance review to determine promotion, job assignment, and salary increases will lower residual resistance to a code's implementation. For example, some firms require certain values, such as an individual's social responsibility, to be linked to performance evaluations. In one firm, relates a director, every employee submits to an annual performance review in which managers are expected to measure that individual's compliance with the company's code of conduct policies in their overall evaluation of his performance. Consequently, the individual's compensation is affected by how well that individual complies with code precepts.

Last, as noted in the British Telecom and Severn Trent experiences, employees need a reasonable time and an opportunity to disengage from the present state.[6] Communication of the importance of accepting the code, explanation of the code contents through education, and establishing means to secure interpretations and resolutions of their own questions about what effect the code will have on their tasks and business conduct are effective in disengaging employees from the pre-code implementation state. Similarly, notes M. A. B. Judge, Peugeot Talbot Director of Personnel and Industrial Relations, 'the firm developed a "consensus" which nurtured a modicum of respect for the Peugeot Charter and Procedure, which naturally reduced resistance'.

Following the motivation steps, the firm's top management can capably control the transition state,[7] first by developing and communicating a lucid image of the future (how acceptance and adherence to the code will enhance the firm's health and environment). For instance, David Packard, co-founder of Hewlett Packard, believes corporate executives should, in this regard, articulate a value-oriented vision of the firm's objectives.[8]

Second, the use of numerous and consistent leverage points, such as changes in social relations and structure, produce lasting effects. Education and training sessions, and the implementation of the varied and essential leverage points comprise an important second action step. The third step useful in managing the transition state includes organizational arrangements for the transition. Such arrangements need to be explicit and useful, and include appointing someone to manage the code's implementation, and assigning resources, such as personnel and financing, to assist the manager in the implementation of the code.

The final action step involves development of a feedback mechanism which provides the transition manager with measures of the effectiveness of the transition. A top executive at Texas Instruments concurs: 'An alternate [as a complement to any "Open Door" policy] feedback mechanism can send confidential or anonymous inputs right to the top of an organization, bypassing the filters that typically exist: our communication line feedback is an extremely valuable source of "grass roots" inputs and provides employees' thoughts, questions, concerns, doubts, and problems that we probably would not otherwise have'. These mechanisms can be numerous, redundant, and sensitive, like surveys, sensing groups, and other less formal channels of feedback.[9]

Another company, an electronic equipment manufacturer, in order to assess progress in its ethics and business conduct training, has utilized employee values surveys to measure attitude changes, interviews with selected persons to determine the progress in code implementation, and contacts with third parties, including customers, suppliers and others.[10]

## ORGANIZATIONAL POLITICS AND CODE ACCEPTANCE

There is also a political dimension in overcoming resistance to change, in this case resulting from the implementation of a new or revised code of conduct or similar policy document. Certainly, gaining and assuring the continued support of a company's key figures and power groups is a pre-requisite for managing change. By including such key individuals or groups as actors in the creation or implementation of the code, the firm's top leadership will either coopt or motivate them, and can eliminate 'lip service' and a high 'snigger' index. For example, although Union Carbide had developed one corporate code which encompasses directives concerning ethical conduct, mission, and values, it allows certain groups to promulgate complementary statements to address issues of relevance to each group.

Likewise, at Dixons, Chairman Stanley Kalms issued a directive that each department or functional unit should draft its own unique code of conduct, and submit it to the group personnel director whose task is to ensure consistent format, style, and publication. Toward this end, top leader behaviour generates organizational energy to support the code's promulgation, while groups of such leaders working in concert have a powerful impact on the organization's acceptance of its code.[11]

The timely use of symbols and language to describe and create support for change defines what some employees may perceive as an ambiguous reality.[12] It is important to place an appropriate title which proactively describes the code's effect on the company culture – such as one firm's 'Five Keys to Self-Renewal', or another's 'Quality Circle'. Moreover, a firm can prominently display the managing director's or chairman's support by reprinting that leader's supportive speech in the company's newspaper; such publication serves as a potent symbol in inducing desired change. One firm deliberately employed 'a striking and attractive format – typesetting and two colours – for the code, and used the format as an affective visual symbol of the code's importance'.

Another highly effective symbol which creates support for code implementation is the managing director's or chairman's personally directing the ethics or business conduct committee. In short, clear, highly visible symbols of support by top executives provide a powerful message of the code's or similar policy document's importance.

Finally, constant change has its deleterious effects. Consequently, the implementation process should include sources of stability (those who implement the code and their location) which act as anchors to steady anxious employees.[13] Some resistance to change may be inevitable, even natural. By realizing how change impacts the psychological contract of employees, and other factors raised in this discussion, top leadership can correctly recognize that resistance, from the employees' point of view, is quite legitimate. Rather than dismissing that point of view as stubborn or rigid, those who wish to promulgate codes should pay more attention, instead, to tactics, including the guidelines for implementing a code or similar policy document appearing in a later chapter. By understanding the forces which nurture resistance to change, and how to address and disarm them, top executives can effectively implement codes of conduct.

## BUILDING A CONSENSUS OF SUPPORT

A consensus as to code content and implementation nurtures a modicum of respect for the code which naturally lessens resistance. Building a consensus of respect for the Meyer Business Aims, whose Managing Director Richard Jewson and Corporate Development Manager Richard Brown helped draft, had high priority for good reason. Another company secured support for implementation of its code through numerous drafts and discussions with group managers, together with other key employees. In this way, a consensus was developed in the drafting and implementation process. The legal counsel and secretary of a large banking firm endorses such a process: 'The exposure of several drafts to a large number of people helps to resolve difficult issues in advance of publication and ensures a good balance of desirable, yet practical, guidelines'. The consequence of such consensus building is that little or no resistance will be manifested.

Several other firms subscribe to the critical nature of cultivation before publication. They make a concerted effort to have the code's principles and philosophies become reality before they are formally published. Such a reaffirmation is often critical to the acceptance process and reduces the potential shock of substantive and procedural change in the organization.

One executive, who also serves as his firm's general counsel, reflects on resistance to change concerning the code and how the company effectively addressed it: 'It is relatively rare that we encounter articulated resistance . . . [however] [w]hen this occurs, we try to deal with it through open and honest discussion'. While the firm recognizes that the 'policy setting should not take place in an ivory tower and we welcome input from all of our employees . . . those employees must recognize that, at the end of the day, senior management has a responsibility to decide the issues and all employees are expected to abide by that final decision'.

When resistance is encountered from individuals who mistakenly believe that deviant behaviour will be tolerated if it maximised short-term results, a firm must deal with it aggressively and openly in the hope that such attention will deter other potentially destructive behaviour.

Strict enforcement of company codes and similar policy statements, including appropriate disciplinary action, quickly dispels attitudes that the code is a mere public relations gesture, and, hence, should not be taken seriously.

According to another company's general counsel, 'there was an initial reaction that the code was too specific and could be construed to prohibit or "second guess" conduct that is appropriate and legal'. Fair and consistent application of the code overcomes such objections, as demonstrated in a subsequent chapter of this book.

# Chapter 12

# Methods of enforcing a code

A business firm creates a code of conduct for a variety of reasons and can realize substantial benefits if the enforcement mechanism is effective, and the code itself is enforceable. In fact, it is probably worse to have a code which employees know is unenforced or unenforceable, than to have no code at all.

There are many reasons to vigorously enforce a code or similar policy document. First, an employee's own personal values may be considerably less lofty than the standards required of him by his company's code; the fact that the code contains provisions for enforcement which the employee believes will be invoked if he violates the code is a good reason for him to exercise those higher principles. Further, employees acutely observe how uniformly and universally the firm's top management enforces the code's standards. If the managing director 'winks' at those standards, his employees may 'wink' back.

Firms which promulgate codes usually possess a high degree of confidence in the ability of the firm's management to regulate itself by employing the enforcement methods used for other firm procedures and policies. Normally those codes which are primarily composed of general precepts are not intended to have strict enforcement mechanisms, but rather seek to achieve their desired results through peer and hierarchical pressures. Reliance on the integrity of the individual and senior executives as role models contravenes the assumption often preferred by auditors, that employee misconduct is best prevented by strict surveillance programmes.

On the other hand, codes which do contain specific rules are usually reinforced by enforcement mechanisms, including fact-finding and adjudication procedures. Certainly, firms which have not instituted compliance or sanction procedures by which to enforce their codes assume personal integrity is a sufficient guarantor of proper or ethical conduct. A number of companies, however, apparently have more trust in formal supervisory procedures, rather than the relatively informal process of recruiting ethical persons and encouraging them to act properly.

Furthermore, an honoured axiom in social psychology posits that behavioural change is almost always linked to structural change within the organization.[1]

Hence, a firm can bolster its code of conduct with internal control mechanisms to make them effective.[2] Therefore, a company enacting a code of conduct should also implement an enforcement mechanism designed specifically to ensure that the firm actively monitors and enforces its code, rather than relying solely on the integrity of individuals. Effective codes clearly specify who is the enforcement authority, the fact-finding agency which investigates alleged violations.

Moreover, open communication and reporting, interwoven in the procedures firms establish for resolution of employee questions and dilemmas, provide a safety-valve channel for the reporting of questionable activities.

## CHOOSING THE ENFORCEMENT AGENCY AND PROCESS

It is important that a code is enforced, since enforcement acts as a deterrent to misconduct. While the nature of enforcement varies from company to company, normally a small body oversees compliance, investigates alleged violations of the code or similar document, and adjudicates the matter. Experience varies as to whether the firm will include outsiders, such as consultants and community leaders, in its enforcement agency, and whether the firm will separate its code enforcement agency from the existing organizational structure.[3]

The advantages and disadvantages of outsider involvement mirror those of public interest representation on boards of directors: while outsiders may enhance the credibility and impartiality of enforcement, they may also be considered as intermeddlers who do not understand the nature of the company's operations, and to whom company executives do not wish to expose the company's 'private' affairs.

The second issue, the process of enforcement, is approached in a variety of forms. Some companies, such as Abbey National, British Steel, Cadbury Schweppes, and Ciba-Geigy, utilize existing firm procedures to enforce the company's code or policy documents. According to Director of Personnel P. J. K. Ferguson, British Steel 'regulates itself by employing the enforcement methods used for other company policies'.

Moreover, Bradford & Bingley, British Telecom, Dixons, ICL, and Norwich Union, for example, find benefit in addressing code or policy statement adherence through job performance reviews. Bibby Corporate Finance Director A. S. Gresty concurs: 'Enforcement is incorporated into periodic personnel evaluations'. Scott Bader Company, notes Operations Manager John Raymond, incorporated code enforcement within its periodic personnel appraisal system in the 1980s. Tying appropriate conduct to promotions and salary increases definitely sends a powerful signal, and acts as a significant deterrent to questionable activities. This procedure reduces the cost of enforcement and, by employing an existing process, obviates the need for a quasi-judicial hearing or trial.

Nonetheless, such incorporation within existing procedures, however comfortable and familiar, does reduce the likelihood of detection. Other companies incorporate surveillance procedures in the code as the primary element of enforcement. Placing enforcement in a special audit function, as is Dowty's procedure, creates a 'superordinate check' on conduct.[4] Some companies employ a combination of the two procedures. Under any method, it is important to assign responsibility of enforcement to senior executives.

The most effective mechanisms are those which are visible, credible, and directly accountable to directors. For instance, Boots has a standing committee on social responsibilities, a sub-committee of the board of directors. According to Boots Personnel Director A. H. Hawksworth, that committee 'is the ultimate "watchdog" body'. Scott Bader Company assigns adjudication of alleged code violations and imposition of sanctions to a specially appointed code violations committee.

The success of any method of enforcement depends on the individual employee's responsibility and the environment of the company. Tesco, relates Company Secretary R. S. Ager, views each employee as the most important enforcement tool, not a committee or surveillance agency, simply the 'personal adherence' of each employee. Dixons, Rolls Royce, and Smiths Industries emphasize to all employees their responsibilities to adhere to codes and policy documents, and, further, to be diligent in assuring that no misconduct is disregarded. At Rolls Royce, Director of Personnel D'A. T. N. Payne notes 'An employee is required to report other employees' violations of the code of business conduct'.

Some commentators, nonetheless, downplay the requirement or expectation that employees report the code violations of others: '[I]n the interests of overall morale, this form of reporting (or informing) should not be stressed or heavily relied on . . . [the] code, however, should contain a tactful and carefully worded statement that the critical violations must be reported and that those who report them will be protected by top management regardless of the outcome'.[5]

## CERTIFICATE OF COMPLIANCE

Cadbury Schweppes, Ciba-Geigy, DEC, Burmah, and Granada emphasize open communication as a check on misconduct and violation of company codes and similar policy statements. Town & Country's Managing Director Ian Bell underscores the benefit of a healthy environment: 'Open communication provides a safety-valve channel for the reporting of questionable activities'. Free and open communication, without punishment, supports any enforcement mechanism. Firms often seek assurance by requiring employees to sign annual certificates that they are abiding by the letter and spirit of the code. These firms reinforce an atmosphere of voluntary disclosure that makes it difficult for employees willing to violate that code to be undetected.

Further, many firms supplement the certificate of voluntary disclosure with other policing mechanisms, but, even standing alone, disclosure decreases conflicts of interest because employees can ask supervisors or others to resolve ethical problems. Disclosure reduces the size of the code. Rather than placing absolute prohibitions on all or a certain class of activities, firms using disclosure techniques create a broad policy position that welcomes discussion in the event of questions of ethical or improper conduct arising.[6]

Many companies require managers or employees, or both, to sign certificates affirming that they have read and understood the code. Smiths Industries, Kingfisher, Scott Bader Company, British Steel, and Burmah Oil have followed this procedure with success. The compliance forms, usually certified annually, may also require the employee to disclose any code violations which he has witnessed, of which he has knowledge, or to which he has been a party.

At least one firm eschews the use of certification, describing it as akin to a 'police state'. Still others are steadfast in extolling the deterrent effect of the certification process. 'I was in a corporation that had people sign a statement every year that said they had not violated the code', recalls the company's former chairman. 'A lot of people had trouble putting their names to that; people put a lot of value on their signatures . . . and they took the code seriously'.[7] A general legal counsel of another firm concurs: 'The annual written certification by employees is likely to deter violations'. Furthermore, when the issues monitored are limited in number, the certification can be a powerful tool.

## OTHER MEANS OF CODE AND POLICY STATEMENT ENFORCEMENT: ATTITUDE SURVEYS, QUESTIONNAIRES, AND AUDITS

Besides written assurances of adherence by employees, companies utilize other techniques to enhance the enforcement of their codes of conduct: surveys, questionnaires, and audits to measure employees' compliance and attitudes regarding codes. Peugeot Talbot, like Yorkshire Bank, Richard Costain, Dixons, and Rolls Royce, employs 'periodic surveys to determine the effectiveness of its character and procedure document', notes M. A. B. Judge, Peugeot Talbot Director of Personnel and Industrial Relations. The Chief Executive of IBM UK, A. B. Cleaver, strongly endorses that company's use of a survey of employees which poses 100 questions or so every two years.

While surveys may be expensive, there is much to gain in production and morale as the company learns a good deal about its employees. One company has employed a series of employee attitude surveys over a five-year period to determine the effectiveness of its code of conduct training programmes. Another company's chairman requires a letter from the top 100 managers in the firm specifying any breaches of the code's policies. A fourth company, according to its director of employee development and communication, uses a similar method to 'develop a sense of how well we are doing with our values'.

Other companies, such as Abbey National, British Telecom, Dixons, J. Bibby, and Wagon Finance, rely on periodic audits to improve compliance with each firm's code or policy statement. Trained auditors bring impartiality, independence, and considerable knowledge of the company's business to the process.

These auditors often already have considerable experience investigating and monitoring various systems within the firm.

Some companies rely on internal or independent auditors and line managers to assure code compliance, even when certification is not used. 'Compliance with the code's policies is measured and assured through audit procedures to review and test the uses of corporate assets and certain business interests and relationships of key employees', emphasizes a large insurance company's general counsel. Special emphasis should be placed on auditing areas identified as sensitive, for example those areas which by their nature appear to present high risk in the context of possible conflicts of interest or improper use of corporate assets.

Similarly, Hewlett Packard's audit group annually interviews the top managers from each of the firm's corporate groups. Auditors ask a battery of questions regarding the manager's familiarity with HP's code of conduct, the frequency and depth of communications the manager has had with other employees regarding the code, and his awareness of any ethical violations or government sanctions against his organizational entity.[8]

Furthermore, Dow Chemical began using an audit procedure in 1976 after the firm drafted its first code of conduct. The Dow Business Conduct Committee, which was responsible for drafting the code, conducts annual audits in all of the firm's major geographic regions. Each audit typically lasts an entire day and involves meetings with seven to fifteen managers who are asked to respond to a list of ten to fifteen questions drafted beforehand by the committee. The committee then discusses any problems that have been identified with the managers, and endeavours to craft solutions to these problems.[9]

# Chapter 13

# Adjudicating violations and imposing sanctions

In enforcing a code of conduct or similar policy document, a business firm should not only monitor the compliance of employees, but also design and institute a system for fairly adjudicating infractions, and imposing sanctions for misconduct. Frank Cagy, when Chairman of IBM, advocated clearly stating in every firm's code 'what kind of conduct it will not tolerate, and what penalties will result'.

Certainly, every company can demonstrate its commitment to proper conduct by disciplining those who violate the company's policies. London Buses Managing Director C. Hodson agrees: 'The company is obligated to demonstrate its commitment by firm discipline and by punishing those guilty of violating those codes'. While it is important to set out in a code or policy statement a brief exposition of various sanctions for misconduct, overemphasis on punishment may send the wrong message: that of emphasizing the 'should nots' instead of the 'shoulds'.

## THE ADJUDICATORY BODY

After an alleged violation is reported, in most cases a specific individual or group within the company is responsible for determining whether a violation actually occurred. For example, according to Severn Trent Company Secretary C. G. McMillan, 'A code violation committee adjudicates violations of the code and vision statement and imposes sanctions'.

At British Steel, like many companies, the seniority of the alleged violator determines which management level will actually adjudicate the matter. Likewise, in one banking firm, 'the adjudication process is overseen by an ad hoc committee which includes representatives as needed from the legal, audit, and human resources departments and decisions as to whether there was an actual violation are rendered by that committee joined by the alleged violator's department or group management'. That firm's managing director imposes sanctions if the violator is a high-level manager, while the same committee which oversaw the determination of actual code violation determines the sanctions imposed on other employees.

Typical sanctions include verbal and written warnings, suspension, termination, and, in the event of law-breaking, reporting for prosecution. 'Without appropriate sanctions, a company's employees will never appreciate the seriousness of code violations or give the code sufficient support to assure its effectiveness', notes another company's chairman of the committee which adjudicates code violations.

A general legal counsel of another company details the central role of the legal department in his company's adjudicatory process: 'Alleged violations surface through the annual questionnaire (from over 320 executives), internal audit procedure, or informants – the legal department directs or supplements the fact-finding process and determines whether an infraction has occurred and the resultant sanction'. Where termination is a possibility, a top executive reviews the matter and determines the appropriate sanction.

In another company, according to its director of human resources, 'alleged violations are channelled to the human resources department'. If the alleged impropriety is not serious, a human resources coordinator, the supervisor, or line manager of the alleged violator, together with the group's managing director, gather facts and adjudicate the matter. However, if the allegation involves serious misconduct, then the director of human resources resolves the matter after the normal consultations, if necessary, with the legal department or other corporate leaders.

Similarly, in a manufacturing firm, allegations of serious misconduct are referred for review by the chairman of the company's oversight committee to the managing director and chairman, while allegations of other misconduct are assigned for resolution to a particular level of management at the group or plant level in which the purported violator is employed.

At an electricity supplier firm, the auditing department attempts to assure uniformity in the application of sanctions through consulting the personnel and legal departments, and, then, determining whether a code infraction has occurred, and by advising of past sanctions for similar offences.

Other companies, rather than appointing a specific person or group to adjudicate alleged code violators, sort out violators via the normal management control process. At Kingfisher, every managing director is responsible for addressing non-compliance of the code of conduct, relates Company Secretary Tim Clement-Jones. Similarly, W. H. Smith's senior management monitor compliance with five core policies in their normal oversight procedures, and apply corrective measures as appropriate.

## ASSURING FAIRNESS

Firms should maintain the integrity of the adjudicatory process, as exemplified by one banking concern. 'Whether the accusation of violation emanates from my review of the annual survey (about 5,000 key employees surveyed), the internal audit, or an informant, assuring continued confidentiality of those involved is a top priority', indicates that banking concern's senior compliance officer and senior executive.

Any adjudicatory process should ensure that relevant facts be gathered and reviewed, and all circumstances carefully considered. Companies must take reasonable steps, as well, to assure fairness, thoroughness, speed, and consistency in the adjudicatory process. Without an actual and apparent system of due process, a code cannot maintain the confidence of those it addresses. Without sanctions for wrongdoing, a code will be less credible in an organization.

Moreover, due process includes the right of an employee to appeal, and, in this regard, companies often merge the appellate procedure with an open door policy so that an employee may petition a higher authority for relief from a finding or penalty which he perceives as inaccurate or unfair.

Firms vary in their application of penalties for various infractions. No matter what penalties for violations are available, firms should make certain that the degree of penalty is directly related to the nature of the infraction. One executive involved in a company's adjudicatory process notes: 'One of my duties is to assure that any code policy provides reasonable notice to employees that particular sanctions can result from policy violation'. That executive adds, 'In those cases where someone may face discipline in the company grievance and arbitration process, I advise management how to ensure due process, including whether a particular sanction is arbitrary or unreasonable'.

# Chapter 14

# Guidelines for implementation

It is appropriate, before formulating final implementation procedures for the code or similar policy document, to review the following guidelines:

1  Establishing a foundation for change.
2  Effectively managing the transition.
3  Involving operating groups in implementation.
4  Defining penalties for improper conduct.
5  Establishing educational and training programmes.
6  Testing the effectiveness of educational and training programmes.
7  Assessing and modifying educational programmes.
8  Publicizing achievements.

1  *Establishing a foundation for change.* John Menzies Group Managing Director Ranald Noel-Paton recounts: 'Our company established a groundwork for the organizational changes required for effective implementation of our statement of principles'. Constructing such a groundwork could very well include the following actions:[1]

a) Every company should identify and expose to employees problems with the current organization. Firms can build the commitment of their employees for anticipated changes and the code of conduct by explaining existent difficulties and suggesting how the innovations will cure or improve the present difficulties.

b) After exposing the difficulties, a company should ask employees to participate in the imminent change. Requesting employee input in the formulation or revision of the code of conduct and its implementation policies is normally perceived by employees as a positive step.

c) To promote participation, each firm should provide employees with rewards for cooperating in the drafting or revising of its code of conduct and the implementation process. The reward structure reinforces participation by employees during subsequent code of conduct revisions.

d) A company should prepare employees for the upcoming implementation or significant revision of the code. Providing ample warning time enables employees to adjust to the coming changes and to disconnect from the current state of affairs, which the company seeks to modify or dissolve.

2  *Effectively managing the transition.* 'Remploy educated employees about the systems we created to manage the transition to firmly establishing a strategy summary', recounts Chief Executive Tony Withey.

   a)  Every company should communicate to employees a clear image of the future – and inform employees of the reasoning behind the development of the code.[2] Inland Revenue Director General Steve Matheson agrees: 'From a staff morale point of view, it was important to emphasize continuity – that the charter brought together existing instructions, training and best practices'. During the implementation of its code of conduct, the firm should appoint an individual responsible for managing the transition period between the old code and new code, or between the absence of a code and the new code. Moreover, individuals responsible for implementing the code should plan the transition, and assure that adequate resources (time, manpower, and money) are properly allocated to the transition.[3]

   b)  Managers responsible for implementing the code or similar policy document should develop a feedback mechanism to provide them with information regarding the effectiveness of the code implementation programme. Moreover, the feedback provided should be evaluated to identify areas where the code's implementation should be improved.[4]

3  *Involving operating groups in implementation.* Shell, as did British Telecom, Legal & General, and RTZ, organized operating groups to assist in implementation. Shell Head of Communications B. K. Elms recalls: 'The multiple operating groups took planned action steps to prepare the entire organization for putting into effect Shell's general business principles statement'. An effective action plan might include the following elements and principles:

   a)  One of the most important steps is to develop the support of executives and groups that possess the key political power within the firm.

   b)  Important leaders within the firm can create additional support for the code. They can persuade employees and other managers that the code is being implemented in the best interest of the firm. In addition, employees and others are more likely to embrace and promote the code if key leaders, themselves, endorse and adhere to the code.

   c)  Where appropriate, the firm should incorporate symbols, stories, and specific language within the code to create energy and enthusiasm in employees regarding the code's implementation.[5] A company may inadvertently create a false sense of security if its code is not woven into the operating fabric of the firm. Therefore, it is imperative to communicate ethics and proper conduct using a common vocabulary that includes mention of the code and its standards.[6]

d) The communication programme should be incessant[7] since continuity will reinforce not only the commitment of management to the code, but will also ingrain the importance of the code in the firm's culture.

4 *Defining sanctions for improper conduct.* The company should carefully evaluate the disclosure of penalties for violating the code. A spectrum of practice is available from vague disclosure to informing employees of exact punishments for specific infractions. Announcements to employees regarding infractions with only a slight description of the penalty may be confusing and counter-productive. Moreover, too detailed a disclosure of penalties may violate an employee's right to privacy. Therefore, every firm should thoroughly consider its policy of informing its employees of the penalties associated with violations of the code of conduct.[8]

5 *Establishing effective educational and training[9] programmes.* Town & Country (as did British Telecom, Ciba-Geigy, NFU, Avon Mutual, Rolls Royce, Smiths Industries, and The Leeds), notes Managing Director Ian Bell, determined that effective, thorough educational and training programmes would facilitate implementation. An effective programme is characterized by the following elements:

a) Education of employees regarding a firm's code should be brief, foster participation, and be respectful of the experience, intelligence, and commitment of those employees being trained.

b) The training programme should be professional in nature and communicate to employees the seriousness that the company has attached to its code. Two approaches have been used to train employees within larger firms. Specifically, the 'trickle down' approach educates from the top and works to indoctrinate successively lower levels of management. Another approach involves the use of outside consultants to educate employees about the code of conduct.

c) Training sessions for each level of management and all non-managerial employees should occur in two sets. The first training set should instruct everyone except those with unbreakable schedule commitments and conflicts. The second set should be scheduled to educate the individuals who did not attend the first training programme.

d) New employees should be introduced to the firm's code of conduct during regular orientation programmes.

6 *Testing the effectiveness of educational and training procedures.* 'Multiple offices, groups, divisions, and segments of Dixons identified a small test area for the training programme', recalls Group Personnel Director R. E. Andrews. After testing and modification, the entire company can be exposed to the programmes. The programme should be administered to the test area and follow-up questionnaires solicited, or focus groups should be conducted to solicit feedback of the programme's effectiveness. Using this experimental technique improves the overall impact of the final training programme.[10]

7 *Assessing and modifying educational programmes.* This assessment of training programmes must be 'realistic', counsels Smiths Industries Secretary Alan Smith. A pragmatic evaluation reduces speculation regarding the actual effectiveness of the educational and training programmes.

8 *Publicizing achievements.* As J. Bibby & Sons Corporate Finance Director A. S. Gresty notes, the firm should seize every opportunity to publicize its efforts regarding its code or similar document. The J. Bibby personnel policies and mission statement comprise the written compendium of company values, beliefs, and standards of conduct. However, publicity should be sought only after the firm has realized positive results from the code training programmes.

# Chapter 15

# Key success factors identified by companies in effectively implementing codes

The experience of the participating British and multi-national companies in implementing codes of conduct or similar policy documents varies, as has been pointed out in an earlier section. Nonetheless, there are numerous factors which are critically important in implementing a code of conduct or similar policy document.

1 *Since human consciences are often fragile, establishing procedures reinforces employee responsibility to conform to the code and other policy statements.* 'A key success factor is establishment of implementation mechanisms to assure compliance with the company's values and standards of conduct', notes D. A. Sharp, Head of Personnel Division at Bank of England. Top executives of British Telecom, Halifax, M & G, Natural Provident Institution, and Richard Costain concur. These mechanisms include:

a) Management involvement and oversight through the supervisory level.
b) Constant consciousness of those written, codified values and standards in recruiting and hiring.
c) Stressing code values and standards in educating and training employees.
d) Well-designed communication programmes to enlighten and motivate employees.
e) Developing awareness of code values and standards through company publications, management meetings, and executives' speeches.
f) Recognition and tangible rewards for conduct which exemplifies desired values and standards.
g) Ombudsmen or other designated persons assigned to field employees' questions and reporting.
h) Thorough concentration on high-risk jobs and areas in terms of violating code values and standards.
i) Periodic certification and auditing to assure compliance with those code values and standards.
j) Well-defined and fair enforcement procedures, including sanctions.[1]

2 *No critical factor for successful code implementation is more important than support by top executives.* 'Advocacy of our company's corporate principles' implementation by the managing director, chairman, and other top executives is a critical element', notes Ranald Noel-Paton, Group Managing Director of John Menzies. Such advocacy strengthens the reputation of the company for honest and fair business practices. In this regard, the managing director is fulfilling a duty which can improve the bottom-line performance because consumers purchase products and services from companies which they respect. In a number of firms, the managing director or chairman has actually defined or oversaw the definition of core values, often unique to that firm.

As many firms' top executives are personally committed to the code or similar policy document, they explicitly refer to those documents in taking a positive stance on business conduct and ethical issues. 'Top management needs to reinforce their belief in an ethical environment frequently', counsels a top executive and general legal counsel of a large drink and food producing company. Strong leadership from top executives includes applying continuous pressure on lower levels of management to maintain their interest in successfully implementing the code.

Moreover, a company can ensure continuity of values in the leadership of successive managing directors as each new managing director, as the chief articulator and advocate of the firm's values, reasserts his commitment to the values of the code or policy document. When successive managing directors honour the code's or similar document's implementation process through inexorable commitment, employees perceive the document and its implementation processes as stable and upright traditions of the company.

Strong leadership in this manner, as the experiences of AMEC, Meyer, and John Menzies exemplify, commands the attention and resolve necessary for effective implementation of a code or similar document.

Top leadership, by its continuous, indefatigable commitment to the code and its successful implementation, can actually inculcate the code standards and values into the firm's environment. 'Active support from the top in stressing integrity and support for code policies does eventually permeate all levels of the company's culture', reveals another top executive.

Nonetheless, reminds an electrical supplier's director of personnel, 'Leadership by top executives in implementation is hollow if those leaders fail to set examples themselves by not only honouring the code contents but also by setting an active example by deed that they are abiding by the processes of implementation, as well – that is the way to make their leadership credible in establishing the code'.

3 *Use of performance evaluations and incentive systems is a spur to effective implementation.* Such a concept is not strange to free market systems – recognition and reward, including pay and promotion, for exemplary per-

formance are characteristic of successful ventures. To ensure that each successive level of management places high priorities on code implementation and maintaining ethical and proper behaviour, a business firm should tie those desired actions to performance evaluation.

The implementation of the code and its attendant programmes most effectively works by first building senior executives' familiarity with the concepts and problem-solving methods of the programme, and then proceeding to successively lower levels of the organization, after gaining the support of the management level above it.[2] The message of incorporating adherence to code standards in performance appraisals speaks forcefully to potential violators that inappropriate behaviour will be punished and that turnover is not the sole means a firm can use to gauge success. 'At Norwich Union, senior executives have administered the implementation and used performance evaluation to create support for our operating code and corporate purpose statement in line management', relates H. W. Utting, General Manager and Secretary.

Often those being evaluated, such as line managers, are the first level of administering the code; their support of the code's implementation has a ripple effect throughout the workforce.

Moreover, top executives who promulgate the code or values statement help assure the loyalty and commitment of line managers in the implementation process by consulting with those persons in advance.

4 *Broad approaches throughout the company promote behaviour commensurate with code and policy statement standards.* Ciba-Geigy, Save & Prosper, Shell, and Texaco utilize such an approach. Ciba-Geigy Secretary I. E. F. Stewart explains: 'Our implementation programme is a systems approach, implemented across the entire company, and not merely a means of punishing "bad" individuals'. In other words, a code should incorporate standards to which the entire population of the firm can adhere.

Ethics or proper business conduct enhancement is better assured by managing certain systems: communication to, and education of employees concerning company policies and society's laws; employee incentives to achieve adherence to those policies and realization of company goals, and resources to assist employees in that adherence and resolution.[3] Codes of conduct, or similar policy documents, are valid only to the extent that other company plans and programmes, such as business strategies, marketing programmes, and customer relations activities, are consistent with those policy documents. Awareness of proper conduct should permeate all, not just supplemental, activities.

5 *Effective code training and education strategies include many elements and facets.* Tailoring the implementation to the firm's unique culture encases the process with a common currency. 'The implementation process, just as the code contents, should be customized to respond to the firm's culture; for

instance, if a firm doesn't have a purchasing interface, education in this area is not only irrelevant, it signals a poorly designed implementation process to employees', warns one financial institution's legal counsel.

By tailoring training, within guidelines, to divisions or operations in the firm, those divisions become more receptive to implementation. For example, one company has a standard code from which variations can be crafted by various company groups. The function of this decentralization is to make the code or similar policy statement relevant to a particular functional area. Moreover, this need for flexibility often arises in holding companies' dealings with their various units.

Many firms designate line management to conduct the training, including workshop sessions, of employees. 'Using a training programme that involves managers provides opportunities to clarify requirements and expectations and also exposes the "hidden agenda" that all too often may have been contributing to an employee's lack of understanding or which otherwise may have inhibited communication', counsels another company's director of business practices.

Encouraging participation and discussion of relevant case-situations, as well as learning through discussion of the code itself, sharpens employee attention. Employees perceive such training as more germane and valuable when they are encouraged to raise sensitive and even controversial issues without any threat of reprisal.[4]

A standardized format for proper business conduct and ethics training workshops, with video tapes, discussion guides, and workbooks, assures consistency at all levels, conveys the idea that ethics has a common meaning, and provides support for supervisors who lead training sessions for their subordinates.[5] Further, 'By teaching the code pragmatically and connecting its standards with business operations, a company creates a proactive sentiment in employees and imbeds the code in the company's operations', advises a top executive of a large banking firm. Finally, management should immediately respond to potential areas of business conduct or ethical problems which are revealed in the training or education sessions. A special focus on vulnerable jobs and areas preempts misconduct where it is most likely to occur.

6  *Structured and fair approaches to code implementation and monitoring compliance offer numerous benefits.* Implementation of Texaco's statement of visions and values is 'an explicitly defined process', relates Chairman Peter Bijur. One benefit of a well-defined implementation process is that 'it is easier to understand and to apply consistently than unexpressed, informal, and arbitrary procedures', notes Norwich Winterhur Corporate Group Secretary R. E. Townsend. An explicit mechanism, with obvious and substantial authority, can monitor and arbitrate ethical and business conduct problems. In this regard, emphasises a top executive at a pharmaceutical products firm, 'A critical factor for success is the uniform and fair administration of the well-defined implementation and monitoring process'.

Perception that the company's code administration, including adjudication of alleged wrongdoing, is fair and consistent breeds respect. The more explicit the process, the greater assurance of due process. Corporate secretaries, auditors, and legal staff play important roles in lending fairness and consistency to the adjudicatory and sanctioning process.

7  *A dual-element compliance system is best.* As Cadbury Schweppes, Dixons, Dowty, Peugeot Talbot, and Prudential experiences indicate, compliance with a code of conduct or similar policy document 'relies on trust and monitoring together', asserts London Buses Managing Director C. Hodson. Firms with well-developed codes and implementation procedures place a fair degree of trust in their employees to adhere to code principles. If the code implementation and enforcement procedures rely on trust and mutual respect, as has been the Hewlett Packard experience, employees will more likely be faithful to the company's values since they believe the company trusts and relies on them to do so.[6]

While it is important to stress every employee's good faith and voluntary adherence to the code, surveillance is invaluable in deterring individuals with less moral urgency from improper conduct. 'A firm can have a well-designed code and all the good intentions imaginable, but without the element of "scrutiny" there is no effective implementation', declares a high-level executive of a food products company. Moreover, the fact that employees, who respond in writing in compliance statements, know their answers are carefully reviewed is a powerful surveillance and deterrent tool. A company must ensure that it practises what it preaches. For many employees, a certificate or questionnaire regarding compliance revives an interest in the contents of the code or similar policy document.

The existence of many checks and balances in the implementation process, such as surveillance, certification, and sanctions, erects a formidable wall which conditions proper conduct for all but the most unethical people. Multiple checks and balances in a control network which supplements trust can more easily identify and terminate those persons with unacceptable character traits, such as dishonesty. A special counsel for an energy supplier reflects: 'Changing standards by which people are judged, with money and material possessions growing substantially in perceived importance, require that compliance be monitored closely – unfortunately in today's climate there is pressure to secure material advantages by any means, ethical or legal or not'.

In this compliance process, strict and sure punishment for company-adjudicated violations of law or code policy sends a signal to upright employees that their conduct is the proper standard for the firm. Only when management is willing to take clear, decisive action to seek out and to sanction non-conformity to code standards does the often initial, natural scepticism of employees fade. Some companies publish in their newspapers descriptions, without mention of the name and location of the offender, of the sanctioned offences as an instructive exercise for employees.

8 *All work groups should be mobilized in the code's implementation.* 'Effective implementation requires the continued commitment and participation of personnel at every company level', counsels Touche Ross Managing Director Michael Blackburn. The beneficial effects of this participation include: employees' more pronounced understanding of the firm's principles and their important roles in the firm, through discussions of company values and goals; higher levels of trust in associates and pride in the firm, as employees interact and discuss those matters important to them and the firm; and, employees' focusing on job-related improvements in product design and quality, due to a perceived greater involvement in the company and its future.

9 *A multi-faceted approach to implementation enhances and reinforces employee acceptance.* 'Administration of the company philosophy at Trusthouse Forte is ongoing and multi-dimensional', notes John Robbins, Head of Press and Public Relations. Establishing many points of leverage to influence and support proper conduct and administration of code procedures is a key factor in any successful implementation. Business conduct committees, hotlines, ombudsmen, and resources to answer employee questions are prime examples.

Successful code implementation is usually characterized by the availability of many channels by which to resolve an ethics or business conduct question or dilemma, as well as a climate that encourages the airing of such matters.[7] Those resources for resolution include personnel departments, legal staff, line managers, and top executives.

A corollary is the necessity to communicate the importance of code values and standards, as well as their implementation, repeatedly and in different ways. Communication programmes which inform and motivate employees are especially valuable. In this fashion, for instance, the managing director, chairman, or other senior executives demonstrate continued support of the code and its successful implementation, because implementation is a dynamic process without an end. For example, top management, by issuing a steady stream of communications supporting code implementation, signals persistence and continuing interest in the implementation process. Moreover, by constantly integrating the principles and standards suggested by codes and similar policy documents, management clothes such documents with a credibility and a sense of priority. The higher the visibility regarding code implementation the more importance employees attach to the very process of implementation. Toward this end, there must be a constant renewal of effort to implement the code – to inculate its values and standards in the company's operations.

For example, one engineering company maintains complete programmes of continual communication concerning its statement of standards, including: awareness workshops for all employees; requiring line managers to review periodically each employee's understanding of the code; publishing articles about implementation in the company newspaper; placing posters concerning code compliance in conspicuous places; integrating a concern for its standards in employee publications; and circulating, on a monthly basis, anecdotal and statistical data concerning the calls made on the company's hotline. Another company has electronically incorporated its code guidelines in the desktop computers which are available to many of the company's employees.

10  *Code implementation and open communication are mutually supportive.* Executives at British Telecom, Cadbury Schweppes, Granada, Legal & General, and Peugeot Talbot stress this key success factor in implementation. So does Remploy Chief Executive Tony Withey: 'Implementation procedures which enhance open and candid communication breed healthy work environments and strong value systems'.

Processes of code implementation which encourage communication strengthen the very standards the code endorses. In addition, unhindered communication creates a climate in which employees cannot easily conceal questionable activities. In this regard, annual disclosure statements and ethics training encourage communication and discussion. When employees discuss decision-making in the sunshine, they invariably make correct, proper, ethical decisions.

Moreover, the reverse is true – climates of trust and open communication are receptive to the acceptance of code values and standards with which the firm expects every employee to comply. A computer company's human resources chief concurs: 'I really don't believe a firm can reach its potential without a belief in vision and trust in others' integrity and professionalism, and it is just such a climate of trust and enhanced communication which accepts and reinforces those standards and values which are codified in a written statement or booklet'.

11  *Encouraging the reporting of improper or unethical activities is a valuable implementation tool.* Executives at Dixons, Granada, Smiths Industries, and Rolls Royce stress the benefits of responsible employees who police themselves and others. Rolls Royce Director of Personnel D'A. T. N. Payne cites as an aid to implementation 'the reporting of improper or unethical conduct which reporting is encouraged and protected by the company'.

As noted earlier, many firms provide hotlines or certification procedures which allow employees to disclose improper or unethical activities of others. Such procedures serve as safety valves for managers to receive valuable information, the transmittal of which would normally encounter organizational roadblocks. One company requires every employee to reveal instances where he has knowledge that an alleged violation of the code has been reported and no action has been taken to correct or resolve the matter reported. The process is strictly confidential; the employee receives a written or oral report as to the disposition of the matter reported.

12  *Revising the code invigorates it.* 'Reviewing and revising TSB Trust Company's Standards and its implementation procedures assures relevance

and enhances credibility', advises TSB Secretary L. H. W. March. D. A. Sharp, Bank of England Head of Personnel Division, concurs, 'Our ethical guidelines statement is brought up to date as the need arises – for example, inside dealing standards'.

Revising the code contents and their implementation procedures responds to changing employee attitudes, and it demonstrates continued support by top management of the attendant reviewing of procedures.[8] A particular firm's ethics and standards are not rigidly fixed in time; rather, standards of behaviour and ways to implement the code values evolve. Consequently, management can respond by updating code practices and principles which govern behaviour in the firm.[9] By revising and recirculating the company's policy document, that firm ensures its vitality. Codes and similar policy documents, as living documents, should respond to new circumstances.

Further, a firm can employ attitude surveys and interviews to measure changes in employee perceptions. 'The annual four-page questionnaire which every officer completes has provided much needed input to help us periodically address new issues and effect revision in the code – maintaining the relevance and currency of code provisions is certainly a critical element for successful implementation of the code', notes a top executive.

13  *Senior management evaluation and orientation programmes for employees assist effective code implementation schemes.* A senior management committee's evaluation of the code's or similar document's ramifications in policy areas such as divestitures, acquisitions, and redundancy provides a nexus between the written word and company strategy. Also, by conducting orientation programmes for employees, the company gains valuable feedback as to what the code or policy document means to employees. Moreover, appointing a committee of company elders, such as former chairmen or members of the board of directors, to critique the effectiveness of the code within the organization provides avenues for needed changes in implementation procedures.

# Chapter 16

# Introduction to codes of conduct and policy documents

In business, as in personal decisions, there is a general set of ethical and proper standards by which decisions should be made. An introduction to a code of conduct provides a company with the opportunity to highlight the importance of those standards by which managers and employees should base their decisions and activities.

Many firms use the introduction to codes or policy documents as a general summary of the ethical character of the firm in the form of a personal letter from the managing director. Other firms employ an introduction by the managing director or chairman as a way of summarizing the history of the firm, and the people and ideals behind its success. It is appropriate, also, for an introduction to discuss briefly the reasons why every employee should follow the code's standards.

The following excerpts of managing directors' and chairman's introductions provide examples from some of the United Kingdom's most successful firms, as well as from several of the world's largest international corporate concerns.

## Coats Viyella

This document outlines the general business principles by which Coats Viyella will conduct its affairs. They apply to the conduct of employees as well as to the corporate approach.

The statement outlines the standards, legal and ethical, on which the commercial and personnel matters of the Company will be conducted.

Coats Viyella is a diversified UK based company with worldwide operations and the Group is typified by a dedication to a decentralized approach in which individual operating companies are given considerable freedom of action in conducting their business. However, the reputation of Coats Viyella can be maintained only by the integrity of its employees and the proper approach to affairs in corporate and subsidiary decision-making. It is acknowledged that the reputation of Coats Viyella is upheld around the world principally by the conduct of the individuals working for it.

This statement outlines the standards which it is believed will best serve the interests of Coats Viyella, and it should be available for wide distribution within the Group throughout the world, in order to ensure that the underlying principles of the business are recognized by all its employees.

## Legal & General

We live and work in a highly competitive, complex business world, where decisions often have to be made under pressure. Much of Legal & General's success is built on public confidence about the way we do business. Under these circumstances it is important to remember the trust and confidence the public place in us, and to know the principles on which we stand in the conduct of our business. Integrity, honesty, and quality contribute to our reputation and success.

For this reason we have formalized our codes of practice in An Assurance of Ethical Standards for which the company and all of us as individuals take responsibility. These guidelines set out a number of principles as standards of conduct for UK employees of Legal & General. The term 'employees' extends to all members of staff, including management.

The guidelines are the result of research and consultation on the part of representative employees and managers within the Business Units who have worked together to codify the principles on which we base the conduct of our business. In most cases we are building on principles we already hold and have expressed through personnel manuals and other forms of policy communication. In some instances practice has been standardized.

Maintaining the good reputation of Legal & General demands a continuing commitment on the part of every employee to ensure that high ethical standards are both respected and acted upon. While no written code can be a substitute for personal integrity, these standards provide the ethical basis on which Legal & General does business. It is essential that individuals acknowledge the trust and confidence placed in them by their employer, customers, and the community, and act responsibly to deserve that trust.

Legal & General's success is a direct result of the commitment shown by the people who make up the company. Our employees are our key resource. To achieve future success it is essential that we sustain our integrity and quality of service to our customers. Accordingly, the company acknowledges a responsibility to develop fully the potential of our staff. We select for all jobs without discrimination based on race, religion, sex, or age. We strive to ensure that our people receive appropriate support, encouragement and rewards to perform to the highest standards.

Legal & General naturally expects all employees to observe professional or statutory codes of conduct relevant to their employment. In addition, it is the company's aim that the individuals within it abide by the spirit and not just the letter of the law. The formalized set of principles which follows will assist everyone not only to protect but also to enhance the reputation of Legal & General.

We see this booklet as marking the beginning of a constructive dialogue with staff about ethical issues. If you have any constructive comments to make or queries about the contents, please complete the sheet inside the back cover. The booklet will be subject to regular review.

An Assurance of Ethical Standards has the full approval of the Managing Directors of all of our Business Units. It is intended to identify consistent standards that everyone will recognize and understand. Adherence to its principles is the responsibility of every one of us.

## Taylor Woodrow

Since its formation in 1921, the Taylor Woodrow Group has set for itself high standards of workmanship, integrity, and relationships with both society as a whole and members of its own worldwide team.

The principles of this policy are well documented in publications by the Group, and in The Taylor Woodrow Way we outline our commitments and policies towards our clients, shareholders, and the communities in which we work.

Please accept this booklet with our compliments. The knowledge that you are aware of our business philosophies will help to maintain our high standards.

## Abbey Life

Since being established in 1961, Abbey Life has enjoyed an outstanding record of growth and achievement through pioneering and selling unit-linked products in the Life Assurance and Pension fields.

This booklet spells out our objectives for the future and our underlying company values and philosophies, recognizing that our success is dependent on the skills and commitment of our staff. We are aware that words and policies do nothing alone – our aim is to establish constantly actions which back up our aspirations for Excellence.

Our priorities for the future will continue to be: to provide our customers with exemplary service and products; to recognize that everyone is important, and to help all Abbey people develop to the full extent of their abilities; to be efficient and profitable; to adopt an open, participative management style; and at all times to do business honestly and fairly, balancing the needs of the task, individuals, and team.

This booklet spells out these objectives in more detail, particularly in terms of our employment policies, so that all staff can better understand our philosophy and the actions which result. It is an amalgam of the views of management and of staff, gained through Opinion Surveys, Excellence in Action checklists, and feedback from Putting People First courses run in 1985.

Looking to the future, we must strive to promote the spirit of this book through actions, recognizing the likelihood that we will sometimes fall short of these standards of excellence, and the difficulties of balancing occasionally conflicting needs in an environment which will be constantly changing, increasingly competitive, and forcing us to question our traditional way of doing things.

We need to be flexible, open to new ideas and willing, on occasion, to admit mistakes and put them right in order to achieve Excellence.

## TI Group

I therefore thought it would be helpful if current policy statements were brought together in one document. Senior managers are responsible for ensuring that the Group Policies are communicated to their operation units and key staff functions in an appropriate way and for ensuring compliance, those to whom it applies must be aware of the contents. Any failure to comply will be entertained only after specific relief has been obtained. In a diverse international group, individual compliance problems will inevitably arise. In such cases, application for relief must be made to the TI Group Secretary and any agreed waiver must be recorded in writing.

TI Group Policies are not intended to place any unnecessary restraints on the freedom of action of members of the Group. Their purpose is to ensure that we can all march to one drumbeat worldwide with clarity of purpose. However, uniformity is not an objective and is only applied where it is appropriate or necessary and thereby reaffirms the principle of decentralization in other respects, subject to one very important commonsense rule. Policy Statements cannot anticipate every conceivable eventuality so – 'if in doubt, refer it'.

## Cadbury Schweppes

Cadbury Schweppes earns its living in a competitive world. It needs to do so successfully to meet its obligations to all those with a stake in the enterprise and to make the Company one to which people are proud to belong.

We are in business to meet the needs of consumers internationally for products and services of good value and consistent quality. Our success in doing so is measured by the profitable growth of Cadbury Schweppes and by the advancement of its reputation.

The basis of our business is the good will of our customers, since we depend on literally millions of repeat purchases daily. The Company's main commercial assets are its brands and it is our responsibility to develop the markets for them. Cadbury Schweppes' brands are a guarantee to consumers of quality and value and we must invest consistently in building their reputation.

In setting out what the Company needs to become, I find no conflict between the values and characteristics we have inherited from the past and the actions we have to take to ensure a successful and independent future for Cadbury Schweppes. We cannot, however, depend on our history to carry us forward. The realities of the marketplace are tough and demanding and the Company has to be able to respond rapidly to them. We need to build on the Company's undoubted strengths and to apply them in ways which are appropriate to overcoming the challenges ahead.

## The Boots Company

The Boots Company is based in Nottingham, with a turnover which places it among the largest UK-based commercial enterprises. It employs over 60,000 people in the twenty countries in which it has its own companies. Much of the equity capital is provided by institutional shareholders such as pension funds and insurance companies, but there are also over 107,000 individual shareholders.

The Company's principal activities are two-fold: the research, manufacture and marketing of pharmaceuticals and consumer products throughout the world (which is the concern of the Industrial Division), and the retailing of chemist, health care, and other merchandise and services (which is the concern of the Retail Division).

The term social responsibility recognizes that business and society are interdependent. Over the 100 years of its history, from its small beginnings in Nottingham to a company with worldwide interests, Boots has established its reputation as a company of integrity, able to provide society with reliable, good-value products and services. Its policies and practices are based on fair dealing and its staff are expected to follow them.

For Boots' people, therefore, this sense of social responsibility has always been fundamental to the way they have carried on business. In more recent years Boards of Directors generally have been expected to formulate and publish the principles they recognize as setting standards for their companies' operations. In line with this trend, in July 1978 the Board of The Boots Company published a document called Social Responsibilities. However, social responsibility is not a rigid formula, which applies for all time: for a company it is part and parcel of the way in which it carries on business. As the social and economic environment changes, so it is necessary for us to review the way in which we have set out our policies and practices in the areas of social responsibility. We have recently completed such a review and we offer the revised document to all who are interested in our Company.

What we have said in the document is based on the Company's policies and practices in the United Kingdom, but the underlying philosophy applies worldwide. Whilst the Company's business must at all times be conducted within the laws of the countries in which it operates, the Company must also be sensitive and responsive to a great variety of social and economic conditions. It is in this context that local management has a particular responsibility, which is to see that the Company contributes to the maintenance and development of standards of good practice wherever it operates.

I am confident that staff throughout the Company's operations will play their part in maintaining our reputation as a socially responsible Company.

## Yorkshire Bank

In today's rapidly changing marketplace it is more important than ever before that we all have a clear view of our future path.

At an operational level, priorities must be amended quickly to keep pace with market conditions. However, the values and principles on which our approach is based remain constant.

This booklet sets out the philosophy of the way in which we wish to carry out our business. Some of the objectives are extremely demanding and will not be achieved overnight. However, they can be used as a guide to action at all levels.

Every member of staff has an important contribution to make to the Society's future – this statement applies to us all. If we apply the principles to the best of our abilities, the Society will continue to face the future with confidence.

## Control Data

These Business Conduct Guidelines outline Control Data's standards for ethical behaviour. However, our reputation for ethical behaviour will be determined not by our words or policies, but by our performance every day.

Our ethics are based on a belief in the dignity of the individual, and the ability of each of us to be accountable for our actions.

Although we are expected to obey the law and to abide by our agreements, our basic ethical standards require more. We must deal fairly and honestly with those whose interests we affect, and treat them as we would expect them to treat us if our situations were reversed.

We must be careful not to abuse the resources and power given to us as Control Data employees. We should create an environment that supports ethical behaviour: an environment where questionable practices are challenged.

The ability and willingness of each of us to raise ethical concerns is our best guarantee of ethical behaviour.

The challenge for each of us is to have the courage to make the right choices no matter how difficult the situation. This is not something we expect you to do without assistance. These guidelines will help you make the right choices.

However, guidelines cannot cover every situation, and guidelines have exceptions. You should seek help from your manager or other Company resources.

Ultimately, however, the responsibility to act ethically lies with you in your independent thinking, questioning, and judgement. If you have any doubt about the legality or ethical appropriateness of any act, you should not do it.

We rely on you to do the right thing. With your continued dedication, I am confident that the reputation of Control Data is in good hands.

# Chapter 17

# Sound business dealings and relationships

A significant portion of the British public views with disfavour the standards of honesty of businessmen and firms. Integrity and trust are vital elements in business relationships. If business people, groups, and entities do not nurture and maintain trust, there is no credibility. Without credibility, business relationships cannot effectively endure. Immanuel Kant wrote of the mutual trust necessary for social intercourse: '[E]xchange of our sentiments is the principal factor in social intercourse, and truth must be the guiding principle' in as much as '[w]ithout truth, social intercourse and conversation become valueless'.

A corollary of this view was reflected as long ago as 560 BC when the Greek philosopher Chilon indicated that a merchant should accept a loss rather than gain a dishonest profit. Why? Because dishonesty is damaging forever while a monetary loss is temporarily painful. Many managers believe that an organization's culture is the most decisive determinant of sound business dealings and proper conduct.

Each day, a business faces difficult choices in dealing with competitors, suppliers, customers, and the government. Often, rules of conduct differ. It is through the use of a code of conduct that managers and employees are able to reference the firm's considered criteria for making proper decisions necessary to ensure honest interactions. A code of conduct provides guidelines for any business firm's environment by which managers and employees can structure sound ethical relationships with each of the above groups.

A code of conduct should first begin with a general outline of acceptable, ethical business conduct. British Petroleum sets out straightforward principles that incorporate a general code of ethics. In this way, a code of conduct provides a general reference for both managers and employees when determining correct behaviour in business dealings.

A related topic is fairness in dealing. In earlier decades, many firms' management believed deception, bluffing, and puffery were the best ways of dealing with groups outside the firm. This type of improper or unethical pursuit of profits is inconsistent with nurturing a healthy environment necessary to enhance profitability and revitalize businesses in the climate of the 1990s. Only through ethical dealing in all relationships can firms develop the trust necessary to succeed. Tesco advises its managers and employees 'that we wish to be a positive and socially responsible member of the community and to be open in the operation of the business'.

Internal control is of vital importance to all businesses. Without complete records and independently audited books, firms are open to scandal. Aish and Company discovered this fact when Company Financial Adviser Jim Smith reported to the Ministry of Defence the excess profits made by Aish. Aish was subsequently forced to refund £463,000 and reduce future billing by £500,000. A thorough and complete internal control system requiring ethical dealings could have, and should have, prevented such unethical practice, and the resulting scandal, from occurring. Firms must create ethical checkpoints within the firm to help create an atmosphere of proper conduct and ethical dealing.

A firm must also determine principles on which it will base its dealings with outside groups. One of the first groups to consider is competitors. United Biscuits provides its managers and employees with an explicit, yet elegant, proviso. 'We compete vigorously, energetically, untiringly but we also compete ethically and honestly. We have no need to disparage our competitors either directly or by implication or innuendo'.

A common business practice is that of tangible and intangible inducements by the firm, and by groups dealing with the firm. ARCO provides its managers and employees with a clear mandate, 'Employees may not accept nor offer gifts or favours that create, or suggest, an improper business relationship'. Providing or accepting payments that will 'grease the rails' is not only unethical behaviour, but is deleterious to effective competition and good business practice. Every firm, and employee, should, instead, preserve and enhance the integrity of the firm and of the economic system by pursuing profits honestly.

Firms must also deal with domestic and foreign governments in an ethical manner. Royal Dutch Shell and Hewlett Packard both have extensive sections in their codes dealing with political involvement and contributions by both the firm and its employees. Firms must also set out explicit guidelines for dealing with government officials and agencies that are in accordance with the UK Prevention of Corruption Act. General Electric plainly states, ' "kickbacks" or "bribes" intended to induce or reward favourable buying decisions and governmental actions are *unacceptable* and *prohibited*'.

As to suppliers, firms must also deal ethically in order to develop long-term, mutually beneficial relationships. The John Lewis Partnership believes in 'making dealings with itself pleasant and advantageous in all proper ways to all its suppliers and their staffs and shall wish not to cause them any needless inconvenience'.

Perhaps most critical to the firm's success are those dealings with customers. Digital Equipment Corporation believes that 'We must be honest and straightforward with our customers and be sure that they are not only told the facts, but that they also understand the facts'. Ethical dealings with its customers provides a business with the requisite trust to engage in further or repeat business with its customers.

Another topic affecting customers is that of product and services: quality and pricing. Cadbury Schweppes mandates, 'The key characteristic we aim for in every aspect of the Company's activities is quality'. Gateway believes 'that price is important to everyone and that "good price + good quality = good value" '. It is clear that firms must provide their customers with both quality and value.

By establishing and publicizing standards of honest dealing in its code of conduct, a firm can create a culture of integrity and encourage standardization of such principles in its industry.

The following excerpts from major firms' codes reflect the necessary emphasis on ethical business dealings, honesty, and integrity.

## STANDARDS OF CONDUCT

### Halifax

The Society's traditions and its Conditions of Employment explicitly and implicitly require personal and corporate integrity in the sense of moral soundness and honesty. This applies to Directors, Senior Managers, and all other employees alike. All Directors, Senior Managers, and managers set the example and are expected to guide and advise others.

The General Conditions of Employment contain rules of conduct to ensure that the Society's employees know and uphold high personal standards, and so maintain the reputation and standing of the Society and those connected with it.

Those conditions include the following important requirements:

To serve the Society honestly, diligently and in good faith.

To behave properly and responsibly to other staff, customers, and others *at all times.*

Not to disclose without authority any information about the Society, its business, or its customers.

Not to allow any conflict to arise between personal interest and benefit and duty to the Society.

To report personal financial difficulties.

The General Conditions do not specifically require employees to obey the law. That goes without saying but, in addition, conduct which is within the letter but not the spirit of the law will only rarely be justified, and is a matter of delicate judgement.

It is desirable that the Society's business associates, especially close associates, should as far as practicable be people and organizations who share the Society's values. The Society's guidelines about matters such as conflict of interest, gifts, and hospitality may sometimes have to be drawn to the notice of business associates.

## Granada Group

Granada companies and Granada staff will always adhere to the highest standards of behaviour in the conduct of business. The basic criterion is that the Group will not do anything of which it would be ashamed if it were disclosed publicly. Specific standards of behaviour include:

Honesty in dealing both with staff and with the outside world.

Adherence to all legal and regulatory requirements in countries in which it operates.

Refusal to give or to accept bribes or other inducements in the furtherance of its business.

Great care is required in the conduct of business with suppliers and other third parties. Granada Group staff are expected to decline offers of gifts, non-business travel, unduly lavish entertaining, and so on, which might compromise their position or judgement on business with that third party.

## ARCO British Ltd

As a company committed to ethical standards, ARCO strives for fairness and honesty in all our relationships. In addition to obeying the law, the basic requirement, we work to sustain our reputation as a company that takes its responsibilities seriously.

A company's conduct depends first upon clear direction from senior management but ultimately upon the good faith and judgement of every employee. Personal initiative, common sense and individual responsibility will always be fundamental to our system.

While no code of conduct can anticipate every situation, the guidelines in this booklet are a useful checklist, augmented by specific policies and statements issued on these topics. Careful attention to these principles in our day-to-day activities is essential.

If our intention can be summarized, it is to foster a climate in which employees are encouraged to act freely, ethically, and morally. With everyone's cooperation and assistance ARCO as an organization will continue to be worthy of this high purpose.

## Abbey National

A firm should observe high standards of integrity and fair dealing.

A firm should act with due skill, care, and diligence.

## Scott Bader

We have agreed that as a community our work involves four tasks – economic, technical, social, and political – neglect of any one of which will in the long-term diminish the Commonwealth. We feel that the practical working out of a balance between the four tasks is a continuing study for the membership as a whole.

As members of the Commonwealth we support the basic ideas expressed in the Preamble to the Constitution and reaffirm that the Commonwealth stands for a new approach to the problems of work and society. Therefore we accept that commitment to the principles of the Commonwealth implies an active concern for the expression of these principles both in our working lives and in the other areas of our lives.

## Mobil Oil Company Ltd

Officers, directors, and employees are expected to conduct their operations in a lawful manner which is fully consistent with the highest ethical standard prevailing in the business communities in which they operate. The books and records of the Company must be kept in a complete and accurate manner. The maintenance of the highest reputation for integrity is under no circumstances to be sacrificed for the sake of results.

## British Petroleum

Ethical behaviour is defined in the Chairman's letter as being a matter of spirit and intent, characterized by the qualities of truthfulness and freedom from deception and fraud. It is relevant to a wide range of Group policies on:

business practices,
personal conduct, and
general personnel and other matters.

As the Chairman's definition suggests, ethical behaviour is more than the sum of these various policies; it requires them to be applied in accordance with principles of honest dealing, respect for natural justice, and constant regard for BP's good name.

Senior management have a crucial role in setting standards and ensuring, by their commitment to them and by their example, adherence by all staff. They thus have an obligation to ensure that corporate and 'local' decisions are subject to the same high ethical standards which will thus provide a framework against which individual members of staff should measure their own personal conduct.

All staff should be aware that adherence to the principles of ethical behaviour is a fundamental part of their duty to shareholders, management, and colleagues. Management must ensure that these principles are clearly enunciated in a manner designed to ensure staff take them seriously, that they are complied with, and are regularly reviewed for update as necessary.

Within BP the general principles of individual ethical behaviour include:

1  the scrupulous avoidance of deception, sharp practice, fraud and of any

behaviour which is or might be construed to be less than honourable in the pursuit of the Group's commercial interest;

2  honesty in dealings with BP as employer, and loyalty to BP above any and all temptations to pursue personal gain or advantage;

3  honesty and loyalty in dealing with fellow employees;

4  respect for the trust placed in the individual including proper use of Group resources or information;

5  avoidance of behaviour or situations which may reflect badly on BP.

## Rolls Royce

The Company has always been concerned that high standards of conduct should be maintained in the transaction of business both to ensure compliance with legal requirements and to maintain its reputation for fair dealing with its suppliers and customers.

For this reason, the Company has, over the years, issued guidelines on particular issues to various groups of employees, but increasing government and public interest in the integrity of business conduct now makes it appropriate for the Company to issue this code to all employees whose duties involve them in business relationships.

All employees to whom this code is issued should read the code carefully and observe it in their conduct of business on the Company's behalf. Further, as the code provides, the Company will make provision for monitoring compliance and for employees to report any infringement of the code which may come to their notice.

## British Coal

The rules set out below apply to all non-industrial staff. They are in addition to rules specified in an individual's contract of employment, to rules made known through national or local instructions from time to time, and to those general obligations of an employee to his/her employer not otherwise referred to specifically.

Certain of the rules set out below are followed by notes, shown in brackets, which explain Board policy and the need for the particular rule.

Certain rules refer to detailed regulations and instructions. These are made known to staff through individual letters or office notices, induction and training courses, the Board's Standard Conditions of Employment for non-industrial staff available at each workplace and held by the Staff Manager or local representative, and the Board's Standing Instructions. Staff should familiarize themselves with and observe all such regulations and instructions, in addition to the rules set out below. If staff are in doubt on particular points they must consult their supervisors or the management officials to whom they are responsible, or their Staff Managers.

As is recognized in the ACAS Code of Practice, any set of rules is unlikely to be exhaustive or to embrace all the circumstances which may arise. The underlying principle therefore which should govern the conduct of Board staff is the need for the Board's business to be conducted in an orderly and efficient manner and for the behaviour of staff to be above reproach. Staff must at all times act in a lawful manner: the particular emphasis placed below on certain statutory requirements, which may be particularly relevant to the workplace, is not intended to detract from this general obligation, and breaches of certain rules may give rise to criminal charges.

Staff will forward the Board's business and interests in matters forming part of their duties to the best of their ability and so far as is within their power cooperate by carrying out their duties in accordance with general principles or instructions given from time to time.

## London Buses

London Regional Transport intends to conduct its affairs, and wishes to be seen to conduct its affairs, with a high standard of integrity, behaviour, and business practice with regards to its customers, suppliers, and staff.

Staff should not use their authority or office for personal gain but should seek to uphold and enhance the standing of London Regional Transport by observing the following precepts:

1  maintaining an unimpeachable standard of integrity in all business relationships both inside and outside LRT;
2  fostering the highest possible standards of competence amongst those for whom they are responsible;
3  optimizing the use of resources for which they are responsible to provide the maximum benefit to LRT; complying both with the letter and the spirit of:
    a) the law of the country in which they practice
    b) such guidance on professional practice as may be issued by the various relevant Institutes from time to time
    c) good business practice
    d) contractual obligations;
4  rejecting any business practice which might reasonably be deemed improper.

## Kingfisher

The group expects a high standard of conduct from its employees, which will not bring any group company into disrepute. If in doubt about any particular course of action, an employee should check first with his or her supervisor. Breach by an employee of any aspect of this code may be treated as gross misconduct under that employee's contract of service resulting in summary dismissal.

## Dow

Our conduct demonstrates a deep concern for ethics, citizenship, safety, health, and the environment.

## Hewlett Packard Ltd

1 *Pay as you go – no long-term borrowing*
Helps us maintain a stable financial environment during depressed business periods.
Serves as an excellent self-regulating mechanism for HP managers.
2 *Market expansion and leadership based on new product contributions*
Engineering excellence determines market recognition of our new products. New product ideas and implementations serve as the basis for expanding existing markets or diversifying into new markets.
3 *Customer satisfaction second to none*
We sell only what has been thoroughly designed, tested, and specified.
Our products have lasting value – they are highly reliable (quality) and our customers discover additional benefits while using them.
Best after-sales service and support in the industry.
4 *Honesty and integrity in all matters*
No tolerance for dishonest dealings with vendors or customers (e.g. bribes, kickbacks).
Open and honest communication with employees and stockholders alike. Conservative financial reporting.

## Pearson

Pearson companies will observe high standards of business ethics and will deal in good faith with customers, suppliers, employees, and employee representatives.

## FAIRNESS IN DEALING

## Abbey Life

A company representative shall exercise due skill, care and diligence in his business dealings and shall deal fairly with investors.

## ARCO British Ltd

Treat customers, suppliers, and competitors fairly and honestly, and in compliance with the antitrust laws. The company's antitrust policy contains the specifics of expected employee conduct.

## Tesco

On a more general plane, this note closes by reminding you that we wish to be a positive and socially responsible member of the community and to be open in the operation of the business. Throughout the business we will avoid prejudice on the grounds of sex, race, colour, and creed.

## Control Data

Control Data expects you to be fair with everyone you deal with on behalf of the Company. Sometimes, however, it may be hard to define what is fair.

In some situations, the law will determine what is fair. Control Data will abide by all applicable laws wherever it does business. Be aware, however, that many of our policies ask more of us than is required by the law. Another way to look at this area of fairness is to imagine yourself in the other person's place. How would you expect to be treated?

## IBM UK Ltd and IBM USA

Everyone you do business with is entitled to fair and even-handed treatment. That should be true no matter what your relationship with an outside organization may be – whether you are buying, selling, or representing IBM in any other capacity.

## Procter & Gamble

A third principle central to the character of P&G is a total commitment to honesty in all our business dealings . . . inside the Company and out. Our decision-making process has been described as a 'democracy of ideas'. This helps insure we can choose the best decision from among *all* the possible alternatives that the organization can generate . . . not just the ideas of one person or a few people. For this democracy of ideas to exist, we must deal honourably and openly with others. We simply cannot tolerate bending the facts or withholding information in order to make a sale. We can't operate with other P&G departments on the basis that 'what they don't know won't hurt them'.

Similarly, in our dealings outside the Company, we strive to be honest and fair. We must try to do the right things with our suppliers. We are a major purchaser of goods and services, and depend upon our suppliers to conduct our business successfully. We may well be tough bargainers, and we never spend money needlessly. However, we should be prepared to pay a fair price for value received, and then expect first quality. And, in all our dealings we never tolerate kickbacks, bribes, or conflict of interest to make our business dealings easier or clear away apparent obstacles. As these practices are increasingly subjected to public scrutiny, we can be very proud of Procter & Gamble's record. It is, perhaps, the best in all industry.

## INTERNAL CONTROL

### TI Group

Strong worldwide financial control is an essential element of the Group's management style and organization. Financial Controllers (and all equivalent appointments) throughout the Group have a functional responsibility, ultimately to the Finance Director of TI Group, for the integrity of financial reporting and for maintaining professional standards.

The Financial Management of each company is responsible for complying with the Group's financial management and control procedures as set out in the Group Statements of Financial and Accounting Policies and for ensuring that cost effective internal control procedures are implemented within its operation. Written statements of these systems of internal control must be maintained.

Good legal title to all our assets, whether fixed, tangible or intangible (such as intellectual property), must be obtained and maintained so that rights of ownership in respect of their use and commercial exploitation can be fully enforced.

A record must be maintained listing each company's assets and their values.

In addition to the details of land and property maintained on each company's asset register, a central Group Register of all properties is maintained by the Group Property Director. He must be notified, therefore, of all acquisitions and disposals and in significant cases in advance of commitment.

### Alcan

To refrain from the offer or receipt of improper payments and to ensure that all financial transactions are properly recorded in the books of account, that books of account and accounting procedures are supported and reinforced by a comprehensive system of internal controls and that they are available for inspection by the directors and auditors of each unit.

### Abbey Life

A company representative shall treat all information given to him by an investor as confidential, but this paragraph shall not prohibit the passing of information from a company representative to the Member.

A company representative shall:

1 keep a record in the form required by the Member of all transactions with investors which involve the transmission of money; and
2 keep such other records as the Member may require of his dealings with investors; and such records shall be kept for such period as the Member may specify.

A company representative shall acknowledge in writing receipt of all money (other than cheques) received from an investor and shall forward promptly to the Member all money due from him to the Member.

### ARCO British Ltd

Accurate and reliable records are critical to the operation of any business. Every transaction between ARCO and those with whom it deals must be reflected on the books of the company promptly, accurately, and in accordance with company accounting practices as well as legal and acceptable accounting standards. Undisclosed or unrecorded funds, assets, or accounts are unacceptable. Deliberately false or misleading reports are inexcusable.

### Control Data

Control Data will not, directly or indirectly, offer any kind of payments or contributions for reasons such as to:

Influence customers, suppliers or governmental entities, including their officials or employees.
Get or keep business.
Persuade any officials or employees of another company to fail to perform, or improperly perform, their duties.
Influence legislation.

Control Data will not submit to extortion as a cost of doing business.

Information that you record and submit to another party, whether inside or outside of Control Data, must be accurate, timely, and complete. Present it so you provide an accurate picture of the material. Reports should not be used to mislead those who receive them, or to conceal anything that is improper.

### General Electric

General Electric Company has ethical and legal responsibilities for the proper use and protection of its assets and for reporting financial information to investors, government agencies, share owners, and others. In addition, the Board of Directors, officers, and managers at all echelons require various financial reports to assist them in the discharge of their responsibilities. The Company has established and must maintain high standards of accuracy, integrity, and completeness in its financial records and reporting. There is thus a need for a Company policy with respect to (1) the nature of the required financial records, reports, and controls and (2) assignment of appropriate responsibilities.

Uniformity in certain basic accounting definitions, classifications, and control practices is necessary in order to meet Company requirements and to provide financial statements for various components and affiliates on a comparable basis. In addition, the financial function uses information derived from sources outside the Company's accounting system and process. Therefore, there is also the need for:

1 a Company statement with respect to establishment of uniform financial reporting procedures and control practices;
2 defining responsibilities of people in nonfinancial functions for initiating information and protecting the assets of the Company;
3 guidance to employees of the Company responsible for relations with affiliated companies with respect to affiliate financial records, reporting, and controls.

It is the policy of the General Electric Company, on its own behalf and in connection with the operations of its controlled affiliates, that:

1 accounts and records shall be maintained and financial reports shall be prepared in a manner which conforms with generally accepted principles, authoritative standards, and legal requirements for accounting and financial reporting;
2 release of financial information outside the Company will be made only after consideration of the Company's interests as a whole and only by those designated to release such information.

Specifically, the accounting, financial reporting, and accounting control system of the Company shall be sufficient to provide reasonable assurance that:

1 accountability for assets is established, assets are adequately protected, the effectiveness of routines to safeguard assets is confirmed periodically, and any significant weaknesses in these activities are corrected promptly;
2 transactions involving the Company are appropriately authorized, and an adequate record and appropriate reports are made with respect to such transactions;
3 adequate record and appropriate reports are made of other events which result in acquisition or disposition of assets or the incurrence or satisfaction of liabilities;
4 financial statements and reports, issued for the Company and its individual organization components, present fairly their financial position, the results of their operations, and/or other financial data in conformity with generally accepted accounting principles appropriate in the circumstances and with other applicable requirements.

Employees of the Company responsible for relations with controlled affiliates shall take such action as may be required to ensure that such affiliates establish accounting, financial reporting, and accounting control systems consistent with those required under this Policy.

Employees of the Company responsible for relations with affiliated companies which are not controlled shall encourage adoption of accounting, financial reporting, and accounting control systems similar to those required under this Policy.

## Procter & Gamble

All official records of the conduct of the Company's business must be accurate, honest, and complete without any restriction or qualification of any kind. This means that the accuracy of any record involves both factual documentation and ethical evaluation/appraisal.

Company employees involved in the preparation, the evaluation/appraisal, and the maintenance of Company records should keep in mind that the Company considers the accuracy of its records of critical importance.

All employees should also understand that the Company does not maintain nor does it countenance any 'off-the-books' funds for any purpose. This means, without exception, that all Company funds must be accounted for in official Company records, and the identity of each entry and account will be accurate and complete.

The Company does not condone the concealing of any payment by means of passing it through the books and accounts of third parties, such as agents or consultants.

As in their other responsibilities, employees are expected to be honest, objective, and loyal in the performance of record keeping responsibilities. However, because loyalty includes never knowingly being a part of any illegal or unethical activity, there is never an excuse for a deliberately false or misleading Company record.

## Quaker Oats

All books and records throughout the Company must be accurate and fairly reflect the underlying transactions. It is each employee's responsibility to ensure that documents supporting the accounting records (receipts, disbursements, journal entries) contain wording which clearly describes the reason and purpose for the transaction.

## Tenneco

The Company and its employees and agents shall comply with all applicable legal requirements and the highest ethical standards of the United States and each foreign country in which business is conducted.

The use of assets of the Company for any unlawful or improper purpose is strictly prohibited.

No undisclosed or unrecorded fund or asset of the Company shall be established for any purpose.

No false or misleading entries shall be made in the books and records of the Company for any reason, and no employee shall engage in any arrangement that results in such prohibited act.

No payment on behalf of the Company shall be approved without adequate supporting documentation or made with the intention or understanding that any part of such payment is to be used for any purpose other than that described by the documents supporting the payment.

Compliance with generally accepted accounting rules and established internal controls is required at all times.

## COMPETITORS

### Kingfisher

The policy of the group is to compete vigorously in the marketplace. In any event acting in collusion with competitors in many cases is in contravention of UK and EEC competition laws and would have serious consequences for the group.

Employees and directors of the group companies must be constantly alert when in contact with employees of competitors and suppliers, whether in the course of business or social life, to the need to avoid (whether deliberately or inadvertently) revealing trading information or any other information which could be of use to the competitor in question.

Employees must at all times be scrupulous in observing legal and ethical standards in the way that they seek to obtain information about a competitor's plans and operations. If in doubt they should consult their supervisor.

### Digital Equipment Corporation

We never criticize the competition publicly. We sell by presenting the positive features of our own products. We want to be respectful of all competition, and collect and analyse all public information about competitors. When we hire people from competitors, we should never ask them for confidential, competitive information, nor should we use confidential literature they may have taken with them.

These ethical and moral concepts must be the same for our business lives as they are for our personal lives. There is no separate or less restrictive business morality. Additionally, there are a number of legal restrictions on how we may conduct business covering many diverse subjects such as financial reporting, competition, pricing, employee relations, etc. Our Corporate or Area Law Departments are available to assist you in complying with these.

We compete vigorously, energetically, untiringly but we also compete ethically and honestly. Our competitive success is founded on excellence – of product and of service. We have no need to disparage our competitors either directly or by implication or innuendo.

In any contacts with competitors, employees will avoid discussing proprietary or confidential information.

No one may attempt improperly to acquire a competitor's trade secrets or other proprietary or confidential information. 'Improper' means are activities such as industrial espionage, hiring competitors' employees to get confidential information, urging competitive personnel or customers to disclose confidential information, or any other approach which is not completely open and above board.

## Burmah

Enterprises should, while conforming to official competition rules and established policies of the countries in which they operate:

1 Refrain from actions which would adversely affect competition in the relevant market by abusing a dominant position of market power, by means of, for example:

   a) anti-competitive acquisitions;
   b) predatory behaviour toward competitors;
   c) unreasonable refusal to deal;
   d) anti-competitive abuse of industrial property rights;
   e) discriminatory (i.e. unreasonably differentiated) pricing and using such pricing transactions between affiliated enterprises as a means of affecting adversely competition outside these enterprises.

2 Allow purchasers, distributors, and licensees freedom to resell, export, purchase, and develop their operations consistent with law, trade conditions, the need for specialization, and sound commercial practice.

3 Refrain from participating in or otherwise purposely strengthening the restrictive effects of international or domestic cartels or restrictive agreements which adversely affect or eliminate competition and which are not generally or specifically accepted under applicable national or international legislation.

4 Be ready to consult and cooperate, including the provision of information, with competent authorities of countries whose interests are directly affected in regard to competition issues or investigations. Provision of information should be in accordance with safeguards normally applicable in this field.

## London Buses

While bearing in mind the advantages to LRT of maintaining a continuing relationship with a supplier, any arrangement which might in the long term prevent the effective operation of fair competition should be avoided.

## Tesco

To attract more customers by fulfilling their needs with a wide range of quality products and courteous service in an attractive shopping environment.

## IBM UK Ltd and IBM USA

If you work in a marketing or service activity, IBM asks you to compete not just vigorously and effectively but fairly as well.

It has long been IBM's policy to sell products and services on their merits, not by disparaging competitors, their products, or their services. False or misleading statements and innuendos are improper. Don't make comparisons that unfairly cast the competitor in a bad light. Such conduct only invites disrespect from customers and complaints from competitors.

## Monsanto

General business information about competitors is important in our efforts to maintain and improve upon our competitive position both in terms of products and technology. However, no circumstances can exist which justify the use of improper means to develop competitive information.

It is Monsanto's policy to use only ethical and legal means for gathering information about present and future competitors.

Full use may be made of competitive information available in trade and other publications, and information obtainable by analysis of a competitor's product where it is available in the open market.

Information disclosed in formal presentations at public meetings may be used freely. However, when information is received privately or in small group discussions, care must be exercised to ascertain that there is no notice that either the information is secret or a confidential relationship is being breached. If there is such notice, receipt of the information should be avoided.

All actions to acquire competitive information from governmental agencies under the Freedom of Information Act or similar state or local laws must be based on prior review and approved by the Patent and/or Law Departments. Monsanto employees are not to induce, through social relationships or otherwise, present or former employees of competitors to disclose any proprietary or confidential information. Any such information offered gratuitously should be refused and Monsanto's employees should avoid having any confidential obligation imposed upon them, unless in writing, with the approval of an appropriate authority. In addition, Monsanto employees are not to question any fellow employees in a manner which is likely to result in confidential information of a previous employer being disclosed.

Employees of competitors will not be recruited or hired for their knowledge of proprietary information of present or former employers. A new employee should not be assigned work in an area where there is likelihood that use of proprietary information of the former employer would be required. New employees should be advised against disclosing or using any confidential or trade secret information of their former employer, and Monsanto supervisors should take action to see that they do not. However, all employees can and are expected to otherwise make full use of the skills, experience, and general knowledge learned in their previous employments.

### Quaker Oats

As a competitor in the marketplace, we continually seek economic knowledge about our competition. However, we will not engage in illegal or improper acts to acquire a competitor's trade secrets, customer lists, information about company facilities, technical developments or operations. In addition, we will not hire competitors' employees to obtain confidential information or urge competitive personnel or customers to disclose confidential information.

### 3M

Relations with Competitors: In competitive situations, no officer, manager, or employee shall agree in any form to an arrangement with a competitor or competitors regarding price, terms or conditions of sale, distribution of products, profits, production capacity, facilities, market share, territories, or customers. Even informational exchanges and trade association memberships should be avoided unless the guidelines of the Management Guide are met scrupulously and General Counsel is consulted.

## USE AND RECEIPT OF GIFTS, OTHER BUSINESS INDUCEMENTS, AND HOSPITALITY

### Halifax

Business gifts other than items of small intrinsic value (such as business diaries or calendars) may not be accepted without the consent of a General Manager, Regional General Manager, or Branch Manager as appropriate.

Personal gifts require even more care. It is reasonable to *exchange* personal gifts of similar value with friends who are also business connections if the gifts are paid for personally by the donor. There are obvious dangers if the value of gifts exchanged is very different. Gifts provided by the Society or a donor in a business capacity should be offered or accepted only within the general guidelines set out in this note. They should therefore be of small intrinsic value such as a single bottle of spirit.

No gift must be one which could be seen as a bribe. That means any corrupt inducement or reward for any act or forbearance or for showing favour or not showing disfavour in business. Offering or accepting any such gift is a criminal offence with a maximum sentence of two to seven years imprisonment and is a serious breach of discipline. Therefore no gift which might reasonably be thought to influence judgement may be offered or accepted.

Good turns and favours also require care. It is better that no good turn or favour should be expected in return. No 'good turn' or 'favour' should be offered or accepted if it could create an obligation which it would be wrong or uncomfortable to fulfil.

No gift should be offered to or accepted from a person at the time of a negotiation with him or her.

## ARCO British Ltd

Employees may not accept nor offer gifts or favours that create or suggest an improper business relationship.

Paying or taking bribes is dishonest, unfair, and usually illegal. The practice is forbidden in ARCO. The Foreign Corrupt Practices Act provides additional guidance in this area.

## The Automobile Association

Similarly, employees should not accept inducements from any business with which the Association has a connection.

## British Steel

British Steel expects from its employees the highest standards of integrity and conduct in all matters concerning the Company. An employee must not subordinate his duty as a company employee to his private interests, or place himself in any position where his responsibilities as a Company employee might conflict with his private interests or give grounds for suspicion in this regard. The Company looks to its employees to exercise scrupulous care at all times in these matters, and particularly in those which are covered in more detail in the succeeding paragraphs.

No gifts (other than advertising matter of modest value such as calendars and diaries) or favours should be accepted by a Company employee, or his close family, from people or organizations with whom the employee has, or it is reasonable to expect may have, business dealings on behalf of the Company. Similarly, Company employees should not offer gifts or favours to business contacts or their close families.

Offers to a Company employee, or his close family, of hospitality or entertainment of a frequency, type, or scale which the Company would not wish to reciprocate, should not be accepted. Rigid definitions are not possible but the Company looks to its employees to exercise commonsense and judgement and, if in any doubt, to decline an offer.

Any offer of an unreasonably generous gift, favour or hospitality that is received should immediately be reported by the employee in writing to his Director (or equivalent).

It is important for employees to be aware that corruptly soliciting or receiving any gift or favour (including an attempt) is a criminal offence.

## British Gas

It is a criminal offence to accept or solicit any gift or consideration from anyone as an inducement or reward for showing favour in connection with the Company's business.

To avoid any possibility of misunderstanding, all such offers should be politely but firmly declined. Gifts delivered should be returned to the sender with an appropriately worded letter and the matter reported to your superior. The only exception is that gifts of a trifling nature, such as calendars or diaries, may be accepted.

Any approaches from contractors, suppliers or traders, seeking favoured treatment in consideration of any offers of benefits or hospitality, must be firmly declined and the circumstances reported to your superior.

Business entertainment should be on a reciprocal basis and on a scale consistent with that which you, when host, would be authorized to arrange.

If you have the slightest doubt about accepting any offer of benefits or hospitality you have clearly recognized a potentially dangerous situation and should seek guidance from your superior.

Similarly, you should not send any gift, other than of a trifling nature such as a calendar or diary, to anyone employed by an outside organization, Government Department, or Local Authority or anyone else with whom the Company has or may have a business relationship.

## Digital Equipment Corporation

Modest entertainment of our customers is regarded as one phase of establishing an effective relationship. Entertainment at dinners and sporting events is appropriate, and should be conducted tastefully and in a manner to promote good communications between the customer and our Company. A small gift may also be appropriate for the same purpose. Any entertainment that bestows valuable benefits upon the recipient is definitely not allowed.

Digital employees and their family members must not accept any gratuities or gifts that go beyond the common courtesies, or which exceed a nominal value from a customer, supplier, or anyone else having a business relationship with the Company. Anyone receiving such a gift should immediately turn it over to his/her supervisor so that the appropriate action can be taken. Our agents and representatives must follow the same practice.

## Rolls Royce

There have been instances of employees coming under suspicion of improperly accepting favours from firms carrying out or seeking work with the Company. In some cases this ultimately led to court proceedings.

Employees are entitled to the protection of guidelines as to what is acceptable and what is not.

In principle, casual gifts of value offered to employees in the context of their work by outside bodies or their employees should be refused. Exceptionally, at Christmas time, it is entirely reasonable to accept single gifts of modest value (generally bearing a company's name or insignia) typically a calendar, diary, inexpensive pen. Other than at Christmas, you are advised not to accept any gift except on reciprocal basis (e.g. exchanging Company ties) because the act of acceptance, without a similar gesture in return, may be perceived as placing you under an obligation to the giver. Any such gifts should be politely refused or returned.

If, exceptionally, you consider that such a gift can be properly accepted without risk to your reputation (e.g. in the context of collaboration, or at the time of your retirement, after a long working relationship) you should seek authorization so to do through your manager from his/her manager. In your own interests you are recommended to put this in writing.

Similar principles apply to the acceptance of hospitality. This should only be accepted (apart from lunch in a normal working day) in the context of a prior arrangement to carry out or discuss business.

### London Buses

Modest business gifts are an acceptable courtesy of a business relationship. However, recipients should not allow themselves to reach a situation whereby they might be, or might reasonably be deemed by others to be, influenced in making a business decision as a consequence of accepting such business gifts; the frequency and scale accepted must not be significantly different from that which LRT would expect to provide. The gift should be advised to the responsible superior.

Modest hospitality is an accepted courtesy of a business relationship. However, the recipient should not allow him or herself to reach a position whereby he or she might be or might be deemed by others to have been influenced in making a business decision as a consequence of accepting such hospitality; the frequency and scale of hospitality accepted should not be significantly greater than LRT would be likely to provide in return. Hospitality received and given should be reported to the employing Manager.

When it is not easy to decide between what is and is not acceptable in terms of gifts or hospitality, any offer should be declined on the grounds that it is against Company policy.

### Halifax

Hospitality (including entertainment, travel facilities, and holidays) is a kind of gift and the same principles apply to it.

Reasonable hospitality is, however, an accepted part of business. Hospitality offered and given must be within the limits of style and cost agreed by the

Society's senior management from time to time. Hospitality received should be within similar limits so that hospitality accepted should not be more lavish than the Society would offer in similar circumstances.

The return of hospitality requires some care. On the one hand repeated unreturned hospitality is to be avoided, but on the other hand the direct return of hospitality without any proper business justification may be the subject of a charge to tax by the Inland Revenue.

Particular care is needed over the offer or provision of hospitality while in negotiation. Hospitality must not tie or appear to tie the Society or any employee to any business connection or vice versa.

## Legal & General

To maintain Legal & General's business integrity at all times, we need to make decisions which are in the company's best interests. To be seen to be receiving any form of personal gain from any customer or supplier could seriously damage the reputation for integrity which is so important to us.

Employees may not solicit gifts or benefits of a personal nature from any customer of Legal & General or any person or organization which does business with Legal & General, or accept gifts other than those recognized by the company as normal business practice.

In practice it is necessary to distinguish acceptable from unacceptable behaviour. The following types of benefits or entertainments are examples of acceptable business practice:

1 Reasonable and appropriate hospitality.
2 Paid trips where the employee is formally representing the Legal & General and prior company approval has been granted.
3 Gifts up to a cash value decided by the Business Unit.
4 Unsolicited promotional or advertising matter of low value.
5 Monetary compensation received from an organization in which an employee holds an official position, for which the line manager has given approval.
6 If there is any question about the propriety of a particular gift or benefit, appropriate guidance must be sought.

We must avoid putting ourselves in the position where it becomes obligatory to offer payments or gifts in order to do business. To pay money or offer gifts which could be considered bribes would have a profoundly adverse effect on the trust our clients place in us and damage the public perception of the company.

Employees of Legal & General may not offer inducements of a sort that would be considered bribes in the course of doing business – either to obtain business or to retain it.

No payment of any kind which is or could be construed to be a bribe may be offered in the pursuit of business. However, certain types of payments should not be confused with bribes. The following points describe practices which fall within normal business conventions:

1 Any normal marketing incentives offered to agents or consultants on behalf of Legal & General in the course of doing business, such as the loan of computers, which are not personal but are considered part of normal business practice, are not improper.
2 Commissions, which are taxable and offered as part of a remuneration package, are ordinary payments and not improper.
3 Promotional items, such as the Legal & General umbrella, do not fit into the category of bribes.

## Ford Motor Company Ltd and Ford Motor Company USA

No employee may solicit, directly or indirectly, for such employee's benefit or for the benefit of any relative or friend, any gift or favour from an organization with which the Company does business or that seeks to do business with the Company.

No employee may accept, directly or indirectly, from an organization with which the Company does business, or that seeks to do business with the Company, for such employee's benefit or for the benefit of any relative or friend, any gift or favour, other than:

1 one of nominal value and involving normal sales promotion, advertising or publicity, or
2 one involving an appropriate social amenity, provided there is not even the appearance of a compromise of sound business principles in the relationship.

No employee or Company organizational activity may make or grant, directly or indirectly, to an owner, employee, or other representative (including any relative or friend on such person's behalf) of an organization with which the Company does business or seeks to do business, any gift or favour, other than:

1 one involving Company-approved sales promotion, advertising, or publicity and (a) directly related to the sale or service of products sold by the Company, or (b) of nominal value; or
2 one involving an appropriate social amenity, provided there is not even the appearance of a compromise of sound business principles in the relationship.

No employee or Company organizational activity may solicit or accept any gift, favour, support, or sponsorship from an organization that does business or seeks to do business with the Company in connection with any Company athletic event or other Company recreational activity, such as a Christmas party or other Company sponsored gathering, consisting principally of Company employees.

An employee who solicits donations on behalf of a charitable or other outside organization should endeavour to avoid creating the basis for an implication of influence or pressure by the Company.

## GOVERNMENTAL AGENCIES, OFFICIALS, AND POLITICS

### Abbey National

A firm should deal with its regulator in an open and cooperative manner and keep the regulator promptly informed of anything concerning the firm which might reasonably be expected to be disclosed to it.

### Royal Dutch Shell

Shell companies endeavour always to act commercially, operating within existing national laws in a socially responsible manner, abstaining from participation in party politics. It is, however, their legitimate right and responsibility to speak out on matters that affect the interests of employees, customers, and shareholders, and on matters of general interest, where they have a contribution to make that is based on particular knowledge.

As a policy, Shell companies do not make payments to political parties, organizations, or their representatives.

Where employees, in their capacity as citizens, wish to engage in activities in the community, including standing for election to public office, favourable consideration is given to their being enabled to do so where this is appropriate in the light of local circumstances.

### ARCO British Ltd

Under the law, corporations cannot contribute to candidates for federal office. The same is true for many state offices. If a contribution is illegal, it cannot be made, either as a direct donation of corporate funds, or an 'in kind' gift of corporate goods or services.

ARCO's corporate values can and should be applied worldwide, yet certain precautions are in order with respect to overseas activities. Do not assume that foreign antitrust, consumer protection, environmental, and other legal standards are the same as in the United States. They are not. Remember that ARCO must comply with US laws governing foreign operations of American firms. The Foreign Corrupt Practices Act prohibits payments to foreign government officials. The Anti-Boycott Statutes bar American companies from joining boycotts aimed at Israel and other countries. And US Antitrust laws may impact foreign transactions affecting American commerce.

### Hewlett Packard Ltd

HP employees shall comply with the legal requirements of each country in which HP conducts business and shall employ the highest ethical standards. Use of HP assets for any unlawful or improper purpose is strictly prohibited.

No undisclosed or unrecorded HP fund or asset shall be established for any purpose.

No false or misleading entries shall be made in HP's books or records for any reason.

No payment (regardless of form) shall be made on HP's behalf without adequate supporting documentation or for any purpose other than as described in the documents.

HP employees shall comply with generally accepted accounting rules and the following business control practices:

1  Transactions shall be executed in accordance with HP policies and procedures.
2  Only authorized persons shall have access to company assets.

No HP funds or assets shall be used for party political contributions without the prior written approval of HP's Executive Committee.

The above prohibitions are not intended to discourage employees from making personal contributions to candidates, parties, or political committees of their choice. Employees, however, will not be reimbursed by HP in any way for personal contributions.

HP's relationship with all government agencies and their officials and personnel shall be such that the public disclosure of full details thereof will not damage HP's reputation.

HP's policy forbids direct or indirect payment of HP or private funds to government agencies, officials, or employees in furtherance of HP business. Gifts of value or entertainment beyond that customarily extended in ordinary commercial transactions are not permitted. All government restrictions on the receipt of gifts or entertainment must be observed.

## Mobil Oil Company Ltd

The Company will not make political donations to any political party or candidate. The Directors will continue to affirm annually that no such contributions have been made.

The Company may, however, from time to time take stands on issues of public policy when, in the opinion of the Management, the interests of the Company, its shareholders, employees, and others associated with the Company are involved. In such cases the Company may decide to spend funds to make public its views, and to give support to organizations that advocate essentially the same position as the Company has taken. Each proposal must be referred initially to the General Manager, Public Affairs, who after consultation with the Legal Department, will seek the approval of the Chairman.

## Control Data

It is Control Data's policy not to use its resources to support political parties or candidates. Therefore, the Company avoids making political contributions, even when these contributions may be legal. Any exceptions to this rule require specific Corporate approval.

Individual employees, of course, may support their own parties and candidates as long as they do so on their time and do not use Control Data resources.

## SUPPLIERS

### John Lewis Partnership

The Partnership shall aim at making dealings with itself pleasant and advantageous in all proper ways to all its suppliers and their staffs and shall wish not to cause them any needless inconvenience.

... Every payment shall be made immediately upon its becoming due. ...

Although the Partnership may profit from a trader's apparent ignorance of the value of goods in which he normally undertakes to trade . . . it shall take no advantage of his ignorance of the value of goods outside his normal business.

It shall punctiliously keep faith with its suppliers.

Should it regret a bargain made in good faith on both sides, and the supplier does not consent to renegotiate, the Partnership shall perform its own part of the bargain punctually and with good grace.

### United Biscuits

UB's size gives it considerable power as a purchaser. This power must never be used unscrupulously.

All suppliers are entitled to fair treatment and every potential supplier should have a reasonable opportunity to win our business. However, we value the long-standing relationships built up over the years with our established suppliers who will not be replaced unless significant benefit to our company can be demonstrated.

All information about the relationship between UB and a supplier is confidential.

Products and services can of course be bought from a supplier who also buys from us. We will not, however, make any conditional or reciprocal agreements – UB's purchasing decisions must be totally independent.

Employees must not allow themselves to become in any way beholden to a supplier. They must avoid doing anything which might create the impression that a supplier has a 'friend at UB' or that special influence may have been exerted on a supplier's behalf.

No buyer may knowingly induce or receive a preferential price for his personal benefit.

Suppliers will be paid on time, in accordance with agreed terms of trade.

## Taylor Woodrow

Our shareholders and clients should be made aware of our policy of using only such subcontractors and suppliers whose services or materials conform to our requirements for high standards of workmanship and quality.

As a large trading group, we recognise that many of our subcontractors and suppliers may lack financial reserves, and we must always ensure that our debts to them are met promptly.

## The Boots Company

In its dealings with suppliers it is the policy of the Company to ensure that:

1 the terms of business are clearly stated and unambiguous, that they are honoured in accordance with good commercial practice;
2 there is no abuse of economic power in dealing with a smaller concern.

The Company realises that it has an interest in the prosperity of its suppliers and contractors, and seeks to develop a close working relationship with them.

It is the Company's policy to meet its UK requirements from UK suppliers, subject always to goods and materials being available at a competitive price, to the right design and specification and to meet required delivery dates.

## The Automobile Association

Staff are warned not to use their position within the AA to pursue any personal grievance against a supplier.

## Digital Equipment Corporation

We wish to be viewed by suppliers as a desirable customer. Business transactions with suppliers will be conducted on an honest, fair, and open basis. Suppliers and potential suppliers will be treated courteously and given an opportunity to present their goods and services for consideration. Competition is encouraged. Our business ethics require that our employees do not accept from suppliers any gifts, gratuities, or entertainment that exceed common courtesy or are of nominal value.

As defined in our Purchasing Policies, business transactions with suppliers and subcontractors should be conducted on a free and open basis. Alternative suppliers should be permitted to compete openly and fairly, so that the procurement choice can be objectively established as the one most favourable to Digital.

We want suppliers to view Digital as a desirable and fair customer. Any employee who has any personal relationship with a supplier should disqualify himself/herself from the decision-making process with respect to that supplier.

## Kingfisher

It is important to the group that first class relationships with suppliers are developed. However, it is not group policy for employees to accept anything other than modest hospitality from suppliers (which for this purpose includes professional advisers, consultants, and property developers, and other organizations doing or wishing to do business with group companies) such as lunch or dinner. Before acceptance of any greater level of hospitality (e.g. overseas trips), employees must advise and obtain written authority from a director of their company who should ensure that the hospitality in question is for the benefit of the group's business.

Gifts (including free services, prizes, cash, or competition entry forms) may not be solicited or accepted from suppliers in any circumstances or for any purpose.

Unsolicited gifts (including free services, prizes, cash, or competition entry forms) to employees of any group company from suppliers should only be accepted on the basis that they are placed into a staff draw.

## Tesco

To maintain and develop long-term relationships with our suppliers to our mutual benefit.

## Procter & Gamble

The Company bases its worldwide supplier relationships on fundamental concepts of honesty, fairness, mutual respect, and nondiscrimination. We encourage continued supplier support of all kinds which will enhance our, and their, prosperity and build sound, long-term relationships. At the same time, we respect and value healthy competition for our business, believing it is essential in a sound business system.

Because the great bulk of the Company's purchasing is handled by various Corporate and Divisional Purchases organizations, these organizations have operating guidelines for dealing with suppliers. These guidelines are available for use by other departments in the development of appropriate guidelines covering direct relationships they may have with suppliers. The appropriate purchases organization should be consulted if any department feels a need for advice on proper handling of supplier relations.

All employees who deal with suppliers or potential suppliers – whether occasionally or infrequently, directly or indirectly – should be guided by the following:

1 Purchases of materials and services are based on the merits – on a total value basis – of the purchase opportunities available from competing offers.
2 All discussions with an existing or potential supplier should be restricted solely to the Company's needs and the materials/services being offered by that supplier. There should be no reference or inference about present or potential relationships with other suppliers.
3 The Company does not countenance reciprocity with suppliers in any part of the business. The materials/services the Company requires are purchased solely on their merits, just as the products the Company sells are sold solely on their merits.
4 P&G employees who make purchasing decisions should not be involved in the solicitation on behalf of charitable, civic or other organizations of gifts of money or time from current or potential suppliers.

## CUSTOMERS

### Abbey National

A firm should seek from customers it advises or for whom it exercises discretion any information about their circumstances and investment objectives which might reasonably be expected to be relevant in enabling it to fulfil its responsibilities to them.

A firm should take reasonable steps to give a customer it advises, in a comprehensible and timely way, any information needed to enable him to make a balanced and informed decision. A firm should similarly be ready to provide a customer with a full and fair account of the fulfilment of its responsibilities to him.

Where a firm has control of or is otherwise responsible for assets belonging to a customer which it is required to safeguard, it should arrange proper protection for them, by way of segregation and identification of those assets or otherwise, in accordance with the responsibility it has accepted.

### John Lewis Partnership

Each . . . retail branch shall offer its goods or services to customers at prices which are unlikely to be undersold by any real competitor . . . . If the Partnership can undersell the cheapest of its real competitors and obtain a sufficient profit, it shall give the benefit of any doubt in favour of lower rather than higher selling prices.

. . . It shall deal promptly and courteously with the customer about any complaint or claim and be generous if the claim is believed by it to have been made in good faith and to be not grossly unreasonable.

. . . It shall take no advantage of any customer's ignorance, and if it finds it has transgressed this Rule and can identify the customer, it shall make good the transgression.

## Gateway

Gateway is dedicated to the shopping convenience of its customers. Gateway will operate stores of different sizes in a wide variety of locations. It is committed to serving small and rural communities when this can be done economically, in addition to major towns and cities. It will adapt and improve its stores, noting customers' wishes as expressed through suggestions, complaints, customer panels, and market research.

Gateway stores will be clean; they will also be interesting and appetizing. They will have a cheerful market place atmosphere, being lively rather than clinical. There will be strong, attractive promotional displays. There will be demonstrations, opportunities to sample products, and store activities to help the community.

Gateway stores will project variety and abundance. There will always be a wide range of brands, including plenty of the old favourites. There will also be new products and new ideas, including Exclusive Brands, the latter representing outstandingly good value.

## Meyer

Through a focused marketing approach we have chosen which customers to serve. If we fail they will go elsewhere. In addition to our trade customers, we also have our shareholders. We must meet their expectations by enhancing the long-term profitability and growth of our company. Only in that way can we ensure personal career security and reward.

We must really know our customers and what they want and expect even before they ask. That means carrying out more research and taking the time, trouble, and effort to work with them and retain their loyalty and support.

## BMW

BMW aims to provide the highest possible level of customer satisfaction to ensure continuing loyalty.

Whilst the primary responsibility for customer satisfaction rests with the dealer network, customer satisfaction and care are the responsibility of all BMW staff.

Customer satisfaction must extend throughout the total ownership.

## Digital Equipment Corporation

We must be honest and straightforward with our customers and be sure that they are not only told the facts, but that they also understand the facts.

To the best of our knowledge and ability, we want to be sure that the products we sell solve the needs of the customer, even when the customer is inexperienced.

We want our products and services to meet the customer's expectations, and to do this we must clarify in advance all of those expectations in a way that the customer will understand. When we sell a product to a customer, we want to be sure that the Corporation fulfils the obligations we took on with the sale. We sell our Corporation, its products, and its services, not a single individual. You must be sure all Digital commitments are met.

## Abbey Life

A firm should not, in the course of its investment business, treat a customer's interests as subordinate to its own, or take unfair advantage of a customer who has placed reliance on or trust in the firm.

A firm should seek from its customers, wherever it is appropriate to do so, any information about their circumstances and investment objectives which it might reasonably expect to be relevant in enabling it to fulfil its responsibilities to them.

A firm should avoid misleading or deceptive representations or practices and should take reasonable steps to ensure, wherever it is appropriate to do so for the purposes of enabling customers to take informed investment decisions, that their customers are properly informed about deals envisaged, their implications, and any other relevant fact.

## Coats Viyella

We are committed to providing our customers with the best possible service. Our service and products only bring returns to the degree that they serve the customer and satisfy his needs. We must strive constantly to reduce our costs in order to maintain reasonable prices, whilst ensuring our suppliers and distributors have an opportunity to make a fair profit. Customers' orders must be serviced promptly and accurately. We must compete vigorously but fairly and strive to develop confidence in our products through good marketing practice and a thorough understanding of and dialogue with our customers.

## Peugeot Talbot

Customers and suppliers are a number one priority. But to give the concept of customer satisfaction the right emphasis we have to redefine what we mean by the terms. 'Customers' are not only our dealers and the people who buy and drive our vehicles but also those colleagues within the Company to whom we 'supply' a service. In this sense we are all 'customers' and all 'suppliers'. In short, we are all interdependent. All departments should be precise, quick, and efficient in dealing with their 'customers' whether inside or outside the Company.

## The Boots Company

The Company's relations with its customers are, of course, of paramount importance to its business, both in the Retail and Industrial Divisions. Its policy is to build up a relationship of confidence through the quality, safety, and (where appropriate) the durability of its products, through a pricing system which represents value for money and with high standards of customer service. In its presentation of goods and services the Company takes great care to:

1 avoid misleading its customers over descriptions or statements whether about price, conditions of supply, terms of payment, or any other matter.
2 deal promptly and courteously with a customer about any complaint or claim.

## United Biscuits

UB's reputation for integrity is the foundation on which the mutual trust between the company and its customers is based. That relationship is the key to our trading success.

Both employees and customers need to know that products sold by any of our operating companies will always meet their highest expectations. The integrity of our products is sacrosanct and implicit in this commitment is an absolute and uncompromising dedication to quality. We will never compromise on recipes or specification of product in order to save costs. Quality improvement must always be our goal.

No employee may give money or any gift of significant value to a customer if it could reasonably be viewed as being done to gain a business advantage. Winning an order by violating this policy or by providing free or extra services or unauthorized contract terms is contrary to our trading policy.

## ICL

Our business objective is to apply information technology to provide high-value, high-volume solutions to customer problems. That is now the driving aim of the entire company and everyone in it.

We cannot begin to achieve that aim until all our thinking is directed towards the marketplace, towards developments that are taking place in the marketplace, and towards the evolving business needs of our customers. Only by concentrating on these can we anticipate and plan the integration of future technology and future market needs. And only then can we set in motion our own programmes to meet those needs with brilliantly conceived solutions and the finest possible service.

The over-riding importance of the needs and expectations of our customers should condition all our thinking and govern all our planning. We are now a company driven by the business needs of our market. We all have to become steeped in the concept that 'there is nothing too good for our customers'.

We owe them 100 per cent quality, 100 per cent reliability and 100 per cent service. Our 'zero defects' standards illustrate this commitment to our customers. We cannot be satisfied with less.

All work units within the company also have to adopt the same attitude towards their in-house 'customers'. Staff people towards their field customers; development divisions towards the sales force that will sell their systems and provide them with market intelligence; these too should adopt an attitude of 100 per cent service.

The customer matters most, and comes first in everything we do. We must never allow our own problems to distract us from understanding and solving his.

## Thomas Cook

We will develop customer relationships that inspire trust. Our customers are International Leisure and Business Travellers particularly those who prize quality and value – and those business partners who deliver our products and services to their customers with a quality consistent with our Brand.

Every encounter between ourselves and our customers will enhance the trust that our customers place in us. For in these encounters we will consistently deliver the values of reliability, responsibility, and knowledge.

Our continued growth will come from the repeat business of customers who, from experience after experience, know that they can trust us above all others.

But the ability to develop relationships will depend on our recognizing that we cannot be all things to all men, and that some people – those who value price above quality, for example – are not our customers.

## Control Data

A relationship of service and trust with our customers is vital to our success as a company. Control Data exists to serve its customers.

We must provide quality products and services to our customers. This is not something we can do once. It is a continuing process.

In addition we must accurately represent our products and services in all our marketing, advertising, and sales contacts.

## Dana

Because Dana is a market-oriented company, it is essential for Dana people to anticipate our customers' needs for total quality products and services. Once a commitment is given to a customer, we must meet that commitment. We believe that our customers' success is our success, and that serving our customers' needs is the best way to make them want to do business with us.

The ways in which Dana operations focus on serving the customer include:

1  Building long-term customer relationships through cooperative partnership agreements.
2  Cooperating with the customer on engineering, design, manufacturing, and marketing support.
3  Manufacturing products to the customer's proprietary design where appropriate, and sourcing wherever customer cost and market needs dictate.
4  Placing regional production and distribution facilities near the customer, to supply customers on a just-in-time basis.
5  Meeting all customer order fill and servicing requirements.

Developing the market strategies for focusing on customers is the Policy Committee's responsibility. Developing the products and tactics to serve customers is a divisional responsibility.

Dana people throughout the organization are expected to know our customers and their needs.

### General Electric

It is the policy of GE to understand its customers' needs for products and services, as well as all related requirements, and to put its best effort into responding to those customer needs before, during, and after every sales transaction.

It is the policy of GE to make reasonable commitments to its customers which reflect GE's true ability to serve and to make every effort to meet these commitments.

It is the policy of GE not to serve market segments whose requirements we cannot meet consistently and well.

### Procter & Gamble

Procter & Gamble's obligations to its customers throughout the world go beyond the delivery of quality products in accordance with contractual commitments. These additional obligations are reflected in certain basic principles of the Company which should guide the actions of all employees who have dealings with those businesses which buy from Procter & Gamble. These are:

1  We treat all of our customers fairly and without discrimination or deception.
2  We deal with our customers as our equals. We try to convince them to buy our products and promote their resale on the basis that this is in their own interests. They are free to purchase any one or more of our products even though they choose not to handle others.
3  We do not try to influence unfairly their decisions with respect to purchasing and promoting competitive items.

## PRODUCT AND SERVICES QUALITY AND PRICING

### Cadbury Schweppes

The key characteristic we aim for in every aspect of the Company's activities is quality. Our products sell on their quality and their reputation is in the hands of each individual and unit throughout the Cadbury Schweppes business. An early Cadbury statement of aims read:

> Our policy for the future as in the past will be: first, the best possible quality – nothing is too good for the public.

We must always be searching to improve quality and to add measurable value to the goods and services we market. But quality applies to people and to relationships, as well as to our working lives. We should set high standards and expect to be judged by them. The quality we aim for in all our dealings is that of integrity; the word integrity means straight dealing but it also means completeness. Both meanings are relevant in this context, because the quality standard cannot be applied in part; it must be consistently applied to everything which bears the Company's name.

### Meyer

To meet our customer needs we must provide not just quality products but even more important, quality services. That means being professional in the advice we offer, delivering what is wanted when it is wanted, having opening hours which suit the customer, not our own convenience. The introduction of quality systems such as BS5750 across the Group and the emphasis on branding are important commitments to delivering a consistent quality service.

### BMW

All at BMW have a vital responsibility to protect and maintain brand values.

The key areas concern the product image and integrity.

BMW products have a customer perception of quality performance and technological innovation. They are aspirational and exclusive.

All at BMW have an obligation to ensure that customers' experiences of BMW products and services meet their high expectations.

### Rosehaugh

There is a commitment to achieving quality in urban design and architecture. Rosehaugh has always recognized its responsibility to provide buildings which are well designed, efficient in their function, and which enhance the environment. The Group supports the initiatives being taken to combine art with architecture in new developments. This is not only socially responsible, but commercially beneficial. Quality adds value.

## Gateway

Gateway believes that price is important to everyone and that 'good price + good quality = good value'. Price is particularly important as far as branded goods are concerned. Gateway is proud of its prices and especially of its promotions; these will represent a real bargain.

## AGENTS AND CONSULTANTS

### Hewlett Packard Ltd

It is both customary and necessary in industry to employ agents or consultants, for example to advise on business opportunities, the status of particular customers and local conditions, to provide services in support of a negotiating team, and generally to promote and protect the good reputation of the Group overseas; and to remunerate these agents and consultants for the contribution which they make to the Group's business. In most cases this is done by means of a commission commensurate with the value of the contract concerned. The terms of their appointment, like any other personal contract, are confidential to the parties and confidentiality is often needed too because of the classified nature of the transaction with which they are concerned, frequently insisted upon by the customer.

It is essential that all such agency and consultancy arrangements are properly regulated and recorded and that they conform with normally accepted business practices. More detailed procedures governing the appointment and remuneration of agents and consultants will be issued from time to time by the Company Secretary who will report thereon to the Audit Committee of the Board. Under no circumstances will the Board of the Company countenance corrupt practices including payments or other inducements being given by employees to political parties, government officials or a customer's executives, nor will the Board tolerate any conduct which constitutes a criminal offence.

The payment of an agent's or consultant's remuneration should, as a general rule, depend on the Group being paid for the goods or services which it is supplying, and will always be subject to any applicable Treasury or other regulations of HMG.

### Control Data

The use of consultants and agents on Control Data's behalf must be approved in writing by your management. A written contract must be agreed to by the consultant or agent.

In general, these agreements have provisions to make sure that people working on behalf of Control Data are retained in good faith to perform jobs for which they are qualified.

Consultants and agents may not be hired to do anything that is illegal or improper. What you may not do directly, you cannot do indirectly by acting through another party.

# Chapter 18

# International business

External trade has for centuries been the linchpin of profitable business conditions in the United Kingdom. Britain's borders have lost commercial significance as the world moves towards a global market. It is clear, given the disappointing ranking of the UK in the World Competitiveness Report released in the summer of 1989, that the British business sector must enhance its ability to compete internationally. Shorter product life cycles necessitate early and effective global marketing. There is no room for the inefficient in a global market.

When a firm decides to compete internationally, it moves into an arena involving complex regulations and laws, as well as foreign practices that sometimes offend an ethical firm's standards. A fitting example is that of the ethical uproar that surrounded the Lockheed corporation of the United States when it was found to have proffered bribes to officials of certain foreign governments. Yet, in many countries, bribery is commonplace and an accepted, and expected, business practice.

Beyond the ethical issues of international business lie the logistical issues. Often, firms must forego payment in currency and accept goods (countertrade) because of problems in the currency markets. For instance, the currency of the former Soviet Union was not traded on the world market, and therefore had little value outside that country. Thus, businesses which wished to trade with the former USSR were forced to accept quantities of vodka, or merchant marine ships, for example, in exchange for their goods. This barrier to trade began to disintegrate with the Soviet Union's dissolution in 1991, as new republics established their own currencies.

Another important issue in international business is that of employing competent people. Often, firms enter a foreign market without being aware of local customs or taboos. Unfortunately, this type of blind entry can end in product marketing failure and monetary loss. Those firms that prudently choose which markets to enter, hiring people familiar with the local customs, may overcome these societal hurdles and barriers, and, therefore, have a greater chance of success.

In many cases, developing a code of conduct for international business must encompass not only the domestic issues, but those issues specifically germane to the foreign market. This challenge may result in having to retrain foreign employees in ways of ethical dealing to which they may be unaccustomed. It is also important for firms to remember, unlike Lockheed in the early 1970s, that ethical dealing extends beyond one's borders.

A special issue regarding international business is that of South Africa. In recent years, the international outcry against apartheid has been a nearly unanimous one, and has caused many international businesses to divest their holdings in, and cease trading with, South Africa. But, with the election of F. W. de Klerk, and the apparent dedication to reform in 1992, and the release of ANC leader Nelson Mandela, international opinion is turning once again to open trade with South Africa.

A recent study completed by RTZ entitled *EC Code of Conduct for Companies With Interests in South Africa* involved that firm's interest in several South African businesses, involving approximately 5 per cent of RTZ's worldwide operating assets. RTZ's creative solution to the South African problem was to do what other international firms did not. Instead of caving in to international pressure to leave South Africa, resulting in economic punishment for both blacks and whites, RTZ instead employed the same ethical hiring and operating guidelines it used in all of its business dealings. For black South African RTZ employees, their employment was an oasis in a desert of apartheid. RTZ's ethical standards and compliance with the EC Code of Conduct allowed it not only to benefit from trade with South Africa, but also to convey a benefit to those most detrimentally affected by apartheid.

Two additional issues affecting international trade are those of the actual dealings in host countries and foreign currency. Alcan's aim, when dealing with a host country, is 'to the greatest extent practicable, to employ and develop nationals of the countries where we operate'. Alcan's dealings in foreign currency are 'only to the extent necessary to conduct the business and protect Alcan's interests'. Alcan represents an ethical firm's attempt to nurture and benefit the foreign countries in which it does business.

There is no easy, straightforward formula for economic and ethical success in international business. However, the following examples demonstrate how several major international concerns have attempted to successfully combine ethical business behaviour with compliance with complex foreign trade regulations and laws. Excerpts are also provided from RTZ's report as an example of what ethical businesses can do if they wish to trade and invest in South Africa.

## INTERNATIONAL TRADE

### Chevron UK Ltd and Chevron USA

Chevron conducts its business in more than 90 countries around the world. And, each of these countries has a unique set of mores, customs, and business practices, along with its own distinctive laws and regulations. To compete effectively and harmoniously, and to satisfy the expectations and needs of our customers, the Chevron companies in these countries have been tailored to respect and conform to the local environment. We are proud that we've been able to adapt so successfully to individually complex and often divergent business settings without sacrificing our high standards of good management control and business integrity. A great deal of the credit goes to our national employees in each country who bring to us their intimate knowledge of local law, customs, and business practices and who have been steadfast in their loyalty both to their countries and to the company.

We realize that special problems can come up when business transactions involve more than one country. In those cases care must be taken to assure that in complying with the laws of one country we do not violate the laws of another.

With increasing frequency, the company and its employees are being requested, and in some cases ordered, to furnish information or documents to government agencies, legislative committees, courts, or other bodies investigating operations conducted in other countries. However, many countries, including the United Kingdom, the Netherlands, Switzerland, Saudi Arabia, Australia, Canada, and South Africa, place restrictions on the furnishing of such information by the companies and individuals within their jurisdiction. Some nations, such as South Africa, prohibit the furnishing of such information to any person or entity outside the host nation without prior written consent of the government. Other nations, such as Australia and Canada, limit such restrictions to orders or directives of foreign courts and legislative or administrative agencies.

All requests for such information should be forwarded immediately to the secretary of the parent company and no information should be furnished until authorization has been obtained from the secretary. This is the same procedure followed for requests for information or documents located in the United States.

## SOUTH AFRICA

### RTZ

RTZ practices non-discriminatory employment policies. All the companies' workplaces are desegregated, as are their associated social facilities. Neither 'contract' nor 'migrant' labour is employed by any RTZ Group company. All employees are paid according to their job grades on an integrated salary structure and, without exception, the pay and conditions of all employees of Group companies exceed the requirements of the EC Code of Conduct. Considerable developments were undertaken in broadening opportunities and advancing facilities in the communities around the operations.

All these aspects are detailed in the reports on employment and community practices which have been prepared on the basis of the standardized reporting format adopted by the Governments of the Member States of the European Community (CMND 9860: July 1986).

In addition to being submitted to the Department of Trade and Industry in compliance with the requirements of Her Majesty's Government and the EC Code of Conduct, copies of the report are freely available to RTZ shareholders, employees, and others interested in this aspect of RTZ's worldwide natural resources and related industrial activities as noted in RTZ's Annual Report and Accounts.

The original 1,356 houses provided in Namakgale by the central government for the sole use of Palabora employees have been renovated and upgraded at company expense. Improvements include renovation and painting, complete electrification, the installation of electric stoves, and the installation of new sanitary fittings and hot and cold water plumbing.

In addition, the company has built 774 homes of a high standard for its employees. Of these, 210 were jointly financed by Palabora and the South African Development Trust.

The company operates home-ownership schemes for its black employees. Employees have the opportunity of either buying their homes from the company at attractive prices with subsidized loans from the company, or building or buying their own homes with loans from financial institutions and subsidized by the company.

Training and development is undertaken to improve the work performance of employees and to prepare them for levels of responsibility commensurate with their abilities. In doing so, skills needed to ensure both the employees' and the company's continued progress are being developed.

Palabora conducts a wide variety of training programmes for all levels of employees and consistently monitors staff performance, personal attributes, and potential abilities in order to identify and develop potential to ensure that future manpower needs are filled from within to the greatest extent practicable.

## DEALINGS IN HOST COUNTRIES

### Burmah

Take fully into account established general policy objectives of the Member countries in which they operate.

In particular, give due consideration to those countries' aims and priorities with regard to economic and social progress, including industrial and regional development, the protection of the environment and consumer interests, the creation of employment opportunities, the promotion of innovation and the transfer of technology.

Favour close cooperation with the local community and business interests.

When filling responsible posts in each country of operation, take due account of individual qualifications without discrimination as to nationality, subject to particular national requirements in this respect.

Not render – and they should not be solicited or expected to render – any bribe or other improper benefit, direct or indirect, to any public servant or holder of public office.

Unless legally permissible, not make contributions to candidates for public office or to political parties or other political organizations.

Abstain from any improper involvement in local political activities.

### Alcan

To the greatest extent practicable, to employ and develop nationals of the countries where we operate.

## FOREIGN CURRENCY DEALINGS

### Alcan

To engage in foreign exchange dealings only to the extent necessary to conduct the business and to protect Alcan's interests with respect to foreseen needs in accordance with prudent practice, and not to engage in currency transactions for the sole purpose of speculative profit.

# Chapter 19

# Executive management concerns

Executive management finds itself in the unique, and often unenviable, position of having to balance shareholders' demands for profit and the ethical standards that can curb profit maximisation in the short term. As agents of the shareholders, management must juggle shareholders' needs and the needs of employees within the confines of ethical behaviour.

The managerial style utilized by executive managers will determine the effectiveness of their responding to the needs of the organization. One prominent British firm's managerial style strives to be 'open, participative, and sensitive both to needs of individuals and to the various businesses and supporting services within the company'. This style provides a nurturing environment that improves the overall productivity of the organization.

Another concern of management is that of staffing. Abbey Life's code of conduct provides explicit guidelines for managers to follow regarding: internal promotion, outside recruitment, manpower planning, career progression, and gradual harmonization of changes in the organization or staffing requirements. Proper principles of staffing reach the core of organizational productivity, and guidelines should be well defined in any code of conduct.

The success of a firm's staffing strategy is substantially dependent upon the firm's internal organization. Abbey Life believes that the firm should have 'adequate arrangements to ensure that staff are suitable, adequately trained, and properly supervised using well-defined procedures'. Internal organization involves not only training and development of employees, but also providing an environment conducive to maximising productivity and effectiveness.

Counterbalancing these concerns for employees are management's responsibilities to shareholders. Two important shareholder requirements are increased share value and greater profits. By expending money to create a pro-employee environment, management works towards increasing share values and profits by improving employee productivity and morale. Taylor Woodrow management believes, 'It will always be our aim to employ the capital provided by our shareholders profitably, courageously, and wisely with enterprise, and we acknowledge their right to expect a fair return upon their capital, whilst having due regard to ensuring the security of their investment'.

Management must also concern itself with its product and services markets. Abbey National makes it a practice to 'observe high standards of market conduct'. Directly linked to a firm's market presence is its competitive ability. Cadbury Schweppes sharpens its competitive edge by 'competing on quality, value, and service, and making the most of all the assets of the business'.

For many firms, research and development plays a key role in determining market and competitive strategies. Alcan's goal is 'to improve our competitive position through continuing research and development'. To foster research and development, ICL includes a section on innovation in its code of conduct because it believes 'innovation is the key to managing change and to meeting our commitment to excellence'.

Management must then look beyond these short-term objectives, and provide the firm's managers and employees with long-term goals and targeted performance. One of J. Bibby & Sons' objectives is 'to be amongst the most efficient producers and suppliers of high-quality products to all our customers'. Cadbury Schweppes' code of conduct provides this guiding direction: 'Everyone in the Company should understand what their individual and team objectives are and how they fit into the wider purpose of the business'.

The following code excerpts address the key management issues of:

1  managerial style;
2  staffing;
3  internal organization;
4  management responsibilities to shareholders;
5  markets;
6  targeted performance, returns, long-term growth and objectives;
7  research and development;
8  competitive ability; and
9  innovation and creativity.

## MANAGERIAL STYLE

### Anonymous

The style of management adopted in the Group of Companies is open, participative, and sensitive both to the needs of individuals and to the various businesses and supporting services within the Company.

A participative style of management requires visible and decisive leadership, which in turn requires moral courage, integrity, vision, and effective communication. The training of managers must emphasize the principles and skills of leadership.

We believe that the Group's business objectives are most likely to be achieved if a management style is adopted which is based on two fundamental principles.

The first is that managers should be given as much freedom as possible to make decisions affecting their own area of responsibility. Freedom emanates from discipline, and in order for managers to have freedom they must know and observe, absolutely, two disciplines. They must know and understand Company policy in relation to their area of responsibility, and they must know the limits of their authority. As long as managers observe these disciplines they have freedom of decision and action.

If this style of management is to work well it is essential that the rules are clear, and that there are not too many of them. It is also vital that at all levels, directors and managers encourage their subordinate managers to decide and to act. There are two aspects to encouragement: there is the coaching role, an essential role of management; and, equally important, is praise and appreciation for a job well done. All subordinates should be helped and encouraged to make decisions and take action.

Mistakes will be made, and they are an essential part of the development and experience of a manager. Mistakes which are made in spite of diligence are excusable and generally without blame. Culpable mistakes are those which are repetitive, careless, reckless, or negligent.

The second principle is the encouragement of the participation in the decision-making process by those affected by decisions. Participation is not always appropriate nor does it relieve managers of their role as the final decision-maker wherever they have the responsibility. However, there is little doubt that on many occasions better performance will result from people who have been consulted before they are involved in action or change.

If the principles and skills of effective leadership and management outlined above are understood and practised, managers will be developed who have discipline, independence, courage, and a sense of achievement.

## ICL

High performance objectives will be realized only if accompanied by an equally strong commitment to self-assessment. Managers must continually challenge and appraise their own management actions and the way they as individuals, and their work units, contribute to the business results.

A manager must measure his own effectiveness as a people manager, for his ability to provide leadership is particularly important. Time must be allocated to people management in order to create the balance of attitudes, commitments, and business effectiveness which constitutes the ICL way.

Recognizing difficult issues and facing up to them quickly is a basic obligation, essential to every effective manager. By openly and constructively discussing problems as soon as they arise, a manager can dramatically reduce the risk of negative impact and more severe long-term effects.

To ignore or hide problems is poor management; the ICL way is to confront and resolve them.

The effective manager walks his offices and workshops, talks frankly with his people, listens, counsels, communicates, understands; he is able to eliminate problems before they can do us harm.

Positive action of this kind creates the atmosphere of openness and trust necessary for an enjoyable and productive work environment.

ICL managers must meet the challenge of being effective business (operations) managers and effective people managers.

Management success in ICL is about optimizing results not just achieving targets. It is an ICL belief that unless a manager is an effective people manager, his business results must fall short of the maximum attainable.

In our industry in particular managers must understand that profits are made by people, not by products. Consequently they must effectively manage, invest in, and develop their people if they and ICL are to enjoy long-term success.

ICL managers are required to set the pace and lead by example. Their 'can-do' attitude to tackling tasks must be infectious, influencing others to adopt the same willingness and positive approach.

The successful manager thinks in terms of opportunities rather than problems, uses his initiative to pick up 'loose balls', and willingly volunteers relevant skills to help others achieve their objectives. When a commitment is made it is invariably carried through.

Such an attitude is essential if we are to meet the challenging, constantly changing demands of our industry.

## George Wimpey

To ensure that management at all levels within the group provides leadership, establishes policies and plans, controls their execution, and communicates decisions and information to all levels of employees.

## Scott Bader

We are conscious of a common responsibility to share our work among ourselves in such a way that it becomes a meaningful and creative part of our lives rather than merely as a means to an end.

## Cadbury Schweppes

Change is constant – in markets, in ideas, in people, and in technology. In an uncertain and changing world we therefore need decisive leadership and trading units which are quick on their feet. We have to look ahead to the opportunities which change presents and to use the past only as a staging post on the way forward. We must accept the risks which attend new ventures; above all we need people with enquiring minds, restlessly searching for new and better ways of advancing the Company. Meeting the challenge of change requires us to adapt to new patterns of work, new jobs and new careers and to seek the training which will make the best of these changes, in our own and the Company's interests. The aim is to encourage openness to new ideas and a readiness to adapt to changing needs.

### Abbey Life

To ensure that all employees know what is going on in the company and have the opportunity to influence decisions which may affect them.

It is a key responsibility of management to supplement formal communication channels with direct, ongoing manager/employee dialogue since this is recognized as the most effective form of communication.

Formal channels of communication will be provided downwards throughout the organization through team briefing, company newspapers, etc., and upwards from individuals and groups through suggestion schemes and other media designed specifically for the purpose.

An informal, participative approach to communication will be adopted in line with our overall management style, with the aim of informing staff about our business to the maximum extent commercial confidentiality allows.

While the responsibility for running the company rests with management, we believe staff have a great deal to offer. We therefore promote a general spirit of involvement amongst staff and take account of their views on issues of direct concern to them, particularly improved working practices and efficiency.

### Peugeot Talbot

All divisions of the Company and all employees have their part to play in the achievement of these objectives. All of us are equally concerned by the subjects covered below.

Nothing is more important in a company than the attitude of its employees. If attitudes are negative or complacent the company will decline and eventually collapse.

Our Company, therefore, places great emphasis on its personnel policies. As well as providing decent pay and conditions, these policies seek to ensure that employees are properly trained, are treated with respect, are listened to, and are kept informed. The policies aim also to encourage employees as individuals and as members of a team to suggest methods of improving the quality and effectiveness of the work they do.

In these ways our working lives can be made more satisfying, the Company's performance better, and the prospects of a prosperous future more secure.

### BBA Group

1  Grit and gumption are preferable to inertia and intellect.
2  The Victorian work ethic is not an antique.

3 One man can only serve one master, to whom he is responsible for a minimum number of succinctly defined tasks.
4 Most companies owned or yet to be acquired possess adequate people waiting to be transformed by dedicated leadership.
5 The effectiveness of an organization is in inverse proportion to the number of hierarchical layers.

## The Boots Company

A special responsibility rests on managers at all levels in formulating and implementing the Company's policy. They should optimize the use of resources available to them in the attainment of the Company's objectives. They also have a personal duty to set a high standard of integrity in all their dealings and both loyally and honestly to carry out the policy and instructions of the Company and to safeguard its good image and reputation.

Managers are responsible for their own work and that of their subordinates. They are, therefore, required to:

1 Keep abreast of new developments in good management practice.
2 Ensure that their subordinates are aware of their duties and authority.
3 Train those under them as appropriate to become qualified for higher positions.

In all these matters a very special responsibility naturally rests with the Board itself, which is ultimately responsible.

## Control Data

The policies, actions, and processes needed to build the kind of work environment we want have been distilled into five principles. Control Data's commitment to you is to pursue:

1 Management practices that ensure fair and just treatment of all employees.
2 Management practices that place a high value on reward for performance.
3 Corporate benefits and support services which recognize that the personal quality of life impacts performance.
4 An environment for continued self-growth and achievement that goes beyond the training and experience required for an employee's present position.
5 A policy that provides an increasing level of employment security for the greatest number of its employees.

Within this work environment you are encouraged to achieve your highest level of productivity, satisfaction, and quality of life.

In return for Control Data's commitment, you are expected to avoid situations where your loyalty could be divided, or your interests conflict with those of Control Data.

### Digital Equipment Corporation

We particularly want to be sure that management jobs are clear and well defined. Because so many people are dependent on the plans of managers, it is very important that their plans have regular automatic measurements built into them. Meeting financial results is only one measure of a plan; other measures are satisfied customers, development of people, meeting long-range needs of the Corporation, development of new products, opening new markets, and meeting the commitments made to others in the company. We believe that our commitment to planning assures our freedom to act.

## STAFFING

### Abbey Life

Abbey has an excellent record of developing its staff through internal promotion and has developed well-established procedures for advertising and selection.

We believe in assessing suitability for promotion objectively and being open and frank about this.

Normally, promotion opportunities will be advertised internally but there will invariably be situations where appointments occur either as part of the planned career development or through direct promotion within a division or department.

The Company will recruit from outside where no suitable internal candidate exists or when it is judged desirable to introduce new ideas or experience. Internal and external recruitment will therefore coexist, though Abbey will seek to favour internal appointments where all other things are equal.

The Company will maintain the highest possible standards of administration and selection techniques and select solely on the basis of suitability for the job.

Inevitably there will be errors of selection. Where this happens employees will be treated with sympathy and respect and every effort to retrain or transfer to a more suitable job will be made before dismissal has to take place.

Staff costs represent almost half of the general expense of running Abbey, and staff levels therefore need to be kept to the minimum consistent with providing excellent service and maintaining good morale. Staff numbers will therefore be planned as objectively as possible and appropriate control exercised to ensure costs are contained within budgeted limits.

Abbey believes that individual remuneration should be determined primarily by performance and responsibility rather than by long service or historical anomalies.

Performance is assessed through the twice-yearly appraisal process and on an ongoing basis less formally. Specific objectives agreed with your boss, together with day to day job accountabilities, form the basis for appraisal grading, which is expressed in relation to the gradings of colleagues so that relative performance can be judged and rewards allocated accordingly.

Responsibility is measured through systematic job evaluation. This is carried out by a panel of experienced senior managers, trained to make informed assessments of the demands of jobs based on detailed job descriptions. Where significant changes in responsibility occur, re-evaluation takes place.

Abbey is committed to providing progressive careers for staff consistent with individual abilities and available opportunities. Salary progression other than at the Annual Review will be dependent on promotion to an evaluated job or the upgrading of an existing job.

In any business, changes in organization and staffing occur from time to time. Where these lead to reduction in job responsibilities or the need for redeployment, a gradual change in pay and benefits will take place until they reflect the new grade. Similarly, differences in grade, pay or benefits arising from historical or arbitrary anomalies will be gradually phased out.

**Anonymous**

The Company believes it is fundamental to the continuing success of the business that staff should be consulted on decisions that will affect them, and that:

1 Decisions should be taken by those responsible for them.
2 The views of staff affected by decisions must be taken into account as regards the decision itself and particularly as regards its implementation.
3 By consulting with staff in this way and by keeping them informed of the progress of the business, a greater understanding of and commitment to local and Company objectives and decisions will be obtained.
4 The result will be improved performance and productivity and greater job satisfaction.

It is recognized that participation involves both negotiation and consultation, but that the two are separate from one another, although the decisions resulting from consultation may result in subsequent negotiations taking place.

Negotiation is between management and staff representative bodies and is concerned with wages, conditions of employment and matters arising from these central issues.

Consultation takes place between management and staff on other matters which concern and affect them in their jobs, the workplace, the location, and the Company. It can take place:

On an individual basis.
On a collective basis.
Between management and staff representative bodies.
Verbally.
By the written word.

Management is responsible for making decisions. However, it has a duty to seek the views of staff, particularly over issues on which they can be expected to make a contribution. It also has a duty to inform staff as soon as is appropriate of decisions that will affect them and the reasons they have been made.

Pursuing a policy of Participation does not imply that all decisions are subject to consultation.

Management decides whether an issue is a subject for negotiation, consultation, or communication. If it is a matter for consultation it will decide the most appropriate way to set about it, depending on whether it is:

1  An individual issue.
2  A local issue.
3  An issue concerning a department or group of people.
4  An issue concerning the workplace or location as a whole.
5  An issue which, because of its implications, needs to be discussed with the relevant Staff Representative bodies in addition to the individuals or groups concerned.

When the decision has been made, the responsible manager will communicate it to those involved.

The range of decisions which can be enhanced by consultation can never be finite but as a guide they may encompass:

Changes in organization.
Methods of working and operating practices.
Systems.
Merchandise ranges.
Deployment of staff.
Changes in departmental layout.
Uniforms.
Improvements in the working environment.
Financial targets.

In the total Participation concept, whether the issues are consultative, negotiable, or a matter of information, management must be aware of the necessity to involve middle management at all stages and thus avoid the danger of bypassing them during the decision-making process.


## ICL

Success in a knowledge industry such as ours depends upon an effective sharing of the talent we have in the company.

Through their leadership, managers must stimulate teamwork as a means of obtaining better results. Teamwork is achieved by developing individual talents, building on the ideas and know-how of the team, and gaining commitment by way of listening, involving, and communicating.

Leading by example, being seen, being involved, providing common understanding and direction are essential elements of a manager's role in developing the cooperative teamwork attitudes which are essential to obtaining the best results.

## INTERNAL ORGANIZATION

### Cadbury Schweppes

We must concentrate on the core tasks of the business and justify every support activity and every level of authority on the value which they add to the goods and services we sell. The basic building blocks of the organization are the business units, managed by integrated teams in direct touch with their markets. All decisions should be taken as near their point of impact as possible. This freedom of operating action carries with it the responsibility to use the strengths and resources of the Cadbury Schweppes Group where appropriate and to keep the aims of the units in line with those of the Company as a whole. The more straightforward the organization and the way in which it arrives at decisions, the speedier its response, the more readily it can be adapted, the more satisfying it is to work in, and the lower the cost it imposes on those it is there to serve. Building up informal links avoids organizational arthritis.

### George Wimpey

To provide a developed organizational structure with the flexibility to cope with fluctuations in demand and varying client requirements, and which will ensure maximum utilization of the Group's human and physical resources.

### Abbey National

A firm should organize and control its internal affairs in a responsible manner, keeping proper records, and where the firm employs staff or is responsible for the conduct of investment business by others, should have adequate arrangements to ensure that they are suitable, adequately trained, and properly supervised, and that it has well-defined compliance procedures.

### Scott Bader

We recognize that there are some members in a position of authority. Such members have a greater opportunity and hence a special responsibility to facilitate the building of jobs which are capable of fulfilling us as people; to act as 'catalysts of common effort' and not as authoritarian 'bosses'.

## MANAGEMENT RESPONSIBILITIES TO SHAREHOLDERS

### Abbey Life

A company representative shall on making contact for the first time with an investor and again at any time when asked to do so –

1  identify himself as being a company representative, and
2  state the name of the Member.

If at the time of his first contact with the investor the company representative is not acting as such but at any later time he begins so to act in relation to that investor, this sub-paragraph shall apply at that later time as if it were the first time the contact had been made.

On meeting an investor, a company representative shall give him a business card which complies with paragraph 4 below, unless he has given him such a card at a previous meeting.

A company representative, when making a call, whether in person or by telephone and whether solicited or not – at the beginning of the call –

1  shall state the genuine purpose or purposes of the call, and
2  if the time or place of call were not previously agreed by the investor, shall ascertain whether or not the investor wishes him to proceed and if the investor does not wish him to, he shall not (but he may ask for another appointment).

### Scott Bader

We are agreed that, as the foundation of our Commonwealth abolished here the power of share ownership, we shall strive to discourage our money from being used to profit from other people's work or to control other people's lives.

### Coats Viyella

Coats Viyella has an obligation to its shareholders to provide an attractive return on the capital they invest. In order to ensure growth, we must experiment with new ideas, encourage research and innovation, and invest in new equipment facilities and products.

### Taylor Woodrow

It will always be our aim to employ the capital provided by our shareholders profitably, courageously, and wisely with enterprise, and we acknowledge their right to expect a fair return upon their capital, whilst having due regard to ensuring the security of their investment.

## Ciba-Geigy

We intend to maintain and improve our position in our various fields of activity by creative and competitive efforts in research and development, production, and marketing.

We will consider entering into new fields of activity, as a result of our own research and development, or in collaboration with third parties, or by acquisition, in order to provide for balanced growth and for the distribution of risk. Fields in which a synergistic effect can be achieved will be preferred.

As a member of Ciba-Geigy Group and within the framework of its worldwide policies and objectives, our Company has independence of action. We will, with the means available to us, achieve the short-term and long-term results necessary for the prosperity of the Company.

We will provide our shareholders with adequate information about the Company's operations, plans, and objectives.

We will safeguard the Company's property and assets, and will conduct our operations with a high degree of efficiency and care.

## Cadbury Schweppes

The Company recognizes its obligations to all who have a stake in its success – shareholders, employees, customers, suppliers, governments, and society – and seeks to keep its responsibilities to them in balance. We aim to act as good corporate citizens throughout the world and believe that international companies which follow that approach benefit their host countries. We believe in open competition and in doing business wherever there are suitable markets open to our trade. We seek to maintain the Company's reputation for meeting society's legitimate expectations of the business and for contributing to the life of the communities of which we are a part. We support worthwhile causes related to the Company's place in society and we encourage members of the Company to play their part in trade and public affairs.

## John Lewis Partnership

The Partnership shall never knowingly mislead investors, and shall not avoidably give such information to any investor as would bring him advantages over other investors or dealers in Partnership securities. Where it is necessary to give confidential information, the Partnership shall endeavour to secure that no use will be made of such potential advantage. Investors are not, however, able to acquire any of the Partnership's equity which is held in trust for the benefit of its members.

## MARKETS

### BBA Group

We shall concentrate in markets where:

1 The products are in a state of maturity or decline 'Sunset Industries'.
2 The scale of our presence in a market segment will allow price leadership.
3 The capital cost of market entry is high.
4 Fragmentation of ownership on the supply side facilitates rapid earnings growth by acquisition of contribution flows.

### Abbey National

A firm should observe high standards of market conduct. It should also, to the extent endorsed for the purpose of this principle, comply with any code or standard as in force from time to time and as it applies to the firm either according to its terms or by rulings made under it.

## TARGETED PERFORMANCE, RETURNS, LONG-TERM GROWTH AND OBJECTIVES, AND PLANNING

### BBA Group

1 The longer run belongs to Oscar Wilde, who is dead.
2 The key macro and micro variables of our business are so dynamic that poker becomes more predictable than planning and reactivity more profitable than rumination.
3 Budgets are personal commitments made by management to their superiors, subordinates, shareholders and their self respect.
4 The cheapest producer wins.
5 The investment of money on average return of less than three points above market should be restricted to Ascot.
6 Gearing should not exceed 40 per cent. The location from which funds emanate should be matched to the location from which the profit stream permits their service.
7 We are not currency speculators, even when we win.
8 Tax is a direct cost to the business and, accordingly, should be eschewed.
9 Victorian thrift is not an antique.
10 Nothing comes free; cheap assets are often expensive utilities.

### BBA Group

1 The replication of our day to day tactic provides long-term growth.

2  We need to address 'Monday' this week and what our reaction will be to what may be on 'Monday' for the next three years.
3  Three years is, in the current environment, the limit of man's comprehension of what may be.
4  Long-term growth necessitates:
   a) Resources – notably men and money.
   b) Sustained performance rather than superficial genius.

## Cadbury Schweppes

Effective competition demands clarity of purpose. Objectives must be attainable, but require us to stretch our abilities, not work within them. Objectives need to be built from the bottom up, but set from the top down. When unit or individual objectives have been fixed, the debate is over and the focus is on their single-minded achievement. All objectives end with individuals, who are accountable for results and therefore must know precisely for what they are to be held accountable. But since the success of the Company depends on the sum of these individual efforts, what counts is the way they are coordinated. Everyone in the Company should understand what their individual and team objectives are and how they fit into the wider purpose of the business.

## J. Bibby

J. Bibby & Sons is an international diversified group of manufacturing and distribution companies operating in the UK, mainland Europe, North America, and the Far East. Its principal activities are paper making and converting; the manufacture and distribution of hospital, laboratory, and scientific equipment; the manufacture and supply of animal feeds and farm seeds; and the distribution and servicing of materials handling equipment.

The group's commercial objectives are to be amongst the most efficient producers and suppliers of high-quality products to all our customers throughout the world through a disciplined commitment to meet their needs and to achieve continuous productivity improvements. The Group also aims to retain strong relationships with suppliers and to provide a good and satisfying working environment for its employees.

The Group's financial objectives are to increase earnings and dividends per share, to provide an above-average return on capital employed and to maintain sound financial ratios. The group intends to achieve its growth targets by a judicious balance of organic investment and acquisitions within well-defined corporate plans and policies.

The management philosophy is to encourage broadly autonomous and profit responsible business units to flourish within a professional corporate and financial structure.

## George Wimpey

To retain a high reputation for performance by providing a service to clients based on technical competence, operational efficiency, reliability, competitive pricing, and adherence to contract programmes.

## Abbey National

A firm should ensure that it maintains adequate financial resources to meet its investment business commitments and to withstand the risks to which its business is subject.

## ICL

The greatest challenge facing managers arises from their responsibility for identifying changing long-term business needs and for planning effectively to meet them. In our industry in particular, predicting, managing, and exploiting change are key demands calling for foresight, judgement, and leadership of the highest order.

Managers are expected continually to identify future opportunities, to monitor and communicate risks, and to take corrective action to avoid excessive exposure.

By analysing the critical long-term issues which confront the business, a manager can establish for his team a clear vision of the future. He can also develop the strategies upon which that future will be secured.

Managers must have detailed knowledge of ICL's objectives and strategies. They must understand them in relation to the Information Processing industry, to our competitors, customers, and products. These objectives and strategies must be effectively communicated to all employees. They must provide the basis for determining sub-unit objectives and work priorities. All employees must clearly understand their individual roles and responsibilities and the standards required for the successful completion of tasks.

The performance of all staff must be regularly assessed by way of reviews, formal performance appraisals, and informal one-on-one discussions. These two-way assessment processes help to maintain standards and to encourage adaptability in our ever changing business environment.

## RESEARCH AND DEVELOPMENT

## The Boots Company

The programme of growth is reflected in the Company's research and development work relating to new and improved products. The Company regards itself as having both a business and a social responsibility to seek new products, particularly relating to the alleviation and cure of disease. The latter, of necessity in the light of present human knowledge and legislation, involves the use of animals for the purpose of testing for efficacy and safety. The Company uses animals to the minimum extent necessary for the purpose and in full compliance with official standards for animal care. It constantly seeks to reduce the use of animals and to find alternative methods. The Company does not use animals for testing cosmetics and toiletries because, in general, its cosmetic and toiletry products incorporate well-established and well-tried ingredients whose safety is already clear. Animal testing might, however, become unavoidable by virtue of legal requirements or, in exceptional circumstances, were a human safety factor to become involved.

## Alcan

To improve our competitive position through continuing research and development. To encourage and support innovation in appropriate fields in every country in which we operate. To disseminate relevant technology and know how to all consolidated group companies, having due regard to the protection of industrial and intellectual property rights and the need to give proper recognition for such development and transfer.

## COMPETITIVE ABILITY

### Cadbury Schweppes

Cadbury Schweppes must be competitive in the market place. To succeed, our products and services must maintain their identity and their edge against the competition. We compete on quality, value, and service and so we must make the most of all the assets of the business. This means innovating and taking risks, while using research and analysis to increase the success rate, not to put decisions off. We are competing in the markets of the world, so we need to combine local initiative with dedication to the long-term interests of the Company as a whole. We are competing in today's markets and in tomorrow's, so profit now must be matched with consistent and imaginative investment in the future.

### ICL

Achievement in ICL is about output, not input or effort. More specifically it means high value output . . . output that creates a demonstrable impact on our business results.

ICL Managers must ensure that the work tasks and actions of their staff reflect this basic principle. Managers are obliged to identify and eliminate sub-standard performance and ineffective work situations. High performance of a low-value job provides a poor return for the individual and the company.

## INNOVATION AND CREATIVITY

### ICL

Innovation is the key to managing change and to meeting our commitment to excellence. Managers must consciously strive for improvements in their personal and work unit performance.

They must exploit modern management techniques and information technology as ways of eliminating low-value tasks and increasing output of high-value activities.

It is the managers' obligation to set the framework for creativity . . . a clear understanding of the need; freedom to challenge the traditional and try out new ideas; and encouragement provided by a supportive teamwork environment.

# Chapter 20

# The relationship between employer and employee

Codes of conduct are instituted not only to direct employee and firm activity with outside groups, but also to establish principles of the relationship between the company and its employees. The importance and complexity of this relationship is evidenced by the plethora of UK legislation governing treatment of employees by their employers. Society and laws recognize employee rights of due process. Employees are more skilled and educated than their forebears, and firms must respond to their concerns. Employees owe their employers certain duties of loyalty and obedience.

Beyond the law is the ethical nature of employer–employee relationships. If employees are expected to act ethically, they must also be dealt with properly by their employers. It must be clear in a code of conduct what a firm's commitments are to its employees. Ciba-Geigy is clear in its approach: 'We will strive to create an atmosphere which is conducive at all levels to the effective teamwork which is of great importance for the success of the Company'. Through explicit commitment to its employees a firm develops the requisite trust between employer and employee.

In many recent scandals involving whistle blowers, the operative policy has been to sack the individual, and for many other firms to avoid offering subsequent employment to that individual. Failure to respond to the problem which was revealed, and instead punishing the messenger, has a chilling effect on an internal reward system which promotes ethical and proper business conduct. Moreover, employees may forego acting ethically in order to keep their jobs. Some have suggested a need for a 'Whistle blower' statute, with construction similar to the Employment Acts of 1982 and 1985. Firms may wish to take the lead in this area, and act before required by statute.

As to the rights of the employee, a code of conduct should be explicit. Every employee should have access to the rules of the game, whether the subject is a nondisclosure agreement or criteria for promotion, a code of conduct or similar document can serve as a handy, trusted reference to such matters. ICL and The Boots Company provide 'laundry lists' of employee rights in their codes of conduct in order to ensure employee awareness.

Many times an employee's outside interests cause conflict with his employment. Whether it be membership on outside boards, part-time employ-ment, personal business ventures, or controversial outside activity, a potential conflict of interest can be explained and deterred by a comprehensive code of conduct. It is the firm's responsibility to present clear rules regarding outside interests. Unclear or non-existent rules may lead to employer–employee friction.

Certain outside interests can lead to serious conflicts of interest, as in outside employment or membership on outside boards. Hewlett Packard is clear in its policy regarding conflicts of interest: 'All employees have an affirmative duty to avoid situations where their loyalties may be divided between HP's interests and their own interests'. Other conflicts may result from relationships with com-petitors, suppliers, and customers. An effective code of conduct should prescribe lock-step avenues of action for the firm and the employee to resolve these conflicts.

In many instances, employees are most concerned about issues of salary and benefits. Medical care, life insurance, bonuses, pensions, and other perquisites are important benefits for employees. Abbey Life's objective is 'to ensure that remuneration, including pension and other benefits, is fair to the individual and appropriate to the company in meeting its objectives'. Abbey Life provides specific policies to ensure this general objective is attained.

Firms must also develop procedures for dealing with the media. Often, firms are in positions that require direct contact with the media. 'Loose cannons' cause severe damage, and a firm should have a policy for employees dealing with the media. British Coal instructs its employees to 'act with discretion, bearing in mind the Board's interest and in particular avoiding disclosure of confidential matters, or statements of personal opinions that might wrongly be interpreted'. A good general rule is: 'when in doubt, no comment'.

In British history, trade unions have played an important, often critical, role in the relationship between employer and employee. To provide a more unified voice when involved in vital negotiations, such as collective bargaining agree-ments, firms have formed employer federations. As one prominent British firm notes, 'It is good management practice to establish a sound working relationship with union officials'.

The following excerpts demonstrate how some leading British and multi-national firms have responded to the foregoing and other important employer–employee issues in their codes of conduct.

## THE FIRM'S COMMITMENT TO ITS EMPLOYEES AND EMPLOYEE RELATIONS

### Alcan

In the pursuit of our objectives, and respecting the laws, regulations, prevailing customs, and practices in each of the countries in which we operate, we have adopted the following policies:

1  To promote increased employee understanding of all aspects of their work and the recognition of how this work relates to the success of the enterprise.

2  To be alert to the attitudes and views of all employees.

## Dixons

Employees are not normally allowed to leave their normal place of work during working hours or to receive visitors or receive or make private telephone calls without the permission of their Manager or Supervisor. At certain locations, pay phones are installed for use by employees.

## ICL

The achievements of a manager are dependent on the achievements of those for whom he is responsible.

ICL is committed to developing its employees to the full extent of their potential. Managers must first ensure that optimum use is being made of current skills and that individuals are given tasks which 'stretch' them in their existing jobs. They must then agree on development and career progression plans with their staff and rigorously monitor the implementation of those plans to make sure they are effective. International and interdivisional opportunities must be considered as a way of accelerating career and personal development.

ICL can offer almost unlimited job opportunities. It is the manager's task to match the needs of the business with those of the employee in order to stimulate the fastest possible growth for both.

## George Wimpey

To organize the vital resources of the Group's employees by creating a working environment that produces an efficient and coordinated team effort, and encourage individual effort by providing satisfactory terms and conditions of employment, job satisfaction, and opportunities for personal development and advancement.

## TI Group

Changes in organization structure, appointments, remuneration, conditions of employment, re-assignment or termination concerning personnel require the prior approval of the respective managers at the 'Father and Grandfather' levels in the organization.

## Scott Bader

We try to be open and frank in our relationships with our fellow workers, to face difficulties rather than avoid them and to solve problems by discussion and agreement rather than through reference to a third party.

We are agreed that in the event of a downturn in trade we will share all remaining work rather than expect any of our fellow members to be deprived of employment, even if this requires a reduction in earnings by all.

## Abbey Life

To maintain an atmosphere of cooperation with and between employees in which the company can effectively discharge its commercial, social, and community responsibilities.

Abbey recognizes that employees and the managers responsible for them should maintain relationships based on mutual respect and recognition of each other's rights and obligations.

The employee's rights are:

1  To contribute to decisions likely to affect them individually.
2  To know what is expected of them and how they are meeting this expectation.
3  To have their aspirations considered.
4  To feel that they are fairly treated.

Manager's rights are:

1  To organize and direct employees towards objectives.
2  To expect rules and standards to be upheld.
3  To expect enthusiasm, cooperation, and commitment.

Any employee having a grievance or concern about any aspect of employment will be heard sympathetically by management, who will seek to resolve the problem speedily and amicably, respecting the needs of the individual, team, and the task.

The same balance between the needs of the individual, team, and task will apply to employees who fail to adhere to rules and standards of conduct or performance.

The company will aim to provide a physical working environment which is healthy, safe, comfortable, and pleasant and to develop a range of employee facilities which promote a sense of belonging.

A major feature of Abbey's approach to professional management is to ensure staff's abilities and skills are utilized to the maximum possible extent. The intention is to match as far as possible the developing competence and aspirations of staff to the needs of the business so that employees share in the company's success.

Abbey has an outstanding record of developing people and we are eager to offer progressive careers to able people within the limits of the company's growth and available opportunities.

Job skills training is a key priority so that staff rapidly achieve an acceptable level of performance.

This will be backed up by education programmes like the Life Assurance Technical Certificate which are designed to enhance knowledge, and by development training activities designed to equip able people for promotion.

We believe individuals should bear the primary responsibility for their own career development by keeping up to date and acquiring the skills and experience needed for growth. The company's role will be to identify potential and help fulfil it.

Appraisals will, therefore, concentrate not only on current performance but also on a realistic discussion of future prospects in the light of strengths and weaknesses, and identify areas where training will improve performance and promotability.

Succession and career planning will take place within People Development Panels and employees with identified high potential will be systematically trained and developed to meet future staffing needs.

Abbey recognizes that employees may at some stage reach the limit of their career development. This will be discussed openly and honestly to avoid dissatisfaction and frustration from unrealistic ambitions. We also appreciate that in these circumstances some staff may wish to develop alternative careers outside Abbey and we will seek to facilitate such moves where it is compatible with our business needs.

### Burmah

Enterprises should, within the framework of law, regulations, and prevailing labour relations and employment practices, in each of the countries in which they operate:

Respect the right of their employees to be represented by trade unions and other bona fide organizations of employees, and engage in constructive negotiations, either individually or through employers' associations, with such employee organizations with a view to reaching agreements on employment conditions, which should include provisions for dealing with disputes arising over the interpretations of such agreements, and for ensuring mutually respected rights and responsibilities.

### Coats Viyella

The Company's dealings with its employees must be guided by respect for the individual, for his or her rights and dignity. We must enable employees to share in the Company's success, recognize their individual achievements, help them obtain satisfaction and a sense of accomplishment from their work, and seek to provide job security.

All employees should treat others exactly as they would like to be treated themselves. In pursuing this objective, the Company is committed to the encouragement of informality but respect for others in personal relationships.

We must always seek a spirit of cooperation between individuals and groups and between managers and the staff based on effective communications and the belief in the good faith and integrity of colleagues, managers, and the Company as a whole.

Recruitment decisions, as well as opportunities for personal development, are influenced by individual abilities and achievement, not by race, sex, religion, or any irrelevant means of discrimination. We must endeavour to allow employees to develop their potential by means of training, education, job experience, and performance review. We must provide working conditions that are both healthy and safe.

Our aim is to reward employees well for their contribution and to ensure that this reward is fair in relation to others, both inside and outside the Company. Everyone has the opportunity to be rewarded at a higher level through better performance from the principle that those who achieve more should receive more.

It is the responsibility of management to provide leadership by setting a positive example in the conduct and standards of work and by creating an environment which encourages and enables employees to perform to the best of their abilities.

## Ciba-Geigy

We will strive to create an atmosphere which is conducive at all levels to the effective teamwork which is of great importance for the success of the Company.

We will endeavour to assign jobs, duties, and responsibilities in accordance with the capabilities of the individuals concerned and in such a way that each is encouraged to make the best possible personal contribution. Promotions will be made as far as possible from within the Company.

We will define duties and responsibilities throughout the Company, and encourage participation in decision-making within the scope of an employee's responsibilities. We will also develop and communicate, as necessary, business objectives and policies, and ensure their implementation.

We remunerate employees fairly on the basis of their assigned jobs, their performance, and experience and with due regard to prevailing standards in the industry.

We will progressively provide for the possibility of developing the potential of employees by means of training, education, job rotation, and performance appraisal.

Our employees will be provided with appropriate information regarding the activities of the Company and in particular we will ensure that each employee receives all relevant information necessary for the performance of his duties and for an understanding of how these relate to the activities of the Company as a whole.

While respecting the right of the individual to privacy, we recognize our social responsibility to our employees. We treat them fairly and with dignity and provide safe and healthy working conditions as well as schemes designed to afford protection to the employee and his family in case of sickness, old age, or death.

## ICL

Our commitment to achievement demands a commitment to develop our skills and abilities in every possible way.

We are a people company. Our main strength lies in the quality and skill of the people who work here. So real progress will come about only by constantly developing and improving our skills. Development of this kind – people development – is one of the basic requirements for business success.

The company will constantly aim to provide you with responsibilities and objectives which measure up to your abilities and ambitions – and ideally stretch them a little too. The company is determined to satisfy your need for personal growth and job satisfaction, and to create the supportive environment which enables you to achieve them.

However, individuals have to make a good deal of the running. The most rewarding development is self-development and employees are expected to help themselves by pushing their managers for guidance, for opportunities, for appropriate formal training, and for new kinds of work experience.

The opportunities are all there within the company, but it's up to individuals to seize them and to respond flexibly when new demands are made on them. Real growth will come to those who are willing to adapt, to learn, to enlarge their horizons, and to tackle new challenges. We have to think for ourselves, find our own chances, and set clear objectives for our own personal development.

Managers carry a corresponding obligation to respond to and encourage employees in every possible way, for the company's success in the future is closely bound up with the success and personal growth of everyone working in it.

## United Biscuits

No element of management responsibility is more important, or more satisfying, than to provide for the future of the company. The test of our discharge of that responsibility is whether we leave our business in better shape than we found it. We will therefore never attempt to maximise short-term profitability at the expense of action necessary for the survival of the business in the long term.

Our success depends on our effectiveness as a team. Company interest must be placed above that of a subsidiary, division, or department; cooperation must outrank self-interest.

To achieve the dynamic morale and team spirit based on mutual confidence without which a business cannot be successful, people have to be cared for during their working lives and in retirement. In return we expect from all our staff loyalty and commitment to the company. We respect the rights and innate worth of the individual. In addition to being financially rewarding, working life should provide as much job satisfaction as possible. The company encourages all employees to be trained and developed to achieve their full potential.

United Biscuits takes a responsible attitude towards employment legislation requirements and codes of practice, union activities, and communications with the staff.

We place the highest priority on promoting and preserving the health and safety of employees. Employees, for their part, have a clear duty to take every reasonable precaution to avoid injury to themselves, their colleagues, and members of the public.

## John Lewis Partnership

The Partnership shall assist members to learn as much as they can about its organization and to develop the special skills which enable them to contribute to its team-work. For this purpose it will encourage Partners to pass on knowledge to each other, will provide Staff Trainers, organize classes and conferences locally and centrally, allow leave of absence in approved cases for classes organized by local authorities and manufacturers, and make any other suitable arrangements.

While such facilities shall be provided primarily for young Partners the Partnership shall also provide for older Partners, especially those taking up managerial positions.

The Partnership shall recognize that vocational training shades into general education, and shall be prepared to help Partners to participate in education which may have only an indirect effect on their contribution to the Partnership's permanence and prosperity but will be conducive to their general culture and personal happiness.

## Digital Equipment Corporation

We encourage people to develop technical skills, breadth of knowledge, and expertise in a specific area. We also encourage people to develop supervisory and management skills. We believe that individual discipline should be self-generated.

## THE RIGHTS AND DUTIES OF THE EMPLOYEE

## Cadbury Schweppes

The Company is made up of individuals and its success turns on their collective commitment to its aims. That commitment can only be won through our ability to bring about a convergence of individual, team, and company goals. People should know what is expected of them and be given every help to meet those expectations. Our standards should be demanding and demanding standards require appropriate rewards. Belief in the ability of people to grow means planning to promote from within, except when an outside infusion is needed. Equally it means that where we fail with people, the situation must be faced up to openly and promptly and resolved with the least loss of individual self-respect, because the failure is shared. In the same way the responsibility for the development of people is shared, the drive must come from the individual and the training resources from the Company. Everyone in the Company should be encouraged to make the most of their abilities.

## BMW

BMW aims to recruit the best possible individuals who thrive in a healthy, competitive, and innovative environment and who maintain integrity in all their dealings.

All at BMW are expected to work effectively to achieve objectives as part of a team, and to treat their colleagues with respect.

BMW will be fair, recognize ability, and reward effort. The company will offer training and skill development to help all individuals develop to their full potential.

## Scott Bader

We recognize that since management by consent rather than coercion is an appropriate style for the Company a corresponding effort to accept responsibility is required from us all. This will show in a desire to attend meetings and to participate in the affairs of our community; it will show in increased communication between person and person and between groups and departments; it will show in an effort to understand the problems encountered and the contribution made by those in other areas of our organization; above all it will be seen as a genuine willingness to learn to develop and grow.

## John Lewis Partnership

While the Partnership's ultimate aim shall be the happiness of its members, business efficiency will be a necessary factor in attaining this aim. But the Partnership shall recognize that only fools put business too far before pleasure, especially health and happiness, and that there is almost infinite scope for imagination and energy in the promotion of happiness in the more important sense of that word.

The greatest care shall be taken of the health of all Partners and of their safety from accident and accordingly no position shall be held, except in an emergency, by anyone whom it is thought likely to overstrain.

Every member shall do his best for the Partnership as if it were in the ordinary sense his own business. He shall not attempt to get from it any more than he sincerely believes to be his fair and just dues. All his dealings with it and with its other members shall be scrupulously honest and quite open and he shall be helpful to all of its other members in their performance of their own duty to it.

In all that they say and do on behalf of the Partnership and in all that is so done by other Partners for whom they are responsible, officials shall be careful not to fall at all short of proper courtesy. This applies as much to behaviour to other Partners or to any person from whom the Partnership buys or with whom it has other business relations as it does to behaviour to customers.

Officials shall always put on written record any promises or expectations that they give to Partners for whom they are responsible. Partners, in their turn, shall always ask for such a written record if they have reason to think it may not be forthcoming.

The Partnership shall take pains to assist Partners to develop their earning-power by experimental promotion or other change of function where this seems likely to turn out well and in all other ways.


### Tesco

To be developing our people's skills, advancing their careers, and rewarding them fairly, offering equal opportunity to all.


### Legal & General

A pleasant and productive work environment is created by people being aware of the needs of colleagues, and adapting their own behaviour to take account of the greater welfare of the workplace as a whole.

Individuals should consider the consequences of their actions on others in the workplace, and ensure that their behaviour does not get in the way of their own or their colleagues' ability to perform their jobs effectively.

Views will always differ about the exact nature of considerate behaviour. Some examples, like refraining from smoking in the workplace, have gathered strength in recent years and are now widely accepted. Smoking is now banned in a number of our workplaces.

There are shades of opinion about drinking alcohol during the working day, but moderation should be exercised to protect a staff member's own standing with colleagues and to enable that person to work with full effectiveness.

Other areas of considerate behaviour are also related to respect for individuals. Sexual harassment has been identified as an area where greater awareness is needed, and it is important to realise that thoughtless words and actions can cause offence. The same is true in relations with colleagues of different racial or religious backgrounds.

### Digital Equipment Corporation

We promote people according to their performance, not only their technical ability but also their ability to get the job done and to take the responsibility that goes with the job. Ability is measured not only by past results, but also by attitude and desire to succeed. Performance results are also used to decide whether individuals should remain in their current jobs.

We should be exceedingly careful when hiring employees from customers. Sometimes this is reasonable and desirable; but we should do it with all caution and by being sure that the employee first tells the customer.

### TSB Trust

A reasonable and decent standard of dress should be maintained by all staff whilst on Company premises. Line managers will guide staff, when necessary, on the interpretation of this statement.

All telephone calls should be conducted in a friendly and helpful manner – especially when dealing with customers or members of the public. They should also be informative from the start: when answering a call the following format is recommended:-

'Good morning (or afternoon)'
The name of your Department
Your personal name.

### PERSONAL INTERESTS OUTSIDE THE FIRM

### Control Data

Employees of Control Data may not invest in companies in which Control Data has or is making an investment without prior Corporate approval. Exceptions to this rule include investments in publicly held companies made during public offerings or through a securities exchange at the market price.

You may not market products or services that compete with Control Data products or services. Nor may you work for a competitor of Control Data as an employee, consultant, or member of the board of directors.

### Monsanto

In addition to the foregoing Conflicts of Interest Policy, the following specific limitations are applied to designated employees with respect to outside business and management activities. As used here, 'designated employees' means all employees classified as Selected or Key Managers or in equivalent positions in subsidiaries or other business organizations in which the company owns, directly or indirectly, more than a 50 per cent interest.

Designated employees are expected to devote their entire working time to the performance of their duties for Monsanto. They should avoid outside business or consulting activities that would divert their time, interest, or talents from Monsanto business. Prior approval, in writing, by an employee's supervisor is required before entering into any consulting activity. Such approval shall not be granted for Selected and Key Managers without written concurrence from the corporate vice president most directly responsible for the affected employee, except that such approval for members of the Monsanto Management Council shall not be granted without written concurrence from the Chief Executive Officer.

Except with respect to employees serving at the company's request as directors or officers of companies in which Monsanto has an ownership interest, designated employees may not serve as officers or directors of any other commercial enterprise unless it is pursuant to an exception approved in writing. The term 'commercial enterprise' includes business corporations, banks, trust companies, other financial institutions, and similar organizations. For Selected and Key Managers, such approval shall be by the corporate vice president most directly responsible for the affected employee, except that such approval for members of the Monsanto Management Council shall not be granted without written concurrence from the Chief Executive Officer. Requests for approval by the Chief Executive Officer shall be submitted, with recommendations and reasons for the request, through the appropriate corporate officer reporting directly to the Chief Executive Officer. In the case of banks and other financial institutions, prior agreement will be solicited from the Chief Financial Officer. Approval will be granted where, in the opinion of the Chief Executive Officer, it appears to be in the best interest of Monsanto.

### Scott Bader

We have agreed not to hold second jobs if our doing so is likely to deprive others (in the community at large) of employment or to affect our interest at work adversely.

### Dixons

It is in your own interest that you should devote your full attention and energies to your work with the Company. Should you wish to take any other employment outside the Company's working hours, you should first discuss the matter with your Personnel Manager to obtain the Company's consent. The Company's consent will normally be given provided that such outside employment does not interfere in any way with your employment with Dixons, for example:

1  Causes you to be too tired to perform efficiently in your job in Dixons.
2  Causes you to refuse to work overtime when requested to do so.

Such employment must NOT be in a competitive industry and must NOT entail any possible conflict of interest.

Violations of the Company's rules on outside employment will lead to disciplinary action, possibly to dismissal.

### Legal & General

We expect full-time employees to concentrate their working energies on Legal & General, and not to undertake any activity, paid or unpaid, which would conflict with this. Part-time working patterns, which are becoming increasingly popular, imply a different lifestyle, but once again, we expect part-time employees to give us their full commitment during working hours.

Legal & General does not permit outside employment, whether paid or unpaid, which interferes with an individual's ability to carry out his or her duties.

Employees must in all cases obtain Legal & General's permission before taking up any outside employment, unless they are employed on the understanding of multiple employment.

Employment includes directorships, partnerships, lectureships, trusteeships, a self-employed business, or other employment in companies or organizations whether in insurance or any other business activity.

Legal & General encourages staff to take up certain active voluntary roles in the community such as becoming school governors. There are Group policies to cover such activities.

## CONFLICTS OF INTEREST

### TSB Trust

The Company gives no special preference to applications for employment from relatives of existing employees.

Problems may arise when close relations are working together, particularly in superior/subordinate positions. For this reason the Company will not normally sanction the employment of close relations where there is a line reporting relationship, whether direct or indirect.

### Mobil Oil Company Ltd

Mobil Oil Company Ltd will not permit and has never permitted conflicts of interest on the part of its officers, directors, or employees. Accordingly, no officer, director, or employee shall knowingly allow himself or herself to become involved in a conflict of interest, or, upon discovery thereof, to allow such a conflict to continue. Moreover, there will be situations which, while perhaps justifiable, involve the appearance of a conflict of interest and they should be carefully weighed.

Generally speaking, any direct or indirect interest in, connection with, or benefit from outside commercial activities, which interest might in any way adversely affect the Company, defined for Conflicts of Interest purposes as including Mobil Oil Corporation, its subsidiaries and affiliates, involves a possible conflict of interest.

To present an exhaustive list of actions or interests which would constitute a 'conflict of interest' is virtually impossible. It is important, therefore, that any officer, director, or employee should report immediately in writing to his or her supervisor any facts which might involve the slightest possibility of a conflict of interest. No new commitments with a potential of this nature, particularly those coming within the provisions of paragraphs 1 to 6 below, should be undertaken without prior approval from Management. The supervisor in turn should forward the report through regular channels to Management, who will arrange for such review.

The Company recognizes that there are many borderline situations. It intends to approach each case objectively, giving full recognition to the attendant circumstances. In some instances, full disclosure of the facts by the officer, director, or employee is all that is necessary to enable the Company to protect its interests. In some others, if no improper motivation appears to exist and the Company's interests have not suffered, prompt elimination of the outside interest will suffice. Should the Company find, however, that an inexcusable violation of Company policy is involved, more drastic action will be taken. This may involve termination of employment, or a requirement that the officer, director, or employee pay over to the Company any profit he or she may have realized, or reimburse the Company for any damage it may have suffered.

The Company's determination as to whether or not a conflict of interest exists shall be conclusive. It reserves the right to take such action as, in its judgement, will end the conflict.

Circumstances in which a conflict of interest on the part of an officer, director, or employee would or might arise (and should be reported immediately to Management) include, but are not limited to, the following:

1 Ownership of a material interest in any supplier, contractor, subcontractor, customer, or other entity with which the Company does business.
2 Acting in any capacity – including director, officer, partner, consultant, employee, distributor, agent, or the like – for suppliers, contractors, subcontractors, customers, or other entities with which the Company does business.
3 Acceptance, directly or indirectly, of payments, services, or loans from a supplier, contractor, subcontractor, customer, or other entity with which the Company does business. The foregoing shall be deemed to include gifts, trips, entertainment, or other favours, of more than nominal value, but shall exclude loans from publicly-held insurance companies and commercial or savings banks at normal rates of interest.

4 Use of such information in a manner which will be detrimental to the Company's interest, e.g. utilization for one's own benefit of know how or information developed through Company research activities.

5 Disclosure or other misuse of confidential or unpublished information of any kind obtained through the individual's connection with the Company.

6 Acquiring or trading in, directly or indirectly, oil, gas, uranium, or related mineral interests including, but not limited to, leases, royalty interests, oil payments, etc.

7 Acquiring or trading in, directly or indirectly, other properties or interests connected with the manufacture, transportation, or marketing of oil, gas, uranium, or other commodities manufactured, transported, or marketed by the Company.

8 Ownership or acquisition of property or interests the value of which has been or is likely to be affected by any action of the Company influenced by or resulting from a decision or recommendation of the officer, director, or employee owning such property.

9 Ownership or acquisition of any property or interest where confidential or unpublished information obtained through the Company has in any way been involved in such ownership or acquisition.

10 The appropriation to oneself or the diversion to others, directly or indirectly, of any business opportunity in which it is known or could reasonably be anticipated that the Company would be interested, e.g. opportunity for purchase or lease of a service station, bulk plant site, jobber, or distributor, etc.

11 Ownership, directly or indirectly, by an officer, director, or employee of a material interest in an enterprise in competition with the Company or its dealers and distributors.

12 Acting as director, officer, partner, consultant, employee, or agent of any enterprise which is in competition with the Company or its dealers and distributors.

Ownership, acting, acceptance, acquiring, or trading shall be deemed to include ownership, acting, acceptance, acquiring, or trading by the spouse of an officer, director, or employee, by members of the family or by close relatives and shall be reported by such officer, director, or employee if the facts with respect thereto are known to him or her. (No officer, director, or employee is required to make any investigation as to the action or interest of those who are not residing in his or her home.)

The legal form of ownership will be of no significance in determining whether a possible conflict of interest may exist except that ownership of an aggregate of less than one-tenth of 1 per cent of the securities of any company or corporation which has total assets equivalent to 50 million dollars or more, or the securities of which are traded on the principal Stock Exchange of the country in which it is incorporated, shall not be deemed to involve a conflict of interest under this

Policy and need not be reported unless the circumstances of such ownership come within the provisions of sub-paragraphs (8) or (9).

An interest is 'material' within the meaning of the Policy when it is significant either in reference to the financial position of the individual concerned or in reference to the size of the entity involved. In case of doubt materiality should be presumed.

## Abbey Life

A firm should be vigilant to identify potential conflicts of interest, and, where it cannot avoid conflict, should nevertheless take all reasonable steps, by way of disclosure, internal rules of confidentiality, or otherwise to ensure fair treatment to all of its customers.

Where, in connection with or for the purpose of investment business, a firm has control of or is otherwise responsible for assets belonging to a customer, it should arrange proper protection for them, by way of segregation or identification of those assets or otherwise.

A firm should ensure that it maintains adequate financial resources to meet its investment business commitments and to withstand the risks to which its business is subject.

## ARCO UK Ltd

Employees must avoid any interest, influence, or relationship that conflicts with the best interests of the company. No company asset or resource is to be used for personal gain, benefit, or any other illegal purpose. The company's Conflict of Interest policy gives further guidance in this area.

### The Automobile Association

Advice to staff that they should not use their position as an AA employee to promote any business or to be engaged in any branch of the motor trade.

### Grand Metropolitan

Each operating unit must ensure that its employees are aware they should declare any commercial investment, interest, or association, which might compromise that employee's independence to fully discharge their responsibilities.

### Abbey National

A firm should either avoid any conflict of interest arising or, where conflicts arise, should ensure fair treatment to all its customers by disclosure, internal rules of confidentiality, declining to act, or otherwise. A firm should not unfairly place its interests above those of its customers and, where a properly informed customer would reasonably expect that the firm would place his interests above its own, the firm should live up to that expectation.

## Kingfisher

It is the policy of the group that directors and senior employees should devote all their time and attention to the business of the company by which they are employed. The consent of the group Chief Executive is required in the event of any director or senior employee wishing to engage in any other business activity. The same consent is also required where any such person wishes to have a direct or indirect financial interest in any such business activity. Interests in a quoted or listed company are excluded from such requirements for consent, unless otherwise stated in an employee's terms of employment.

Furthermore, all employees should avoid conflicts of interest between the group's business and their activities or those of their spouses or other close relations. 'Close relations' for this purpose means an employee's spouse, children and step-children, parents and parents' children, and relations by marriage of any such individuals. In the event of such conflicts arising, or potentially arising, they must immediately consult the Chief Operating Officer (Chairman or Managing Director) of their employing company, and obtain his or her clearance in writing.

## United Biscuits

An employee will avoid conflict of interest by making it known that he or she is employed by UB and that views expressed on public, political, or civic affairs are those of the individual and not necessarily of the company.

No director or senior manager or other employee with privileged or financially sensitive 'inside' information may deal in the company's shares without first notifying the directors in writing of their intention and receiving a written acknowledgement of that notification. No employee may make known to any person outside the company material information about the company's operations or performance which could influence share dealing.

No employee should have any financial interest in a competitor or supplier which could cause divided loyalty or even the appearance of divided loyalty. Nor should an employee have any other financial interest which could cause speculation or misunderstanding about why he or she has that interest.

No employee may be involved with activity for personal gain which for any reason is in conflict with UB's business interests, nor may work be solicited or performed which could be in competition with UB. Unless authorized by a director, no outside work may be performed or business or clients be solicited on company time or on company premises. Nor may company owned equipment, materials, resources, or inside information be used for outside work without similar authorization.

No employee or any member of his or her immediate family, will accept from or give to anyone in a business relationship, gratuities or gifts of money or any consideration of significant value which could be perceived as having been offered because of the business relationship or to gain a business advantage.

The company's property is more than physical plant and equipment or product – it includes technologies and concepts, ideas and recipes, business and product plans as well as general information about the business. Misappropriation of the company's property in any form is theft.

## Legal & General

Legal & General's business success depends on gaining and keeping the trust of customers, the public, and the business world in general. As individual employees we are acting as representatives of Legal & General; therefore our integrity must remain beyond question.

Employees must not put themselves in a position where their personal interests conflict with those of Legal & General.

Employees may not enter into any transactions in which they have a personal interest that may conflict with the interests of Legal & General. Where there is any doubt, full disclosure must be made to appropriate authorities within the Business Unit.

Provided disclosure has been made, permission may, in some circumstances, be granted.

It is a criminal offence to solicit anything of value from any individual, business, or company which is hoping to influence or to win business from Legal & General.

An example of a conflict of interest might be a transaction on behalf of Legal & General with a supplier or consultant where the supplier or consultant is: a person related by blood or marriage to the employee; a personal friend; or an organization in which the employee or his/her family holds a material financial interest.

It may happen that a conflict of interest situation already exists. In such a case, the employee must refer it to an appropriate authority.

## British Gas

Anyone who has a personal interest in an organization with which British Gas has or may have a business relationship is vulnerable to allegations of impropriety. If a personal interest or that of a member of one's immediate family might influence the Company's business relationship, it should be formally declared in writing at HQ to the Company Secretary or in a Region to the Regional Secretary, who will record the declaration of interest in a Register maintained for this purpose. Examples of a personal interest that should be declared are a directorship, a large shareholding, promise of future employment, or the employment of a close relative or friend in a position of influence in an organization which may be given business or awarded contracts by the Company.

Some staff in British Gas have access during their work to unpublished information about the Company's activities or future prospects which, if published, might affect the share price. If you are in this special position and you wish to buy or sell British Gas shares, you must first study the separate guidelines on share dealing, which are available from your head of department.

You should not deal in the securities of any company when, by virtue of your position as an employee of British Gas, you are in possession of information likely upon publication to affect the market price of those securities. This includes shares or debentures or options to subscribe for shares or debentures.

In addition to the foregoing, if you are a Senior Officer or within Purchasing Department at HQ or in a Region, you will be required from time to time formally to declare in writing to your HQ or Regional Director or Controller details of any shareholding, involvement, or activity which could give rise to a conflict of interest. Everyone employed in the industry's Purchasing function is expected to abide by the Ethical Code of the Institute of Purchasing & Supply.

In addition to the foregoing, if in any other Department you are in a position to influence the choice of contractors or supplier, you may be required to make a similar formal declaration at the discretion of your Managing Director, HQ Director, or Regional Chairman as appropriate.

## IBM UK Ltd and IBM USA

Your private life is very much your own. Still, a conflict of interest may arise if you engage in any activities or advance any personal interests at the expense of IBM's interests. It's up to you to avoid situations in which your loyalty may become divided. Each individual's situation is different, and in evaluating your own, you will have to consider many factors . . . .

## Quaker Oats

No officer or employee can have any personal interest outside the Company that could conflict or appears to conflict with the interest of Quaker or its shareholders. Conflicts of interest may arise when an employee is in the position where he or she can use the Company connection for personal or family gain apart from normal compensation provided through employment.

## SALARY AND BENEFITS

### Abbey Life

To ensure that remuneration, including pension and other benefits, is fair to the individual and appropriate to the company in meeting its objectives.

The overall pay and benefits policy will be determined by Abbey's business performance.

The cash element of remuneration will be given greater emphasis than benefits in order to provide a higher level of disposable income with freedom of choice on how to spend it.

As far as possible pay and benefits will take account of appropriate market comparisons to ensure competitiveness in order to attract and retain employees of the right calibre.

We are convinced that achieving and maintaining excellent service standards is a major contribution to our success.

Our aim is therefore to achieve a level of service to policyholders and sales intermediaries which is better, and seen to be better than our main competitors, and achieve the same standards of service to each other.

We will also continue to drive towards excellent administration, fast, accurate, and high quality, with staff putting themselves in the customer's shoes.

We recognize that Abbey's success is totally dependent on the commitment and cooperation of our staff.

To this end we aim to support the development of staff to the full extent of their abilities consistent with business requirements.

Our objectives are to provide strong product development and innovation which leads the market, meets the needs of our clients, and maximises the productivity of our distribution channel and to improve our overall market awareness and create an image and stay distinct from the competition.

The development of 'leading edge' computer systems will be a vital contribution to our future success so we intend to continue the improvement of existing systems, balancing responsiveness to user needs with the company's requirement for effective systems strategic planning.

## IBM UK Ltd and IBM USA

We seek motivated, intelligent, educated people who understand and embrace our values, work hard, have fun working, are flexible and often creative. Compensation is based on results, and promotion on results and ability.

## TI Group

Levels of remuneration, benefits, and conditions of employment should be provided which will attract, retain, and motivate people with the necessary ability and experience to achieve the Group's business objectives.

## DEALING WITH THE MEDIA, LECTURES, AND PUBLICATIONS

### London Buses

Staff are encouraged to participate in discussions at technical institutions and meetings of similar bodies which have as their object the advancement of knowledge of the transport industry and its problems. London Regional Transport and its subsidiaries have no desire to formulate any rule on the consent of any such publication by staff, whether it is a book, letter, or article for publication in a newspaper, magazine, or elsewhere, or an address, broadcast or televised interview, talk, or lecture. Members of the staff in exercising their right to free expression of their opinions are expected to remember their responsibilities and are relied upon not to make statements publicly on matters of policy which are not yet public knowledge; not to express personal views in such a form that they are taken by the public to represent official policy; and not to refer to decisions or contemplated decisions, which it may be their duty to carry out, in a manner or in circumstances likely to cause misunderstanding. Permission to use statistics, data or designs not previously published, and guidance on any other aspect of the proposed publication or talk on which the author may be in doubt, should first be obtained from the employing Manager. Any approach from, or contact with, the press and media generally should be discussed with the Public Relations Manager or a senior member of that office's staff prior to commitment.

### Kingfisher

As regards contacts with the Press, group policy is that all enquiries from the national or financial press must be returned to Kingfisher plc who will respond after consultation with the operating company where necessary. In addition comments on trading, profit targets, future strategy, and political issues like Sunday trading destined for other publications such as the trade press or internal house magazines should be cleared in advance with Kingfisher plc. Personal interviews with the press by senior managers should be cleared with Kingfisher plc and approval will only be given where these fit in with the overall communications objectives of the group.

### British Coal

When preparing material for publications, lectures, speeches, broadcasts, or letters to the press on matters concerning the coal industry and the subsidiary activities of the Board, staff will act with discretion bearing in mind the Board's interest and in particular avoiding disclosure of confidential matters or statements of personal opinions that might wrongly be interpreted as an expression of the Board's policies or intentions. The Board's permission must be obtained for any quotation from or reproduction of material the copyright of which belongs to the

Board. Staff undertaking publications, lectures, speeches, or broadcasts otherwise than in their official capacity must not make use of their Board title or description without permission. If permission is given they must make clear that any views expressed are their own personal ones and do not necessarily represent the views of the Board. Staff engaging in such activities in their normal capacity must declare any fee or royalty or other tangible benefit obtained and will surrender it if required by the Board to do so.

(It is the Board's policy to encourage staff to contribute to the general spread and distribution of technical and other knowledge and for this purpose to engage in activities such as writing books and articles, giving lectures, and making speeches and radio and television broadcasts provided that this does not adversely affect their work for the Board. If anyone is in doubt as to what they may safely publish they should consult their supervisor or management official to whom they are responsible.)

### TI Group

Communications with the national media should only be undertaken by a Group Executive Director or with his express authority.

Communications with local media on matters of local interest may be undertaken at the discretion of a site manager. However, care must be taken that there is not a TI Group or wider dimension which could be of interest to the national media. If in doubt, advice should be obtained from Group Public Affairs.

## TRADE UNIONS AND UNFAIR DISMISSALS

### Anonymous

Most companies are members of relevant Employers' Federations and are, therefore, committed to support the principle of collective bargaining with recognized independent trade unions which have agreements with, for example, the NFBTE, or, on jobs undertaken under civil engineering conditions, with the FCEC. Such recognition applies only to hourly paid operatives. Any pressure from unions not recognized by relevant Employers' Federations must be referred immediately to the Industrial Relations Department.

It is the Group policy and good management practice, in locations where trade unions are recognized and well organized, to establish a sound working relationship with the full-time union officials rather than to allow, or encourage, the development of unofficial activity among the site stewards or other site-based groups of employees.

Conditions of employment for hourly paid operatives and the procedures for dealing with grievances and disputes are laid down in the relevant national industrial agreements (e.g. The National Working Rules for the Building Industry). National agreements must be adhered to but may be supplemented by local or site agreements for the maintenance of good industrial relations. In those parts of the Group not covered by national agreements, company or local agreements may be negotiated with the relevant unions after prior consultation with the Industrial Relations Department.

All formal company, local, or site agreements in the UK must be drafted in conjunction with Personnel, Legal, and Industrial Relations departments before signature by the authorized signatory for each specific division in order to ensure compatibility of principles and to avoid unsatisfactory precedents.

Personnel Managers are responsible for advising their management on the implementation and interpretation of this policy, the law, and of national and local agreements with trade unions.

Under the Employment Protection (Consolidation) Act 1978 and subsequent Acts, the dismissal of an employee shall be regarded as being unfair if the reason for it, or if more than one reason the principle reason, was that the employee:

1  was, or proposed to become, a member of an independent trade union;
2  had taken, or proposed to take, part at any appropriate time in the activities of an independent trade union; or
3  had refused, or proposed to refuse, to become or remain a member of a trade union which was not an independent trade union.

An independent trade union is one whose name is entered on the list of trade unions maintained by the Certification Office.

Where a Tribunal finds a dismissal to be unfair, by reason of union membership or activities or non-membership, and the complainant requests the Tribunal to make an order for reinstatement or re-engagement, or the Tribunal makes such an order on its own initiative, should the Employer refuse to reinstate or re-engage then an additional special award will be made by way of compensation. The level of award will be 104 weeks' pay subject to a minimum of £12,550 and a maximum of £25,040 where the individual makes the request, and 156 weeks pay subject to a minimum of £18,795 where the Tribunal takes the initiative. These awards are in addition to the usual awards for unfair dismissal.

If an employer is forced to dismiss a non-union employee as a result of a union-only labour clause in a commercial contract, he can require the Client or main contractor to be a party to any unfair dismissal proceedings if they arise. The Client or main contractor may then be ordered by the tribunal to pay a *full* indemnity to the employer who dismissed the non-union member to cover any unfair dismissal compensation. The Client or main contractor, in turn, can require the relevant trade union in the case to be a party to any unfair dismissal proceedings where he insisted on union labour only as a result of pressure from that union and can recover compensation from that union if an unfair dismissal award is made by the tribunal.

Under the law an employer is required when requested by a *recognized independent trade union* to make his premises available to the union for the purpose of conducting a secret ballot, providing:

1  it is reasonably practical for the employer to do so; and
2  the purpose of the question to be voted upon is one, or more, or the following:

   a) to obtain a decision or ascertain the views of members of a trade union as
      to the calling or ending of a strike or any other industrial action;
   b) to elect workplace representatives or any other officials or representatives
      called for in union rules;
   c) to amend union rules; and
   d) to obtain a decision on an amalgamation or transfer directly involving the
      union.

The law does not compel trade unions to hold secret workplace ballots. It simply
obliges an employer to make his premises available for such ballots if requested
by the union.

There is no obligation to provide facilities of any sort in connection with a
ballot so the basic duty is restricted to that of providing physical space, and,
within the right to time off for trade union activities, time off to permit employees
to vote.

## TRAVEL AND ENTERTAINMENT EXPENSES

### TSB Trust

It is the responsibility of all employees to ensure that the Company's resources
are used with care at all times and no waste is incurred. This applies as much to
expenditure (purchasing goods and services of all sorts) as to the economic use
of supplies and materials.

Expenses incurred by staff whilst carrying out Company duties or furthering
Company business will be reimbursed, providing always that such expenses are
fair and reasonable for the circumstances.

Significant and/or persistent abuse of expenses will result in disciplinary
procedures being taken.

Employees are expected to plan their visits/journeys as economically as
possible in relation to time and cost. A claim may be refused either wholly or in
part in cases where it is considered that the employee has incurred expense which
could have reasonably been avoided.

Employees required to stay overnight while on Company business may find
suitable accommodation subject to the approval of their Departmental manager.
Accommodation should normally be arranged at hotels of a three star category or
below.

It is the Company's policy to reimburse genuine business entertaining
expenses within reasonable limits. Claims made for lavish entertaining will not
normally be met.

Staff must take care when accepting hospitality from, or giving it to, outside
interests: the Company must be seen to be above any suspicion of corruption or

bribery. Before accepting or extending any such invitation staff should clear the matter with their line manager in the first place.

When entertaining visitors or business associates at any of the Andover sites staff should normally use the facilities offered by the Company staff restaurant. Should local commercial establishments be used, the prior express approval of the line manager must be obtained. Authorization of such expenses must be in accordance with the rules laid down in the Cost Control Manual.

The Company recognizes that there are benefits to be gained from 'internal' entertaining (managers entertaining their staff, or other managers) and will normally bear the cost of this. However, it must be kept within reasonable limits, both in terms of numbers involved and the frequency of occurrence. Company catering facilities should be used for such occasions. Wine should only be ordered when visitors to the Company are being entertained. In appropriate cases, managers on the 'A' List may order wine. Orders should be in writing and must be countersigned by their immediate manager.

It is important to distinguish between 'subsistence' and 'entertaining' when completing expense claim forms.

Working lunches will be funded by the Company only when and where they are for bona fide work purposes or the furtherance of the Company's aims. They are not provided as a staff benefit and abuse of the facility may result in it being withdrawn from the offender.

Working lunches may be booked in advance with the Catering Manager by 'A' List managers and by other staff only with the prior express approval of a Department manager.

Drinks cabinets are provided to senior staff for genuine entertainment purposes only. They should only be used on appropriate occasions and then with due moderation.

The facilities and services provided by the Company are primarily intended to make work more efficient and conditions more pleasant for employees. They should not be abused: significant and/or persistent abuse will result in disciplinary procedures being taken. Generally, all Company property and facilities should be treated with the same care with which you would treat your own.

These facilities and materials are provided for the furtherance of Company work. Whilst occasional and small use of them for private purposes is acceptable this must not be abused.

Notice boards located outside of the staff restaurant are provided for general use by staff who wish to advertise social activities, accommodation, etc. All other notice boards are for specified and non-general use: staff should not use them for private, promotional, or advertising purposes. Notices should also not be attached to walls, doors, or screens. Department managers are responsible for controlling their areas in this respect.

Staff are encouraged to use 'Chatterbox' for their advertisements and notices.

Meeting and conference rooms are provided for bona fide work purposes and should not be used for private or non-work related matters. They may be used, if free, by staff studying for exams, providing this has been agreed by the appropriate line manager.

Rooms should be booked in advance with Office Services Department.

In the interests of economy as well as line availability all telephone calls should be kept to a minimum, both in frequency and duration. The Company uses call monitoring equipment as part of its telephone budgetary control measures.

## USE OF COMPANY PROPERTY, RESOURCES, AND TIME

### Legal & General

No company can afford to run a business where its facilities are abused for personal reasons.

Company property and time should be used for business purposes. Employees may only use company property for personal reasons where permission has been given.

Permission from the line manager is required for personal use of company time and property including:

Photocopying
Emergency local telephone calls, or calls such as can only be made during the business day
Use of office equipment and supplies

Examples of abuse would be:

Franking private mail
Making unnecessary private telephone calls
Using company time for private business
Receiving payments from third parties for work done in company time.

Practice in this area depends on a degree of mutual trust and common sense. Permission will usually be given for important phone calls or small amounts of photocopying.

On those occasions when employees have incurred business expenses, they will be reimbursed upon producing the proper records and filling out the correct expense claim form. When making claims, it is essential that everyone gives an honest and accurate account of them.

Sums claimed as expenses must have been reasonably incurred in pursuit of the business interests of Legal & General. Expense payments will compensate employees to the extent that they are out of pocket, and no more.

Employees must keep proper records of expenses incurred and expense claims must be supported by receipts, in accordance with established procedures.

On those occasions when an advance is given against expenses, the advance must be properly accounted for.

Employees may not falsify any record, book, or account, or submit a false personal expense statement, or a claim for reimbursement of a personal expense which is not related to business.

Employees responsible for approving expenditures must do so based upon proper supporting documents, as must those responsible for keeping books. This will ensure that accounting records are kept reasonably detailed, and accurately reflect all transactions.

## REIMBURSABLE EXPENSES

### Tesco

The use of company funds for unlawful purposes is strictly prohibited.

No undisclosed or unrecorded funds or assets shall be established for any purpose.

No payment on behalf of Tesco shall be approved or made with the intention that any part of such payment is to be used for any purpose other than as described by the documents and financial records supporting the payment.

Loans from Tesco PLC or its subsidiaries to its Directors are prohibited under the Companies Acts and so are bridging loans from subsidiary companies to subsidiary company Directors.

There are legal restrictions on the use of credit or charge cards for personal purposes and, accordingly, no such expenditure is allowed. In any case where, by accident, a card has been so used there will be reimbursement on demand.

A company cannot make tax-free payments except to casual staff below the tax paying level, or to a limited extent in respect of relocation expenses supported by invoices.

# Chapter 21

# Confidential and proprietary information

In the 1990s, industrial economies have increasingly relied on information and knowledge, rather than natural resources or raw materials, to add value to their products and services. In fact, as the worldwide best-seller *Megatrends* relates, the entire world has become information and knowledge based, and primarily those firms that obtain, control, and effectively and quickly utilize information and knowledge will succeed in an uncertain future. Consequently, every firm, whether an industrial concern or a software developer, must protect its confidential and proprietary information, including its unique and exclusive ideas and practices. Theft of trade secrets, one form of proprietary information, costs British firms dearly. Through a code of conduct, a company can provide its employees with guidelines on how information is to be controlled and safeguarded within the firm. Every firm has an affirmative duty to acquire and preserve competitive advantages such as commercially sensitive information.

Confidential information is that information regarding business strategy, internal control, and other business information created within the firm. British Steel's approach to protecting such assets is straightforward: 'No Company employee or former Company employee may disclose to unauthorized persons confidential or other classified information to which he has access as an employee of the Company'. Difficulty arises when the code of conduct is vague in its definition of confidential information, so it is wise to be explicit in what is 'confidential information'. British Gas provides its employees with clear instruction: when in doubt 'Seek advice from your superior'. Enlightened firms design internal control measures to shield confidential and proprietary information from those within and without the firm who don't utilize it for the firm's benefit, and to prevent its transfer outside the firm to competitors

Copyrights are a creature of law designed to protect the original work of authorship that is established in a tangible medium of expression from which it can be comprehended, e.g. a computer program, design, or drawing. Many times firms experience friction with employees concerning employee-created copyrights. One prominent British firm is explicit in its handling of copyrights: 'The company as employer owns the copyright for all purposes in all material created by its employees in the course of their employment'. In this regard, every firm should use explicit, unambiguous language to provide employees with notice. By doing so, there is little room for misunderstanding.

Often, a firm includes an overall intellectual property proviso in its code which establishes guidelines to protect copyrights, patents, trademarks, and other types of intellectual property. British Coal provides in its code of conduct that its employees 'must not exploit for their personal gain any inventions, designs, ideas, processes, or methods which they have developed or helped to develop in the course of their work'. A broad statement, such as British Coal's, provides contractual protection where governmental protection might not exist, i.e. processes or methods.

A final category of protected information is that of proprietary information. The international corporation Control Data includes such information as business plans, customer base, pricing strategies, and stockholder identities within its definition of protected proprietary information, and establishes with each employee a firm agreement not to reveal such information to unauthorized parties. IBM's success is built upon proprietary information which it accumulated and protected. One way IBM safeguards its information is through the use of a code of conduct with a specific section that prescribes the correct use and security of proprietary information and lists sanctions to be levied against those who violate this policy.

The following excerpts provide insight into how major British and multi-national companies address the intricacies of confidential and proprietary information. These firms understand that loss or misuse of valuable assets, such as proprietary information, may jeopardize the firm's existence.

## CONFIDENTIAL INFORMATION, PERSONAL DATA, AND COMPUTER SECURITY

### TSB Trust

It is a condition of employment that all staff treat Company data – particularly personal data – as confidential.

Important provisions of the Data Protection Act are now in force and must be strictly observed by all staff. The DPA Briefing leaflet, copied to all staff, summarizes the Act and explains what it means to the Company and to each of us as employees. In particular, staff should note that no personal data must be removed from Company premises and that no personal data acquired in the course of, or in connection with, his employment should be held on his own personal micro at his home. If in any doubt, discuss the matter with your manager before taking a course of action that may contravene the Act.

It is Company practice to clear desks of all working papers at the end of the day; it is essential that all confidential documents, or documents of value (e.g. cheques), are locked away.

Staff must exercise the utmost discretion regarding the disclosure of information: if there is any doubt whatsoever the enquiry should be passed on to one's manager and/or asked to be put in writing. The authenticity of an enquiry should be checked whenever possible by the recipient telephoning the caller back. Should the enquiry concern information about a member of staff, Personnel Department must be asked to telephone the caller back; enquiries from the press must only be dealt with by Corporate Relations Department. Do not pass calls around the Company from extension to extension.

Complaints must be dealt with politely and rapidly. If a complete answer cannot be given at once, an acknowledgement letter must be sent. Complaints should normally be dealt with by Supervisors/Managers. Staff should not discuss customer complaints outside of Company premises.

Should abusive telephone calls be received, staff should not reply in kind but inform the caller that they are not prepared to continue the conversation and that they are putting the receiver down. A written report should then be made of the call and passed to the line manager.

## ARCO UK Ltd

Employees are responsible for protecting proprietary or confidential information, which may not be given to any individual or organization without permission.

## British Gas

We all have a responsibility to safeguard the confidentiality of any information acquired during the course of our work including information kept on computers and a duty never to use it for personal advantage. Such information should not be disclosed outside British Gas. Equally, we should all be on our guard and avoid careless and thoughtless talk which may damage the Company's business or that of any of its customers.

Any disclosure or similar communication made to management in accordance with this Code will be treated as confidential although it may be discussed with your Director or Controller.

## British Steel

No Company employee or former Company employee may disclose to un-authorized persons confidential or other classified information to which he has had access as an employee of the Company.

Classified information from Government Departments to which Company employees have access in the course of their work is also subject to rules concerning unauthorized disclosure and misuse of information. The unauthorized disclosure of such information is an offence under the Official Secrets Acts.

## TI Group

The TI Board requires that there should be a high standard of commercial and financial security in TI Confidential information, whether financial, know how, or indeed any other kind, must be kept secure and protected. It is essential that all employees are kept aware of their obligations and in particular the restrictions on the use of price sensitive information. Employees must not deal in TI shares when in possession of price sensitive information. In cases of doubt the Group Company Secretary must be consulted.

## Dixons

You are not permitted to communicate to any other person, firm, or company, whether during your period of employment or afterwards, confidential details of any of the affairs of the Company or its subsidiary and associated Companies, or their employees, except in so far as such communication is necessary for the discharge of your duties, or is expressly authorized by the Company. Similarly, you must not attempt at any time to use secret or confidential material which you may acquire during the course of your employment in any way to cause loss or harm to the Company.

## London Buses

Staff have an obligation not to divulge confidential information available to them only through their employment. Confidential information received in the course of duty should be respected and should never be used for personal gain; information given in the course of duty should be true and fair and never designed to mislead.

## Tesco

You are reminded that every care should be taken in copying, carrying, distributing, keeping, and destroying documents so as to maintain confidentiality.

## Rolls Royce

Information received by employees in the course of business dealings for the Company must be treated as confidential and not used except for purposes for which it is disclosed. In particular it must not be used for personal gain.

## United Biscuits

Confidential information about our business is the property of the company. Only those people with a business 'need to know' should have access to confidential information and such information may not be disclosed to anyone within or outside the company without the authority of a director.

Information about customers and suppliers, or indeed about any organization or individual, must not be misused.

Personal information about employees must only be collected, used, and retained where it is required for business or legal reasons and will only be available to those with a clear business 'need to know'. Any decision on use of personal information for valid business purposes will be weighed against the individual's right to privacy.

The company's health care specialists are employed as impartial advisors and their actions are governed at all times by their professional codes of ethics. Access to clinical data is confined to the occupational physicians and nurses and no confidential information may be disclosed to any others without the consent of the individual employee.

## Legal & General

The nature of our business requires us to obtain detailed information about hundreds of thousands of private individuals and companies who entrust their business to us. Our customers are entitled to expect that we show responsibility in the way we use this information, much of which will be private and some of which will be highly sensitive. In the same way, we need to observe confidentiality in our dealings within the company, and toward our colleagues.

Prudence and caution must be exercised in using confidential information and in sharing it only with those who have a legitimate need to know.

Examples of confidential information include: information about our customers, suppliers, and employees, and all factual information concerning companies with whom we do business or whose securities we buy and sell. The term 'confidential information' covers trade secrets, business or product plans, systems, methods, software, manuals, and customer lists.

Confidential information should not be used or disclosed to progress any private interest or make any personal gain.

Misuse of unpublished price-sensitive information relating to securities is a criminal offence. If an employee gives another person information of this kind and the other person acts on it, the employee could be held liable for the actions of the other person.

There are a very few occasions when people performing certain functions may be required to exchange confidential information. In such cases clear guidelines must be followed.

## Mobil Oil Company Ltd

All businesses operate through their employees. Consequently, a business must frequently give its employees confidential information or the employees may originate confidential information as part of their job. Under usual circumstances, an employee is legally and ethically required not to give such confidential information to others or to use it for personal benefit or for the benefit of others even after employment is terminated.

Confidential information includes any trade secret or technical information which: 1) is not common knowledge among competitors to whom it may be useful and 2) gives the one in possession some advantage over competition. Some examples in our business might be sales promotions; results of research; scientific studies or analyses; details of training methods; computer programs; new products or new uses for old products; methods used to save drilling costs; investment opportunities or acquisitions investigated, but not implemented; new business or financial opportunities; details of net prices for petroleum products charged to industrial or commercial customers, and the contents of contracts between the Company and such customers. Of course, the list is not limited to these but the above serve as an illustration.

The Company requires you not to give to others, or to use for yourself or for others, any confidential information you may obtain while employed by the Company, until this information becomes generally available to the industry. It must be appreciated that this confidentiality obligation continues even after your employment with the Company has terminated. The obligation also applies to confidential information obtained from Mobil Oil Corporation divisions or affiliates. The only exception to the obligation is if you have Company permission to disclose information.

In addition, if you know of confidential information belonging to any former employer, you may be legally or ethically bound by similar obligations to your former employer. The Company expects you to fulfil this obligation, and to refrain from giving your fellow employees, and from using in the Company's business, any confidential information belonging to any of your former employers. Of course, the Company wants you to use on your job all information which is generally known and used by persons of your training and experience and all information which is common knowledge to the industry.

You are also required to communicate fully and immediately to the Company every invention, discovery, improvement, or secret process in any way relating to the business of the Company (or which is capable of being used or adapted for use in such business) which you may make or discover or which may come to your knowledge in the course of the duties for which the Company employs you. Except as otherwise provided under the Patents Act 1977, all such inventions, discoveries, improvements, or secret processes shall belong to and be the absolute property of the Company. You will, if and when required to do so by the Company (whether during, or after the termination of, your employment) at the Company's expense, execute any documents or do any acts which the Company may consider necessary for obtaining the grant to the Company or its nominees of Letters Patent (or the equivalent protection in the United Kingdom or elsewhere) and to vest all right, title, and interest in such invention, discovery, improvement, or secret process in the Company or its nominees.

Upon the termination of your employment with the Company, you will forthwith return to the Company all records, samples, books, stationery, and other matter in your possession or control which concern the Company's business.

If you have any questions about these matters, consult your supervisor.

## TSB Trust

The Company's business is increasingly reliant on computer processing systems and it is of the greatest importance that the confidentiality and integrity of the data thereon is assured (this applies to micros and minis as much as to mainframe computing). The following is a summary of computer security requirements which all staff must follow. Further detail can be found in the Computer Centre Standards Manual (Vol. 1002).

No staff shall wilfully misuse any computer system, facility, or equipment, encourage or allow any one else to do so, nor attempt to defeat any security system. Any such action will result in Disciplinary Procedures being taken forthwith.

Department Managers are responsible for the proper use of computer equipment in their Department and only authorized users may operate such equipment. Equipment and computer time may only be used for Company business: computer games and any form of private or non-Company business use is forbidden. No additional equipment may be installed or used unless the proper authorizations have been obtained beforehand.

All data, programs, and files developed for, or held by, the Company are for the sole use of the Company and may not be accessed, altered, or copied without proper authorization. Proprietary computer software is copyright and may not be copied or used on machines except that for which it is licensed. Staff may not make copies of any software for private use and conversely private software may not be used on Company premises.

Passwords must be regarded as confidential and should not be disclosed to any other person, nor should any person attempt to obtain and use passwords which have not been issued to them. Any cases of misuse, or suspected misuse, of passwords should be reported to the appropriate Department Manager immediately.

Only authorized staff and visitors who have been cleared and signed in by an authorized member of staff may enter a designated secure area. Identity cards must be displayed by all staff whilst they remain inside a secured computer area. No employee who has been issued with a security entry number shall divulge this to anybody else.

## COPYRIGHTS

### British Coal

Copyright in any writing, design, drawing, or computer program made by staff during the course of, or arising from, their employment belongs to the Board (unless otherwise indicated), who have the right to publish and use the information therein in whatever form they require. All such material belongs to the Board and shall be surrendered by staff when no longer required for the purpose of work for the Board, at any time on request or at the latest on termination of their employment with the Board.

## IBM UK Ltd and IBM USA

In most cases, the copyrights in employee generated works of authorship such as manuals and computer programs are automatically owned by IBM through operation of law. In other cases, title to the copyrights is given to IBM by contractual provisions. IBM considers it important to limit the distribution of copyrightable material within IBM to that in which the copyright is owned by or appropriately licensed to IBM. To assure that material not owned by IBM is appropriately licensed, IBM may request a licence from you before you will be permitted to place copyrightable material into or on any IBM owned distribution channel, including internal mail and electronic channels such as conferencing disks, VM, or PROFS. This licence may be requested whether you or IBM actually owns the material. If there is a question of ownership, you should consult your manager before you distribute material in IBM through any channel. Your manager may consult the legal and the intellectual property law departments to determine whether you will be permitted to place the material in the particular distribution channel.

## INTELLECTUAL PROPERTY, IMPROVEMENTS, AND INVENTIONS

### British Coal

Staff must not exploit for their own personal gain any inventions, designs, ideas, processes, or methods which they have developed or helped to develop in the course of their work, or which otherwise belong to the Board under their contract of employment or the Patents Act 1977.

(Staff who wish to exploit any inventions or copyright for their own purposes, whether for gain or not, must seek the Board's agreement through the Staff Manager, but must understand that permission will only be given in exceptional circumstances. Staff may, however, be eligible for an award under the Board's Scheme for awards for inventions in the technical field.)

### Dixons

Subject to any statutory requirements to the contrary, any discovery, invention, or improvement in the methods, procedures, processes, or products of the Company which you make (whether alone or jointly) during the course of your employment, must be immediately disclosed to the Company to whom it shall belong absolutely. If required by the Company you must, at its expense, do all such things and execute all such documents (including a formal assignment for nominal consideration) as may be necessary to protect any such discovery, improvement, or invention and to vest in the Company the full benefits of your discovery.

## IBM UK Ltd and IBM USA

When you joined IBM, you should have been required to sign an agreement that sets out specific obligations you have as an employee, relating to the treatment of confidential information. Also under the agreement, when you are employed in a managerial, technical, engineering, product planning, programming, scientific, or other professional capacity, you assign to IBM the rights to any ideas and inventions that you develop if they are in an area of the company's business. Subject to the laws of each country, this obligation applies no matter where or when – at work or after hours – such intellectual property is created. The existence of this intellectual property must be reported to IBM, and the property must be protected like any other proprietary information of the company. However, if you believe that your idea or invention falls outside the area of IBM's business interests, you may ask IBM for a written disclaimer of ownership.

## PROPRIETARY INFORMATION

### IBM UK Ltd and IBM USA

IBM has a large variety of assets. Many are of great value to IBM's competitiveness and its success as a business. They include not only our extremely valuable proprietary information, but also our physical assets. IBM proprietary information includes intellectual property, typically the product of the ideas and hard work of many talented IBM people. It also includes the confidential data entrusted to many employees in connection with their jobs.

Protecting all of these assets is very important. Their loss, theft, or misuse jeopardizes the future of IBM. For this reason, you are personally responsible not only for helping to protect the company's assets in general. Here is where your awareness of security procedures can play a critical role. You should be alert to any situations or incidents that could lead to the loss, misuse, or theft of company property. And you should report all such situations which come to your attention. What types of assets should you be concerned about protecting? And what are your responsibilities in this regard?

Proprietary information is information that is the property of IBM and is usually classified under the IBM classification system. Such information includes the business, financial, marketing, and service plans associated with products. It also includes personnel information, medical records, and salary data. Other proprietary information includes designs; engineering and manufacturing know how and processes; IBM business and product plans with outside vendors and a variety of internal data bases; and patent applications and copyrighted material such as software. Much of this information is called intellectual property, and represents the product of the ideas and efforts of many of your fellow employees. Also, it has required substantial investment by IBM in planning, research, and development. Obviously, if competitors could secure proprietary information such as product design specifications without making the same substantial investment in research and engineering, they would be getting a free ride on IBM's investment. Pricing information and marketing plans are also highly useful to competitors.

The value of this proprietary information is well known to many people in the information industry. Besides competitors, they include industry and security analysts, members of the press, consultants, customers, and other so-called 'IBM watchers'. Some of these individuals will obtain information any way they can. No matter what the circumstances, IBM alone is entitled to determine who may possess its proprietary information and what use may be made of it, except for specific legal requirements such as the publication of certain reports.

As an IBM employee, you probably have access to information that the company considers proprietary. Given the widespread interest in IBM – and the increasingly competitive nature of the industry – the chances are you probably have contact with someone interested in acquiring information in your possession. So it's very important not to use or disclose proprietary information except as authorized by IBM and to provide adequate safeguards to prevent loss of such information. The unintentional disclosure of proprietary information can be just as harmful as intentional disclosure.

To avoid unintentional disclosure, never discuss with any unauthorized person information that has not been made public by IBM. This information includes unannounced products, prices, earnings, procurement plans, business volumes, and capital requirements. Also included are: confidential product performance data; marketing and service strategies; business plans; and other confidential information. Furthermore, you should not discuss confidential information even with authorized IBM employees if you are in the presence of others who are not authorized, for example at a trade show reception or in a public area such as an airplane. This also applies to discussions with family members or with friends, who might innocently or inadvertently pass the information on to someone else.

Finally, keep in mind that harmful disclosure may start with the smallest leak of bits of information. Such fragments of information from other sources form a fairly complete picture. If someone outside the company asks you questions, either directly or through another person, do not attempt to answer them unless you are certain you are authorized to do so. If you are not authorized, refer the person to the appropriate source within the company. For example, if you are approached by security analysts or investors, you should refer them to your local communications manager or to the Office of the Treasurer. Similarly, unless you have been authorized to talk to reporters, or to anyone else writing about or otherwise covering the company or the industry, direct the person to the information specialist in your communications department. If you do not know what functional area the questioner should be referred to, ask your manager. Besides your obligation not to disclose any IBM confidential information to anyone outside the company, you are also required as an employee to use such information only in connection with IBM's business. These obligations apply whether or not you developed the information yourself. And they apply by law in virtually all countries where IBM does business.

## Control Data

Proprietary information is information that is not generally known outside of Control Data. A variety of information can be considered proprietary. Some examples include:

1 Control Data technology.
2 Business plans or statistics (other than those already published in quarterly reports, the annual report, or in news releases).
3 Customer base and installation statistics.
4 Unannounced products and services.
5 Pricing strategies.
6 Identification of stockholders.

Control Data will determine which, if any, of its proprietary information can be released.

# Chapter 22

# Communication within and without the firm

Clear channels of communication within a firm may provide both improved information dissemination and increased productivity. Therefore, when a code of conduct is introduced or revised, effective internal communication of the new code guidelines is crucial to their success and implementation. Firms with open channels of communication encourage new ideas, information, and grievances to travel freely between management and employees.

Hewlett Packard incorporates the concept of 'management by wandering around'. This interactive, hands-on management style allows managers to talk openly with their employees, and for executive management to see how the firm works from the perspective of the employee and mid-level manager. HP also has an open door policy that allows every employee to direct concerns and ideas to whatever level of management he feels is appropriate until the concern is resolved. With this policy, there is no fear of violating the 'chain of command' that many overly structured firms have developed. HP's unique 'HP Way' attracts to its culture employees that are motivated, satisfied, productive, and effective.

One prominent British firm uses a more top–down approach to communication, but promotes free and open communication between managers and employees. Whatever course a firm takes regarding internal communication, the emphasis must be on open communication. Firms must create an atmosphere of two-way discussion where managers and employees are encouraged to communicate different ways of approaching a problem. In a flexible, curious environment, there is not a rigid attitude to solving problems that stifles creativity. Rather, creativity and new approaches are nurtured and rewarded.

A second concern firms have is with communication outside the firm. Alcan publishes information regularly to provide a clear picture of the overall structure, activities, and performance of the Alcan group of companies. Openness with the public concerning company operations helps to foster ethical conduct and improve a firm's public image.

The following code excerpts illustrate how progressive firms promote open, two-way communication within the firm, and communicate outside the firm.

## COMMUNICATION WITHIN THE FIRM

### Anonymous

The Company believes that it is essential for its staff to be informed on the progress, policies, plans, and financial state of the Company.

The Company recognizes its staff as important contributors to the business and as such will encourage them to make their opinions known on issues which affect them directly.

In pursuing an effective communication policy, the Company aims to help staff achieve a better understanding of the Company's objectives and policies and to gain their commitment to them.

In all cases, managers will be informed of the progress, policies, plans, and financial state of the Company before the staff.

As a matter of courtesy, Staff Representative Bodies will be informed of the content of Company communications addressed to all staff before such communications reach the staff they represent. Examples of this would be policies, plans, and the financial state of the Company.

It is recognized that:

1 It is important to create a climate within the Company which is conducive to effective communication.
2 Communication is a two-way process and management has the responsibility of ensuring that staff are able to communicate their views as well as communicate to them.
3 The policy has close links with the company's policy on Participation.
4 In certain cases, there may be a need to preserve confidentiality which could impose constraints upon communication.
5 The method of communication must be such that credibility is recognized and maintained and that misinterpretation is avoided as far as is humanly possible.
6 Great care must be taken to explain the Company's financial results and local objectives and results as appropriate.
7 Managers will always communicate direct with their staff and not through Representative Bodies, except on matters concerning pay and conditions of employment which are negotiable.
8 Line management has permanent responsibility for keeping staff informed.

Line management in each business or division is responsible for:

1 Creating and maintaining an effective communication plan within the agreed guidelines.
2 Ensuring that Company communications reach the staff they are intended for.
3 Monitoring the quality and effectiveness of communication within their unit.
4 Recognizing training needs in communication skills and ensuring these are met.

Each business or service division has a manager who acts as Communications Manager and who is responsible for:

1 Establishing with Directors and Managers the best way of getting communications to their staff and, where required, providing the means for them to do this.
2 Advising managers in other SBUs where and how specific communications should be directed within their unit.
3 Liaising with other Communications Managers to recommend improvements in current practice.
4 Ensuring that Company communications reach the managers or members of staff who should receive them. Staff and Training Division is responsible for:

   a) Providing training in effective communication.
   b) Through Staff Managers and SBU Communications Managers, monitoring the effectiveness and quality of the implementation of the policy.
   c) Reviewing and updating this Policy.

## Hewlett Packard Ltd

One of HP's fundamental strengths is effective communication, both upward and downward within the organization. Two key ingredients for making this happen are:

*Management by wandering around, raising concerns and the open door policy*

1 To have a well-managed operation, managers must be aware of what is happening in their areas – not just at their immediate level, but also at several levels above and below.
2 Our people are our most important resource, and managers have direct responsibility for their training, their performance, and their general well being. To do this, managers must move around to find out how their people feel about their jobs and what they think will make their work more productive and more meaningful.
3 Managers are expected to promote a work environment in which employees feel free and comfortable to seek individual counsel, express general concerns or other ideas.
4 All employees have the right, if in their opinion they feel such steps are necessary, to discuss their concerns with the level of management they feel is appropriate to handle the situation. Any effort to prevent an employee from going to higher-level managers, through intimidation or any other means, is absolutely contrary to company policy and will be dealt with accordingly.
5 Using the open door policy will not in any way impact any evaluations of employees or subject them to any other adverse consequences.
6 Employees also have responsibilities. They should keep their discussions with upper-level managers objective and focused on significant individual

concerns. Employees should also keep in mind that there are different points of view in every situation and that they may need to play a role in resolving the issues.

## Cadbury Schweppes

The principle of openness should apply in all our dealings inside and outside the Company. It follows that we should keep everyone in the business as well informed as possible within the legal limits of confidentiality. It also implies a readiness to listen. I believe in an open style of management and in involving people in the decisions which affect them, because it is right to do so and because it helps to bring individual and company aims closer together. The responsibility for decisions rests on those appointed to take them, but if they are arrived at openly, the decisions are likely to be better and the commitment to them greater. Openness and trust are the basis of good working relationships on which the effectiveness of the organization depends. They imply an acceptance of the mutual balance of rights and duties between individuals and the Company.

## Control Data

We all share a responsibility to protect Control Data's reputation.

It takes courage to raise an ethical issue – especially if it involves a situation in your work area. However, Control Data gives you that responsibility and will support you when you exercise it.

Control Data encourages its managers to maintain an open door policy for dealing with employee suggestions and problems.

## COMMUNICATION OUTSIDE THE FIRM

### Alcan

To publish information regularly regarding Alcan and its subsidiary companies on a consolidated basis giving, through comprehensive accounts and otherwise, a clear picture of the overall structure, activities, and performance of the Alcan group of companies.

# Chapter 23

# Anti-discrimination and equal opportunity in employment

The concept of equal opportunity is a vital component of any free enterprize system. Economic growth results from the utilization of all assets at hand to their fullest extent. Many business leaders believe that skilled, dedicated, productive employees are the most important assets of any firm. It therefore follows that maximizing the firm's return on its investment in its employees will ultimately lead to an increasing of the firm's profits. Hiring and promoting the best employees is in the best interest of the firm. Discrimination precludes many of the most qualified and promising people from either being hired or fairly promoted. Not only is this practice illegal under the Race Relations Act of 1976 and the Employment Acts of 1982 and 1985, but it can result in detrimental, uneconomical outcomes for the firm. When merit, not bias or prejudice, is the basis for reward, every person realizes that achievement produces promotion and increased benefits to that achiever.

A more covert and sinister form of discrimination is that of unequal pay. Following the Equal Pay Act of 1970, this type of activity is illegal. Nevertheless, unethical firms can still harass their employees and engage in unequal pay and reward systems by passing over them for warranted promotions, promoting them to undesirable positions, or placing a 'glass ceiling' between an employee and executive management. This type of activity is both unethical and uneconomical.

Firms such as ARCO and Peugeot Talbot have extensive provisions in their codes of conduct which prohibit any discrimination in the hiring or promotion of employees. Discrimination can be based on race, religion, sex, handicap, or other false measures of worth. Every firm should be explicit in its code of conduct that discrimination of any type will not be tolerated. Every firm should institute and delineate in its code severe sanctions against discrimination.

Another positive subject in a firm's code is an equal opportunity section. Equal opportunity involves dealing fairly not only with employees, but also with suppliers, agents, potential employees, and contractors. Just as a firm should try to maximize its personnel resources, it should also try to reach its potential in dealings with competitors, suppliers, and customers. In short, a firm should choose the best suppliers, just as it chooses the best employees, in a manner free from discrimination.

The goal of all firms should be enhancing job performance by eschewing discrimination based on factors other than merit. Some firms, however, go further, and actually seek persons of various groups which have suffered discrimination. A policy employed by many American firms is that of affirmative action. This policy involves first looking to specific groups that have a history of being discriminated against, and that have been unable to obtain the work and promotions for which they might otherwise have qualified based on their representation in the overall population of the community or region where the firm conducts its business. The international firms of Goodyear and Monsanto utilize broad programmes to ensure that categories of victims of past discrimination receive the opportunities they deserve.

The following model code excerpts show how some firms have dealt with discrimination and equal opportunity, as well as affirmative action.

## ANTI-DISCRIMINATION AND SEX DISCRIMINATION

### Peugeot Talbot

Care must be taken that appraisal and training and personal development decisions are not influenced by any unwarranted generalizations . . . . This is particularly important in respect of opportunities for on-the-job training and other planned experience which will develop an employee's capabilities within a section, department, or function.

Aspects of personnel administration which involve a change to an employee's salary or place of work or employment with the Company (including termination/ redundancy procedures) will require observance of the Equal Opportunity Policy.

Managers and supervisors must take care that they do not discriminate in the operation of grievance and disciplinary procedures on grounds of sex, creed, or race (e.g. by ignoring or treating lightly grievances from employees of a particular sex, race, or creed on the assumption that they are over-sensitive about discrimination).

Managers and supervisors must not refuse employment or decline promotion to anyone or otherwise discriminate because groups of employees have indicated that they will not work with or train someone of a particular sex, creed, or racial group, or because they fear that employees will not accept a colleague of another sex, creed, or racial group.

Contact your Personnel Department if you have any queries or if you need to discuss any employment or employee relations problem arising from alleged or suspected discrimination.

Each Personnel Department has access to a member of staff who is familiar with the Race Relations Act and the Sex Discrimination Act and can obtain professional advice upon any problem you may have in respect of legislation or on the Company's Equal Opportunity Policy.

Whilst observance of the spirit and letter of the Company's policy will ensure that obligations created by the Sex Discrimination Act 1975 and the Race Relations Act 1976 are fully met, it is important that Supervisors and Managers are familiar with and understand the legislation. This is because:

1  knowledge of the legislation and its implications complements and adds to a full understanding of the Company's policy;
2  it is important that managers and supervisors should recognize that the law places responsibilities on them as individuals as well as upon the Company. Non-adherence to these requirements can make both individual supervisors/managers and the Company liable to legal proceedings in which both may be ordered to pay compensation.

A summary of the Sex Discrimination Act 1975 and the Race Relations Act 1976 is contained in the Appendix.

It is particularly important to recognize that not only is direct discrimination contrary to Company policy and unlawful but also indirect discrimination.

*Direct discrimination* means treating someone less favourably than another on grounds of sex, marital status, colour, race nationality, ethnic or national origin.

*Indirect discrimination* means applying a requirement or condition which, although applied equally to all persons, is such that a considerably smaller proportion of persons of a particular sex, marital status, or racial group can comply with it and it cannot be shown to be necessary for the satisfactory performance of a job.

For example, neither the Race Relations Act nor the Sex Discrimination Act outlaws the selection of candidates on the basis of their height. If however, an employer rejected all candidates under 6ft tall the effect would be in practice to reject a greater proportion of applicants from some races than others and of women than men. This 'indirectly' discriminating height requirement would be illegal unless the employer could justify it, e.g. in terms of job requirement.

Under the Sex Discrimination Act 1975, sex discrimination is unlawful in the following areas:

employment and training;
education;
the provision of goods, facilities, and services to members of the public.

In employment it is also unlawful to discriminate against a person because that person is married.

Advertisements which indicate unlawful discrimination in these areas are themselves unlawful.

This summary deals with discrimination in employment and not in those other areas covered by the SDA.

The Equal Pay Act 1970 requires employers to give equal treatment in respect of pay and other substantive conditions of employment to men and women doing the same or broadly similar work.

Sex discrimination means the less favourable treatment of a woman or a man, on the grounds of a person's sex. The Sex Discrimination Act makes this unlawful.

Discrimination can take the following forms:

### Direct sex discrimination

It is unlawful if a person is treated less favourably than a person of the opposite sex is treated or would be treated in the same or similar circumstances.

### Indirect sex discrimination

It is unlawful for a person to apply a requirement equally to both sexes, if this requirement has the effect of excluding considerably more women than men, or vice versa, unless it can be justified.

For example, if a technical qualification was demanded which few women possess and which was not necessary for the job, this may well be indirect sex discrimination.

## Gateway

Gateway is committed to employing well-trained and motivated staff who take a pride in their job and who care about the service they give to customers. Staff will be drawn from the community regardless of ethnic origin, sex, marital status, or religion.

## TI Group

In accordance with the legislative requirements of the countries or states concerned, it is Group policy that no decision on selection, terms, and conditions of employment, training, placement, promotion, or remuneration should be decided or influenced by any consideration of sex, race, colour, creed, or ethnic or national origin. Similarly, employment and career development decisions should not be influenced by physical disability, unless such disability demonstrably presents the safe and efficient conduct of the job.

## ARCO UK Ltd

Discrimination in employment is illegal, immoral, and wasteful of vitally needed human resources. ARCO is committed to the belief that such discrimination is to be avoided in all aspects of its business operations.

## Alcan

To be guided by principles of non-discrimination, respect for human rights, and individual freedoms, and to refrain from improper involvement in political activities in the conduct of our business in all countries.

## EQUAL OPPORTUNITY

### Grand Metropolitan

The Group is committed to the principle of equal opportunity in employment, regardless of a person's race, colour, nationality, ethnic or national origins, sex, or marital status. Each operating unit is required to operate employment policies and procedures which are fair, equitable, and consistent with the skills and abilities of its employees. These policies will ensure that all employees are accorded equal opportunity for recruitment, training, and promotion and equal terms and conditions of employment in all jobs of equal value.

### Peugeot Talbot

It is the policy of the Peugeot Talbot Motor Company Limited that the promotion and application of the principles of equal opportunity (non discrimination) will be operated throughout all its establishments.

No individual will be treated less favourably than another on the grounds of sex, marital status, race, nationality, ethnic or national origin, colour, or creed.

Equal opportunity will apply to all areas of employment, including advertising and recruitment, selection, training, appraisal, development and promotion, conditions of employment, compensation, benefits, facilities, and services. It will include selection for redundancy, short time, lay off, shift work, overtime, and work allocation.

Although religious discrimination against a person by reason of his/her religious beliefs is not debarred by legislation it is contrary to Company Policy.

It is the responsibility of the Company to ensure that discrimination does not occur in any area of employment but each individual employee, without exception, is required to observe the requirements of the Company's Equal Opportunity Policy. Failure to observe Company Policy will result in disciplinary action.

## AFFIRMATIVE ACTION

### Monsanto

The company is committed to affirmative action and other programmes to assure fair employment, including equal treatment in hiring, promotion, transfer, training, compensation, termination, and disciplinary action. The company is also committed to programmes to intensively recruit minorities and females. If a supervisor is not aware of the terms of the programme applicable to the facility, the individual responsible for equal employment or the appropriate personnel representative at the supervisor's facility should be contacted immediately.

## DISABLED PERSONS

### Grand Metropolitan

The Group recognizes its obligation towards disabled people and seeks to provide as much suitable employment as the demands of the Group's operations and the abilities of the disabled person allow. The Code of Good Practice on the Employment of Disabled People issued by the Manpower Services Commission is to be used by the UK operating units in the development of their approaches to the employment of disabled people.

# Chapter 24

# Sexual and other harassment

Since the passage of the Sex Discrimination Act of 1975, it has been illegal for firms to engage in sexual discrimination. One of the most insidious forms of sex discrimination is sexual harassment. Usually, sexual harassment involves men harassing women. The results are destructive to the victim and detrimental to the morale of any workforce. Many times, women face harassment directly or through innuendo. Male managers may imply that only sexual favours will lead to a woman's promotion. At many firms, such as Peugeot Talbot, the codes of conduct clearly prohibit and punish any sexual harassment in the workplace.

Moreover, any work environment should be free from other harassment for any reason – race, national origin, or handicap.

With the current legislation in effect, a firm is unwise to allow sexual harassment to continue. As more women enter the workforce, the continuance of sexual harassment will lead to larger numbers of lawsuits. Such lawsuits reflect poorly on the firm, and the current management. Every firm should prohibit verbal or physical harassment based on any reason – race, colour, sex, or similar classifications. Harassment-free environments are more productive and demonstrate respect for every employee's dignity.

The following excerpts from business codes of conduct show how leading firms have addressed the issue of sexual and other harassment.

## Chevron

An essential part of our commitment to equal employment opportunity is to maintain a working environment in which the dignity of each individual is respected and in which employees may perform their job duties without physical or verbal harassment because of race, sex, colour, national origin, religion, age, handicap or veteran status. It is important for all employees to know and understand that no form of harassment will be tolerated.

## ARCO UK Ltd

A positive, constructive environment is essential for long-term productivity and worker satisfaction. Such an environment, grounded in mutual respect, must be free of harassment for any reason – race, colour, national origin, handicap, veteran status, marital status, etc. No such treatment will be tolerated.

## TSB Trust

The Company is entitled to expect employees to maintain reasonable standards of conduct, reliability, efficiency, and competence.

Drunkenness, rowdyism, or indecency on Company premises will be viewed seriously. Such conduct could be classed as gross misconduct and the Disciplinary procedure invoked against staff involved in such behaviour.

A reasonable and decent standard of dress should be maintained by all staff whilst on Company premises. Line managers will guide staff, when necessary, on the interpretation of this statement.

# Chapter 25

# Alcohol and drug abuse

The illicit use of drugs and alcohol on the job is a menacing phenomenon in industrialized societies. In 1989, the *Exxon Valdez* ran aground in Alaska's Prince William Sound. The resulting spill of 240,000 barrels of oil not only damaged, perhaps permanently, the fragile ecosystem, but nearly destroyed the local fishing industry. It was later determined that both the ship's captain and a United States Coast Guard radar operator were impaired by a high level of alcohol in their bloodstream. The *Valdez* spill is yet another example of the havoc alcohol abuse can wreak upon persons, corporations, and society. Alcoholism and drug abuse cost UK businesses dearly – in lost productivity, poor decision-making, wasted material, theft, accidents and injuries, poor product quality, and expensive employee replacement and training. Every firm should establish procedures in its code of conduct that deal specifically with the growing problem of dependency or abuse of alcohol and drugs.

Responsible firms that have their employees' best interests in mind have incorporated substantial alcohol and drug abuse policies within their codes of conduct. National Westminster Bank's code states: 'The Bank will treat dependence on alcohol and drugs as an illness, and encourage appropriate treatment'. A programme of treatment is often more cost-effective from an economic perspective. The cost of recruiting and training replacements for employees terminated for alcohol and drug abuse is substantial, and usually higher than rehabilitating the dependent employee.

Yet, these programmes often rely on the employee's revealing his problem. The concern of many firms is how to encourage compliance with these programmes, when fear of losing their jobs might deter employees from seeking help. Voluntary compliance can be effectuated through two courses of action. First, the firm must have clear guidelines for its policy towards alcohol and drug abuse. Second, by developing the clear channels of communication mentioned in a prior chapter, managers can create an environment of trust necessary for employees to come forward with their problems.

The following excerpts signal a positive approach to addressing alcohol and drug abuse.

### National Westminster Bank

The Bank is concerned about the health and welfare of its staff. The Bank will treat dependence on alcohol or drugs as an illness, and encourage appropriate treatment.

More people in Britain have been drinking more alcohol. In the 1970s the amount of alcohol consumed went up by a third. The main indications that drink problems existed also increased – drink/driving charges, deaths from liver cirrhosis, and drunkenness offences; each of these increased by 25 per cent, while admissions to hospital for alcohol depndence increased by 50 per cent.

There are over 750,000 problem drinkers in England and Wales alone. If we included those affected by problem drinkers, such as their families and work colleagues (many problem drinkers are in employment), that figure would be multiplied several times.

There are no statistics on alcohol-related problems in the Bank, but there is abundant evidence from across society that people of both sexes, all age-groups, and all grades in any large organization are affected.

There is a growing awareness that drinking alcohol in the lunch hour makes staff less effective during the afternoon. It can also leave people vulnerable to drink/driving accident offences after work. Some companies now ban alcoholic drinks on their premises during the working day. It is important to remember the effects of alcohol when dealing socially with customers. The Manager should think twice before offering a drink from the drinks cabinet.

Drug abuse of several kinds is growing. In Britain during the last four years there has been a rapid rise in the number of registered drug addicts and many more are unregistered; at least 50,000 people in this country are addicted to heroin, for example. We cannot afford the comfortable thought that it will not affect Bank staff. Three possible areas are:

Experimentation by young staff. Many young people at school or university try 'soft' drugs such as marijuana. More dangerous 'hard' drugs such as heroin are becoming increasingly available, and their use is far from limited to unemployed youngsters in inner cities.

Drug dependence in adult men and women taking tranquillizers or other legal drugs for years, either with prescriptions or without.

Use of stimulants such as cocaine by high earning and highly pressured finance staff, is not uncommon on Wall Street and could spread to the finance sector in Britain. 25 million Americans have tried cocaine and between 5 and 6 million use it at least once a month.

As well as the damage to health which such drug abuse causes, illegal use of drugs risks police prosecution.

Given the will, treatment for a drink or drug problem works.

As the policy makes clear, the person with the problem must first accept the need for treatment.

Many alcohol or drug dependent people may have approached their general practitioners for help with physical symptoms. They should not hesitate to approach one of the Bank's medical staff; any approach will be confidential.

People with a drink or drug problem frequently try to disguise the fact from themselves and from friends and colleagues. Colleagues may cover up for a person they suspect of having a drink or drug problem. They misguidedly think they are helping.

If the problem is ignored and goes untreated, rehabilitation becomes much more difficult. The effects on health can go beyond the stage where they can be reversed. Heavy drinking, which if tackled early may allow a return to lighter social drinking, can progress to dependence on alcohol from which recovery is only possible by giving up all alcohol for ever.

It is an unfortunate aspect of dependence on drink or drugs that the person often will not face facts.

I have seen careers and lives needlessly and tragically cut short by alcohol and drugs. We must stop this happening.

## PPG

Every PPG associate, as a fundamental tenet of employment, owes the Company his or her best efforts on the job. PPG's people are its most valuable, as well as its most costly, assets. The care, diligence, and creative energy which individuals employed by PPG are expected to provide requires that every associate exercise reasonable care in matters concerning their personal health and well-being.

Deliberate abuse or neglect of the individual's health diminishes that person's value to the Company and therefore undermines the basis of this implicit arrangement. Accordingly, it is contrary to policy for anyone employed by the Company to impair their capabilities through the use of alcohol, drugs, or other intoxicants. In addition to diminishing an employee's own work capability, the use of these substances can seriously jeopardize the safety of others and the welfare of the business. As a result, drug abuse is a matter of legitimate concern to PPG.

### Panhandle Eastern

The Panhandle Eastern Companies will seek to aid in the rehabilitation of employees who suffer from drug and alcohol abuse by:

1 Recognizing alcoholism and drug abuse as conditions which are treatable and which only the affected employee, with appropriate assistance, can control.
2 Offering employees with either of these conditions assistance in treatment and rehabilitation.
3 Recognizing that any action contemplated by the Companies in alcoholism or drug abuse cases should have the dual objectives of restoring the individual to a condition of health and usefulness to himself and his family and to restore his job performance to an acceptable level.

4 Relating continuation of employment to the taking of corrective action by the employee. Refusal to accept diagnosis and treatment or continued failure to respond to treatment will result in appropriate action by the employing Company, including possible termination.

## TSB Trust

Working lunches will be funded by the Company only when and where they are for bona fide work purposes or the furtherance of the Company's aims. They are not provided as a staff benefit and abuse of the facility may result in it being withdrawn from the offender.

Working lunches may be booked in advance with the Catering Manager by 'A' List Managers and by other staff only with the prior express approval of a Department Manager.

Drinks cabinets are provided to senior staff (HO Grade 13 and above; lower grades only where there is a particular business need) for genuine entertainment purposes only. They should only be used on appropriate occasions and then with due moderation.

# Chapter 26

# Employee and consumer health and safety

Since the Industrial Revolution in Britain, workers have been exposed to an increasing variety of health and safety hazards. Present-day dangers, such as exposure to carcinogenic or toxic chemicals, are an extension of problems and dangers of a century and a half ago, when workers suffered from 'brass chills', 'painter's colic', and 'grinder's consumption'.

The health and safety of employees has become an issue of paramount importance to business firms, especially since the passage of the Health and Safety at Work Act of 1974. The economic and social costs of workplace illnesses and injuries are staggering. By inculcating principles of workplace health and safety in its employees, a firm can avoid diverting resources into unrewarding and unprofitable activities, such as antagonistic dealings with government regulators.

The benefits of health and safety in the workplace go far beyond satisfying government rules and regulations. Those firms which have safe work environments are far less likely to be troubled by problems such as employee lawsuits, high levels of employee turnover, low worker productivity, and poor public images. Firms should realize that, ultimately, the penalties for cutting corners with respect to health and safety in the workplace far exceed any short-term savings. By clearly enunciating its policies in a code, a firm can establish workplace health and safety as a high priority. For example, General Electric's policy is to 'take all appropriate measures to protect the health and safety of its employees'.

Another concern for firms is the health and safety of consumers. The public does not tolerate the Roman maxim of two millennia ago, 'Let the buyer beware'. Ford Motor Company suffered huge damage awards in the United States occasioned by locating the fuel tank of the Pinto automobile in a highly vulnerable position which exploded on occasion when the rear of the car was struck. Many other scandals illustrate the folly of ignoring consumer health and safety. Every firm should institute safety and quality programmes to meet rising consumer expectations and global competition of the 1990s.

In today's highly litigious society, firms must provide employees with safe workplaces, and consumers with safe and reliable products, or face the prospect of lawsuits, government intervention, and the public's loss of confidence. The following excerpts reflect how some leading firms have tackled these complex issues in their codes.

## HEALTH AND SAFETY

### TI Group

The Group's policy is to comply with the Health and Safety regulations and establish good practice relating to the working and local environments in the countries in which Group companies operate.

### Grand Metropolitan

The Group is committed to providing safe places of work and safe working arrangements for its employees. Each operating unit is responsible for defining its Health and Safety Policy and for operating appropriate procedures to ensure, as far as is reasonably practical, the health, safety, and welfare of its employees.

### Bank of England

It is the Bank's policy to seek to provide safe and healthy working conditions and to enlist the active support of all staff in achieving these ends.

The objectives of the policy are:

1 To provide standards of safety, health, and welfare which comply fully with the requirements of the Health and Safety at Work Act 1974 and all other relevant statutory provisions.
2 To maintain safe and healthy workplaces and safe systems and methods of work.
3 To protect staff and others, including the public, from forseeable hazards whilst on Bank premises or on Bank business.
4 To provide staff with the information, instructions, training and supervision they need to work safely.
5 To develop safety awareness among staff.
6 To make staff aware of their individual responsibility to take all reasonable care for the safety of themselves and others and to co-operate with management in matters of safety.
7 To encourage full and effective consultation with staff on safety matters.

All employees have a duty imposed by the Health and Safety at Work Act 1974:

1 To comply with agreed safety instructions and directions in current operations and to cooperate in meeting statutory requirements.
2 To take reasonable care of their own health and safety and that of other persons who may be affected by their acts or omissions.

3 To ensure that necessary safety instructions are given to and observed by staff under their control.

Every level of line management, including persons in permanent or temporary charge of offices or sections, can be held personally liable for the health and safety of their staff.

**Anonymous**

To prevent accidents and maintain the health and safety of all employees by establishing the following:

1 That all offices, sites, and other areas of work are maintained in a safe condition.
2 To provide welfare facilities to the required standard and to comply with the provisions of the Health and Safety at Work Act, any of its subsequent enactments, and the policies and procedures laid down within the Group.

Management at all levels is responsible for ensuring that the above objective is, as far as practicable, fulfilled.

The Group Chief Health and Safety Adviser will be responsible for providing an advisory service and for maintaining close liaison with the Health and Safety Commission and Executive.

All offices, sites, depots, and factories will appoint, in writing, a person who will be responsible to the local management for advice on safety, health, and welfare.

Safety training will form part of general employee training. Such training shall include periods on the implications of the Construction Regulations and other statutory requirements and Company policies, and methods of preventing injury, damage, and waste.

Safety will be planned into each construction/production operation.

The Management of the Group regards the promotion of industrial safety, health, and welfare within its business as an essential part of its responsibilities. Furthermore, it regards the maintenance of safety and health matters as a mutual objective of management and employees at all levels.

The Group will:

1 Provide and maintain safe and healthy working conditions in accordance with the requirements of the Health and Safety at Work Act; Factories Act; Offices, Shops and Railway Premises Act; and other relevant statutory provisions.
2 Ensure as far as is reasonably practicable that all working places are maintained in a clean and tidy state especially with respect to means of access and prevention of hazards due to accumulation of rubbish and blocking of fire escapes.
3 Ensure as far as is reasonably practicable that safe systems of work are used

in all working places and that suitable equipment is provided, used properly, and regularly maintained.

4 Provide integrated safety/job training for all employees, and additional safety training where appropriate.

5 Ensure that adequate fire fighting equipment is maintained, and that a suitable fire drill is carried out.

6 Maintain a constant and continuing attention to all aspects of safety, in particular by:

a) Making regular location safety inspections.

b) Seeking contributions from employees on safety matters.

c) Ensuring that each location is given adequate health and safety cover by a person well versed in the safety requirements covering the Group's activities. Such a person will maintain liaison with the Group Safety Department as necessary.

7 Ensure that procedures for reporting accidents and dangerous occurrences are properly implemented.

Employees will:

1 Take reasonable care for the health and safety of themselves and others affected by their actions.

2 Use any protective equipment provided, and observe safe methods of working and statutory obligations.

3 Report incidents that have led, or may lead, to injury.

4 Cooperate in the investigation of accidents with the object of introducing measures to prevent a recurrence.

A basic fire drill operates in all locations and individuals should make a point of familiarizing themselves with the fire drill notices displayed in their place of work.

First aid facilities are provided at all workplaces. Individuals should ensure that they know where these facilities are and who is in charge of them.

Within the overall Group policy statement individual companies should produce a detailed safety policy document and a copy should be available (at each place of work) for inspection by employees. The document should clearly state the name of the person who is responsible for safety at the workplace.

All accidents and dangerous occurrences will be investigated, reported, and recorded in accordance with instructions issued by the Safety Department. All injuries must be reported to the workplace Supervisor as soon as they occur. Where qualified First Aid Attendants are appointed, they, too, must be notified.

A young person is defined in safety legislation as someone under 18 years of age, and certain restrictions and procedures apply, as follows, when they are employed:

1 Not later than seven days after taking on a young person to work in premises

or a process subject to the Factories Act, e.g. a site, factory, depot, details must be sent on form 2404 (obtainable from the group safety department, Woking) to the local careers office of the Department of Employment. Details must also be entered in the appropriate part of the general register held on site or in a factory, etc.

2  In factories and on sites there are strict requirements as to the occupations and hours which young persons are allowed to work.

3  Young persons are prohibited, under specific statutory provisions, to be employed where toxic processes are involved, e.g. asbestos and lead and the operation or maintenance of plant or equipment unless under supervision for training purposes.

4  The general duty on the employer under Section 2 of the Health and Safety at Work Act 1974 may mean that an employer is unable to engage a young person.

Where doubt may exist over the suitability of a place of work or the ability of the young person consult both the Group Safety and Occupational Health Departments.

Under Section 2 of the Health and Safety at Work Act each employee must be given, on joining, a statement of the Group's accident prevention policy.

Safety supervisors who have qualified through a recognized safety course, or are qualified by experience to the satisfaction of the Group Chief Health and Safety Adviser, and are carrying out the duties of site safety supervisors are entitled to be paid an allowance of £5 a week, if weekly paid, or the equivalent amount, paid twice annually, if monthly paid.

The Personnel Manager concerned will be responsible for liaising with the Safety Department in advising the salaries or wages department of staff entitled to receive this allowance.

The main purpose of this scheme is to ensure that the Group has a sufficient number of certificated first aiders whether in the offices or on site, to provide an efficient first aid service and to comply with current legislation.

Qualified first aiders are required to hold a certificate of Training following a course of instruction approved by the Health and Safety Executive, which is valid for three years. In order to encourage employees to take the necessary examinations, the Group makes an award of £20 on first passing the examination and £15 on satisfactory completion of a refresher course.

In addition first aiders who are officially recognized by the Group and who are called upon for duty are paid an extra £182 per annum salary, or £3.50 per week if paid weekly.

Internal courses are arranged from time to time by the Medical Centre and Divisional Personnel Managers will be notified of the details.

The British Red Cross Society, St John's Ambulance Brigade, and St Andrews Brigade run courses at their various branches throughout the country. Employees should inform their appropriate Personnel Department when they have successfully completed a course. To be acceptable for the H & S (First Aid) Regulations 1981, the course must have been approved by the H & S Executive.

The appropriate Divisional Personnel Department is responsible for notifying the employee that he/she is eligible for the award and the increase in salary and seeing that the payment is made.

## PRODUCT SAFETY

### Procter & Gamble

Company documents have detailed the general principles of our product safety policy. In brief:

1 Our products shall be safe for humans and the environment when used as intended and under conditions of reasonably foreseeable misuse.
2 Our safety testing programme must provide practical assurance of safety for the products we sell.
3 Our programmes must be based on an expanding scientific understanding of our products and their components, and input from leading consultants shall be used to ensure that latest scientific judgement is reflected in both our research and our safety conclusions.
4 Any research involving animals shall be done only when no equally predictive alternative testing methods are available, or when required by law, and then such testing will be conducted under professional supervision so as to provide for the humane treatment of all animals and to minimize the numbers used.
5 Findings which contribute to the world's scientific knowledge will be submitted for publication to leading journals.

In the conduct of safety research, it is essential that we adhere to high professional standards for such research in order to assure the Company and the consumer of the best possible safety judgements.

All employees associated with safety research have a responsibility to see that experiments meet the highest scientific standards of design, conduct, documentation, and reporting.

Of equal importance is the responsibility of both manager and scientist to ensure that all responsible views are included in the evaluation of safety data. Managers must avoid actions which in any way discourage or tend to suppress the free exchange of views.

## SECURITY AND SAFETY

### TSB Trust

It is the intention of the Company to do all that is reasonably practicable to ensure a safe and healthy working environment for all employees and to safeguard its business premises in so far as is reasonably practicable from hazards to its employees and to the general public. The provisions of relevant legislation will be observed.

Security and safety at work is very much the responsibility of each and every individual member of staff. Each of us must take all reasonable precautions to protect ourselves, our colleagues, and all possessions and property from risk of damage. Any dangers, or possible sources of danger, should be brought to the attention of your line Manager and of the Company Safety Officer. All accidents must be reported as soon as they occur.

It is the duty of all members of staff to report any matter that may affect the security of the Company and its property to the Assistant Manager, Security.

The Company cannot accept responsibility for loss or damage to staff's personal property or possessions. Desks with lockable drawers are available to all and should be used to secure personal possessions when necessary. The Security Section of the Support Services Department should be informed of any losses and any items found should be handed to them also. In certain circumstances compensation may be paid by the Company to employees suffering loss or damage of possessions.

'The Company security system depends on Company staff and visitors being easily identifiable as such.

All staff are issued with identity cards and are required to wear them in an easily visible position on their person at all times when on Company premises. Loss of an identity card should be reported to Support Services Department for action. Failure to wear an identity card renders the offender liable to disciplinary action.

Reception should be informed when non-Company personnel are visiting premises and they will issue the appropriate identity cards which must be returned at the end of the visit.

Personal visitors (friends, relations, etc.) are not encouraged during work hours; should such visitors arrive they should go no further than foyer/reception areas.

Should it be planned to take business visitors on a tour of the premises, the Department Managers of the areas due to be visited should be given adequate advance notification.

If you discover a fire, immediately operate the nearest fire alarm call point. If possible, attempt to extinguish the fire using the hose reels or hand extinguishers provided. Do not take any personal risks.

On hearing the fire alarm staff must leave the building immediately and report to their nearest assembly point. Use the nearest available exit; do not stop to collect personal belongings; do not re-enter the building until told it is safe to do so by a Fire Brigade Officer; act sensibly and responsibly.

Certain areas of the buildings are for restricted access only (e.g. the Postroom, Switchboard room, and Salaries Section). Staff should also note that entry should not normally be made to any manager's office if it is unattended: the secretary or another member of that Department's staff should be approached before entry is made in such circumstances.

Staff who plan to work after 6 pm or at the weekend must obtain the prior authorization of their Department or Divisional Manager. Security Department must be given adequate notice (for weekend working, by the prior Thursday at latest). Staff should not remain on Company premises (other than at Sports and Social venues) once they have finished work.

In an emergency access can be gained after normal hours to any Company building by contacting the on-duty Security staff at the Computer Centre or at Keens House.

# Chapter 27

# Compliance with laws

The rule of man was evidenced in the England of several centuries ago when 'the dungeons of the barons' castles were full of both men and women put in prison for their gold and silver and tortured with pains unspeakable'.[1]

In present-day British society, the rule of law has supplanted the rule of man. Respect for the law and rights of others is the hallmark of modern Western civilizations.

Governmental statutes, regulations, and ordinances have become more pervasive in the business arena, as a reflection of the increased complexity and sophistication of business transactions. In varied fields such as employee discrimination, health and safety issues, predatory pricing, and unfair competition, parliament has responded to petitions by employees, businesses, and consumers for increased legislation. Usually, firms find it difficult to comply with these voluminous regulations, let alone the numerous changes occurring each year. Moreover, for firms competing internationally, the difficulty with keeping abreast of, and complying with, the multitude and diversity of foreign laws increases geometrically.

Every person has responsibility to develop sufficient understanding of the law in order to act as a responsible member of society. Toward this end, every firm should include in its code or company policy document a summary of those laws most pertinent to its business.

A UK firm interested in competing in the US, Japan, or any other foreign market must seriously consider the 'rules of the game' before entering the new market. For instance, antitrust laws, whose origin can be traced to seventeenth-century England, are an integral part of the United States' economic system. The following excerpts demonstrate how some major UK and multi-national firms have attempted to address in their codes the important and difficult task of complying with both domestic and foreign laws.

### United Biscuits

We believe in and obey both the letter and the spirit of the law, but the law is the minimum and no set of rules can provide all the answers or cover all questionable situations. While it is the responsibility of top management to keep a company honest and honourable, perpetuating ethical values is not a function only of the chief executive or a handful of senior managers. Every employee is expected to take on the responsibility of always behaving ethically whatever the circumstances. Beliefs and values must always come before policies, practices, and goals; the latter must be altered if they violate fundamental beliefs.

## TI Group

Directors and managers are required to make themselves aware of and to comply with their legal responsibilities under the laws and regulations applicable to the territories in which their businesses operate.

## Burmah

Enterprizes should:

Upon request of the taxation authority of the countries in which they operate, provide, in accordance with the safeguards and relevant procedures of the national laws of these countries, the information necessary to determine correctly the taxes to be assessed in connection with their operations, including relevant information concerning their operations in other countries.

Refrain from making use of the particular facilities available to them, such as transfer pricing which does not conform to an arm's length standard, for modifying in ways contrary to national laws the tax base on which members of the group are assessed.

## ARCO UK Ltd

Adherence to the law is not the whole of a corporation's ethical responsibility, but it is the logical starting place. Employees are expected to conduct the company's operations in accordance with the laws of the countries, states, and locales in which we do business.

## Digital Equipment Corporation

Honesty and personal responsibility are the foundation of Digital's operating principles. We will conduct our business in every country in a way that instills confidence in our customers, suppliers, and employees that Digital will fulfil its commitments. In addition, we will refrain from any action that will raise questions about Digital's Business Ethics.

Since Digital, an American-based company, conducts business in many countries, we will conduct all worldwide activities well within the standards of US Business Ethics. We will, of course, comply fully with local laws in all countries.

Each Digital employee represents the Company and must conform to the above principles. When any action seems in any way questionable, the employee should consult with his/her supervisor as to the appropriateness of the action. This process should continue upwards in the Company until the appropriateness of each action is assured by senior managers. In this process, all decisions should be written down, so that there is a clear record of the process.

Digital wants to be proud of every action taken by employees. We want to surface every borderline issue so that decisions are made in an open and conscious way.

Digital will comply with local law, regardless of custom. We want to be good citizens in every country where we operate, and we expect every employee to be so.

We will declare the material imported into every country honestly and correctly by executing the required forms and paying the assessed duties. Digital will not import materials without an appropriate licence. Of course, we will not make direct or indirect payments or bribes to customs agents, regardless of whether this is a local custom that is viewed as normal.

We will comply with all regulations regarding visa and work residency permits, and will honestly declare the presence of our personnel in any country.

Digital will transfer funds in strict accordance with the requirements and restrictions of each country and no employee should become involved in any process to violate these.

We believe in minimizing tax expense in conformance with all tax laws, while paying all taxes, duties, and levies for which we are liable. Every employee has a similar responsibility to pay all taxes and duties that are required in each country. That means that the full measure of employee compensation, including pay and allowances, should be reported to the appropriate government authority, and the proper measure of taxes will be withheld and paid. All required tax returns, to an employee's home country as well as the employee's country of residence, must be filed on time and accurately reflect the full amount of taxable compensation.

# Chapter 28

# Insider trading and share dealing

Insider trading and related disclosure issues have been topics of discussion for many centuries. Cicero, discussing the issue, noted that a vendor who sells a building with a hidden defect should fully disclose that flaw to a potential purchaser. At present, UK laws regarding insider trading and share dealing are a response to perceived wrongdoing and an attempt to maintain the integrity of the financial markets.

Insider trading is defined as the buying or selling of a firm's securities by a member of management, an employee of the firm, or by a person outside the firm, who has knowledge of material, 'inside' information not available to the general public. The buying or selling of securities by an 'insider' is illegal when it is predicated upon the utilization of 'inside' information to profit at the expense of other investors who do not have access to the same information. The prices of most securities reflect available public information about those companies. When one investor acts on inside, non-public information, he essentially corrupts the 'level playing field' vital to fairness and public confidence in the securities market. To avoid any taint of impropriety, British Steel mandates that 'an employee or director should not deal in any of the securities of British Steel at any time when in possession of unpublished price sensitive information in relation to those securities'.

Concerns about insider trading led to the passage of the Company Securities (Insider Dealing) Act of 1985. Recently, the Bank of England was required to revise its code of conduct section regarding insider trading due to the passage of the Insider Dealing (Public Servants) Order of 1989. These two Acts evidence the need for firms to include explicit procedures regarding insider trading in their codes of conduct and similar policy documents in order to protect themselves, and to encourage ethical dealing.

A second issue concerning securities is that of share dealing. Share dealing involves an employee's buying or selling the shares of his or her employer. Many firms such as Kingfisher require prior approval by the firm before employees can engage in buying or selling Kingfisher shares. British Steel enlarges the subject of its prior approval mandate to include any other firms' securities that might be affected by a British Steel employee's inside knowledge. It is clear that firms must construct guidelines for every employee to follow when dealing with both his employer's shares and the shares of other firms transacting business with the employee's firm.

The following excerpts illustrate how many leading UK firms and several international corporations address the sensitive issues of insider trading and share dealing.

## INSIDER TRADING

### ARCO UK Ltd

Employees are prohibited from actively speculating – rapid turnovers, options, trading, etc – in the securities of ARCO or its affiliates. Nor may employees buy or sell these securities if they have inside information which could influence the market price of the securities before that information is made public.

### Tesco

No individual in possession of price sensitive inside information may deal before that information has been made public.

The Guidelines apply not only to Directors and Executives but also to their spouses, infant children, and any other interest (such as a Trust) over which that person could influence investment decisions.

The International Stock Exchange has established a Model Code which changes from time to time and which is thought to constitute an acceptable standard of practice. We will all observe the Model Code. A copy is annexed, up to date; we will issue fresh drafts as these appear.

It is recognized that adherence to the Model Code could cause problems to individuals in certain circumstances or at certain times. In that event, please consult a member of the Advisory Group who will obtain appropriate advice for you.

As the Model Code indicates, there will be times (for example when a bid is contemplated or in process) when Executives have price sensitive information and other people within the senior group then become 'Insiders'. You should endeavour to restrict the number of people who share any price sensitive information. The Secretary will consider at appropriate times the position of individuals in the company and will issue a notification.

There is no restriction in time on the exercise of mature share options but the grant of options and the sale of shares acquired by exercise is subject to these Guidelines.

You are reminded that in order to comply with International Stock Exchange Rules, the Secretary must be informed of any sales and purchases, including price and number of shares, within five days of the transaction. Directors are obliged to inform the Chairman (or in his absence the Managing Director) before dealing in Tesco shares.

Any speculation, or short-term dealing in shares of suppliers of goods or services to Tesco or shares of companies which you are aware are of interest to Tesco as acquisitions, is barred. The issue here again is one of insider information and the Model Code covers this.

If you are aware that a company's results, or share value, could be significantly affected by a Tesco decision, you should not invest. Similarly, if you have a holding and a sale decision would be affected by the same circumstances, this may come within the insider dealing rules. You should seek clarification in any specific instances from a member of the advisory group.

We should not have any financial interest in a competitor or supplier which could cause divided loyalty or speculation or misunderstanding about why that interest is held.

A Register of Directors' shareholdings in suppliers or competitor companies will be maintained by the Company Secretary who should be regularly advised of any sales or purchases.

### British Steel

Attached is a copy of the employees' Additional Guidelines for Transactions in Securities.

These Guidelines apply to all employees who are or may be in possession of unpublished price sensitive information (as described in the Guidelines) who wish to deal in the securities of the company.

You should study them closely and carefully note the provisions. If in any doubt about the meaning of the Guidelines or whether they apply to you, you should consult your Works Manager (or equivalent) before dealing.

An employee or director of British Steel plc or any of its subsidiaries should not deal in any of the securities of British Steel plc or its subsidiary or associated companies ('the Group') at any time when he is in possession of unpublished price sensitive information in relation to those securities.

The same restriction applies to dealings by an employee in the securities of any other company listed on a stock exchange when, by virtue of his position as an employee of a member Company of the Group, he is in possession of unpublished price sensitive information in relation to those securities.

Employees should not deal in the securities of the Group at any time on considerations of a short-term nature.

At other times, an employee who is not prohibited from doing so by the Company Securities (Insider Dealing) Act 1985 can feel free to deal subject to the provisions of the following Rules:

In addition to observing the above principles an employee should not deal in any securities of the Group without first notifying his works manager (or equivalent) and receiving an acknowledgement. A written record will be maintained showing that the appropriate notification has been given and acknowledged.

During the periods of two months immediately preceding the preliminary announcement of the Company's annual results and the announcement of the half-yearly results, an employee should not purchase any securities of the Group nor should he sell any such securities in the absence of exceptional circumstances.

The restrictions on dealings by an employee contained in these Guidelines should be regarded as equally applicable to any dealings by the employee's spouse or by or on behalf of any infant child and to any other dealings in which he is or is to be treated as interested. It is the duty of the employee, therefore, to seek to avoid any such dealing at a time when he himself is not free to deal.

Any employee of the Company who acts as trustee of a trust should, where he is a sole trustee, follow the same procedure as for any dealings on his own account and should deal only if he would be personally allowed to deal under these Guidelines. Where any employee is a co-trustee he should ensure that his co-trustees are aware of his employment by British Steel plc so as to enable them to anticipate possible difficulties. An employee having funds under management should likewise advise the investment manager. However, it is an over-riding principle that under no circumstances should an employee make any un-authorized disclosure of any confidential information, whether to co-trustees or any other person, or make any use of such information for the advantage of himself or others, even those to whom he owes a fiduciary duty.

Any employee who is a beneficiary, but not a trustee, of a trust which deals in securities of the Group should endeavour to ensure that the trustees notify him after they have dealt in such securities on behalf of the trust and should ensure that the trustees are aware of his employment by British Steel plc.

References in these Guidelines to 'securities' have the meanings ascribed thereto by Section 12 of the Company Securities (Insider Dealing) Act 1985. The definition includes any type of class of share, debenture, loan stock, or option traded on a recognized stock exchange and also includes purchases or sales made through an employee share scheme or otherwise.

An exhaustive definition of price sensitive information is not possible. Nevertheless it should be assumed for the purpose of these Guidelines that the following matters are included amongst those so to be regarded if publication of any of them would be likely to affect the share price:

1  Any announcement of profits (or losses) or the recommendation or declaration of dividends or other distributions to shareholders.
2  Any proposed change in capital structure, including rights or scrip issues and the issue or repayment of debt securities.
3  Significant acquisitions or disposals of assets.
4  Any information required to be disclosed and public announcements to be made at the time of a takeover by or of the Company.
5  The notification to British Steel plc of an interest of 5 per cent or more in its equity.
6  Any decision to seek shareholders' approval to a proposal for British Steel plc to purchase its own shares, and if implemented, any such purchases.

7 Any proposed change in the general character, structure, or nature of the business of the Company.

8 Any changes in the tax status of the Company.

9 Any decision to take industrial action in any significant part of the Company.

10 A major claim made against the Company.

Employees' attention is drawn to the general legal position set out in the Company Securities (Insider Dealing) Act 1985 which makes it a criminal offence punishable by imprisonment for up to seven years together with an unlimited fine to deal in the securities of the Company with a view to making a profit or avoiding a loss when in possession of unpublished price sensitive information. There are also similar prohibitions (and sanctions) abroad which may also apply.

Where there are exceptional circumstances, as a result of which an employee wishes to deal in any securities of the Group, or any securities to which Basic Principle (ii) refers, at any time when he would otherwise be prohibited by the Code, he must first notify his divisional or functional head and receive an acknowledgement. Examples of such exceptional circumstances might be where a pressing financial commitment had to be met or where the employee's duty under the Code conflicts with some legal duty imposed upon him.

An employee who wishes to buy or sell shares but who may, through the knowledge he has of certain of the Company's affairs, feel unable to deal within the dealing windows should consult his works manager (or equivalent), who may in turn consult the relevant personnel manager.

Where an employee has co-trustees who are not themselves employees of the Company, he may not be able to ensure that the procedure applicable to his personal dealings is followed in respect of dealings on behalf of the trust. The employee/trustee has to avoid acting in breach of trust and at the same time to refrain from divulging or abusing confidential information, and it may not therefore always be practicable to expect that trustees will refrain from dealing at a time when one of their number is not personally free to deal.

On the other hand, if an employee, whether or not himself a trustee, has, as settlor or otherwise, an important influence over the decision of the trustees, the procedure applicable to his personal dealings ought to be followed and the trustees should not deal when he personally is not free to deal.

A Director should not deal in any of the securities of British Steel plc or its subsidiary or associated companies ('the Group') at any time when he is in possession of unpublished price sensitive information in relation to those securities.

The same restriction applies to dealings by a Director in the securities of any other listed company when, by virtue of his position as a Director of a Member Company of the Group, he is in possession of unpublished price sensitive information in relation to those securities.

Directors should not deal in the securities of the Group at any time on considerations of a short-term nature.

At other times, a Director who is not prohibited from doing so by the Company Securities (Insider Dealing) Act 1985 can feel free to deal subject to the provisions of the following Rules:

A Director should not deal in any securities of the Group without first notifying the Chairman, via the Secretary, and receiving acknowledgement. In his own case the Chairman should first notify one of the other Directors and receive acknowledgement.

A written record will be maintained by the Secretary that the appropriate notification has been given and acknowledged.

During the periods of two months immediately preceding the preliminary announcement of the Company's annual results and the announcement of the half-yearly results, a Director should not purchase any securities of the Group nor should he sell any such securities in the absence of exceptional circumstances.

The restrictions on dealings by a Director contained in this Code should be regarded as equally applicable to any dealings by the Director's spouse or by or on behalf of any infant child and to any other dealings in which for the purposes of the Companies Act 1985 he is or is to be treated as interested. It is the duty of the Director, therefore, to seek to avoid any such dealing at a time when he himself is not free to deal.

Any Director of the Company who acts as trustee of a trust should, where he is a sole trustee, follow the same procedure as for any dealings on his own account and should deal only if he would be personally allowed to deal under this Code. Where any Director is a co-trustee he should ensure that his co-trustees are aware of his directorship of British Steel plc so as to enable them to anticipate possible difficulties. A Director having funds under management should likewise advise the investment manager. However, it is an over-riding principle that under no circumstances should a Director make any unauthorized disclosure of any confidential information, whether to co-trustees or any other person, or make any use of such information for the advantage of himself or others, even those to whom he owes a fiduciary duty.

Any Director who is a beneficiary, but not a trustee, of a trust which deals in securities of the Group should endeavour to ensure that the trustees notify him after they have dealt in such securities on behalf of the trust, in order that he in turn may notify the Secretary. For this purpose he should ensure that the trustees are aware of his directorship of British Steel plc.

The Register maintained in accordance with Section 325 of the Companies Act 1985 will be made available for inspection at every meeting of the Board of British Steel plc.

The Directors of British Steel plc, as a Board and individually, will endeavour to ensure that any employee or Director or employee of a subsidiary company who, because of his office or employment in the Group, is likely to be in possession of unpublished price sensitive information in relation to the securities of any listed company, deals in those securities in accordance with this Code.

References in this Code to 'securities' have the meanings ascribed thereto by Section 12 of the Company Securities (Insider Dealing) Act 1985.

Directors are reminded that Section 323 of the Companies Act 1985 makes it an offence for a Director, together with his associates as mentioned in (iv) above, to deal in the options of any company of which he is a Director.

An exhaustive definition of price sensitive information is not possible. Nevertheless it should be assumed for the purpose of this Code that the following matters are included amongst those so to be regarded:

1 Any announcement of profits or the recommendation or declaration of dividends or other distribution to shareholders.
2 Any proposed change in capital structure, including rights or scrip issues and the issue or redemption of debt securities.
3 Material acquisitions or realizations of assets.
4 Any information required to be disclosed to the Stock Exchange under the provisions of the City Code on Take-overs and Mergers for the time being in force.
5 The notification to British Steel plc of an interest of 5 per cent or more in its equity.
6 Any decision to seek shareholders' approval to a proposal for British Steel plc to purchase its own shares, and if implemented, any such purchases.
7 Any proposed change in the general character or nature of the business of the Company.
8 Any changes in the tax status of the Company.
9 Any decision to take industrial action.

Directors' attention is drawn to the general legal position set out in The Company Securities (Insider Dealing) Act 1985.

Where there are exceptional circumstances, as a result of which a Director wishes to deal in any securities of the Group, or any securities to which Basic Principle (ii) refers, at any time when he would otherwise be prohibited by the Code, he must first notify the Secretary of the Company and receive an acknowledgement in accordance with Rule (i) of the Code. Examples of such exceptional circumstances might be where a pressing financial commitment had to be met or where the Director's duty under the Code conflicts with some legal duty imposed upon him.

Directors who wish to buy or sell shares but who may, through the knowledge they have of certain of the Company's affairs, feel unable to deal within the dealing windows should consult the Secretary, who will in turn consult the Chairman or the Chief Executive.

The obligation of a Director to give notice of his interests in securities of the Group are set out in Sections 324, 325, and 328 of the 1985 Act. Notification of any dealings has to be made to the Secretary within five days, and the Secretary has to inform the Stock Exchange at once.

Where a Director has co-trustees who are not themselves Directors of the

Company, he may not be able to ensure that the procedure applicable to his personal dealings is followed in respect of dealings on behalf of the trust. The Director/trustee has to avoid acting in breach of trust and at the same time to refrain from divulging or abusing confidential information, and it may not therefore always be practicable to expect that trustees will refrain from dealing at a time when one of their number is not personally free to deal.

On the other hand, if a Director, whether or not himself a trustee, has, as settlor or otherwise, an important influence over the decision of the trustees, the procedure applicable to his personal dealings ought to be followed and the trustees should not deal when he personally is not free to deal.

## Hewlett Packard Ltd

The Companies Act makes it a criminal offence for any employee to disclose, outside the normal course of that employee's duties, information which is unpublished and of a price sensitive nature – that is to say, information not generally available which is likely to affect materially the market price of the Company's shares. Additionally, any such person may not buy or sell the Company's shares whilst in possession of such information and this prohibition extends to six months after employment terminates. Nor may an employee buy or sell the securities of another company while he or she is in possession of insider information relating to any transaction (actual or contemplated) involving the Company and that other company. Penalties under the Companies Act are severe.

Employees who qualify as 'insiders' (as broadly defined above) may not advise or procure others to deal in securities or pass the information on to others who they know will use it for such purposes. Disclosure to the Company's own professional advisers in the proper course of their duties is permitted.

These restrictions apply also to an employee's immediate family.

Even the premature announcement of a substantial order may affect the price of the Company's shares.

Employees must therefore exercise extreme caution and discretion when dealing in shares or handling insider information and, quite apart from any general legal consequences, the Board of the Company will view any breach of these rules with the utmost severity. Dealings by an 'insider', even when permitted by the above guidelines, must first be notified in writing (as appropriate) to the Secretary of the Business Unit concerned or the Company Secretary and acknowledged in writing.

Directors are bound by the same requirements and even more rigorous constraints concerning dealings with the Company's shares; certain employees who, by virtue of their role in the Group, are regularly in possession of price sensitive information are similarly required to accept such further constraints in relation to dealings in the Company's shares by them or their immediate family.

The Company Secretary is available to advise on the interpretation and application of these rules as they affect any individual employee.

## SHARE DEALING

### Control Data

No Control Data Director or employee may buy or sell options on Control Data stock at any time.

### British Steel

During their work, employees may gain access to unpublished information about the Company's activities or future prospects which, if published, might affect the price of the Company's shares or other securities. Employees who obtain such information and who wish to buy or sell British Steel shares or other securities, must first study the additional guidelines on share dealing which are available from their Works or Personnel Manager.

No employee of the Company may deal in the shares or other securities of any other company when, during his work, he has in his possession unpublished information which, if published, might affect the price of that company's shares or other securities.

No Company employee (or, with his knowledge, his close family) should hold shares or otherwise be financially involved in any outside business if his activities on behalf of the Company could materially affect the fortunes of that business. This includes businesses which are or which may become Company suppliers, customers, or significant competitors. If any such interests are already held the employee should declare these through the normal channels, to his Director (or nearest equivalent), who will advise whether any disposal of shares or other action is necessary. (It may, for example, be possible to transfer responsibility for negotiating particular contracts to another employee.)

Interests of a non-pecuniary nature can be just as important as pecuniary interests. Kinship, friendship, membership of an association, and many other kinds of relationship can sometimes influence an individual's judgement or at least give the impression to other people that he may be acting from personal motives. It is therefore in an employee's own interest, as well as that of the Company, that he should declare any such non-pecuniary interests which might in any way be thought to affect the proper discharge of his duties as a Company employee.

If in any doubt about the interpretation of the above paragraphs, the employee should consult his Director, through the normal channels, for advice on the appropriate action in the circumstances concerned.

If a Company employee wishes to engage (whether or not in working hours) in any outside business as a proprietor or director, he must first obtain written permission from his Director. He must also obtain such permission before becoming involved with any outside business as an employee, or in some other capacity, if there could conceivably be a conflict with the Company's own interests. Each case will be considered on its merits.

Before undertaking any such outside business activities in normal working hours, employees also need to obtain permission under separate rules governing extramural activities – even where there is no possibility of a conflict of interests. Permission may be conditional upon the employee accounting to the Company for all remuneration or benefits received by him in respect of such outside business or undertaking.

Members of senior management require written permission in all circumstances.

### Kingfisher

Any dealings in the shares of Kingfisher plc by any relevant employee or director of Kingfisher plc or any group company require prior approval. 'Relevant employees' means those who have access to financial results or other confidential information of Kingfisher plc or any group company, whether they have managerial or non-managerial status. Such employees will be informed that they are considered relevant employees.

The Stock Exchange Code of Practice (a copy of which is attached and which will be taken to apply to both directors and relevant employees) also contains restrictions on dealings in shares by certain third parties (for example spouses who are connected with directors or relevant employees).

Approval must be obtained via the Company Secretary of the company of which they are a director or an employee, who will route the request through Kingfisher plc. Approval will not be given for dealings falling outside the Stock Exchange Code of Practice, but it may also be withheld in other circumstances at the discretion of the group Chief Executive.

A decision by the group Chief Executive will normally be given within two days of receiving a request for approval. The 'other circumstances' where it is envisaged that the group Chief Executive may withhold his approval are where although an employee or director may not be aware of an impending transaction or other state of affairs, it is important in the group's own interests and for his own protection that he should be told not to deal in the shares of Kingfisher plc.

Furthermore, it is a criminal offence to deal in the shares of any quoted company whilst in the possession of information which has not been published and which, if published, would have a material effect on the price of such shares.

# Chapter 29

# Commitment to society and the local and international community

A business firm and its environment interact in many ways. Commercial activities not only deliver economic benefits to society and local communities, but also affect conditions of community living. Increasingly, business firms, as loci of power, authority, and responsibility, shape the moral and intellectual tones of the age.[1] Companies derive their existence and rights from society. These rights can be revoked or amended when companies do not sufficiently direct their activities and conduct toward the benefit and protection of society.

Social responsibility, in the context of a business firm's operations, means that a firm has responsibilities to society beyond production of goods and services. In the modern view of a firm's proper role, a firm has a broader constituency than merely its shareholders and owners. Practically speaking, as society and local communities prosper, additional consumers with increased disposable incomes are available to purchase greater amounts of goods and services. By helping to ameliorate social problems, firms improve those environmental conditions advantageous for long-term prosperity and profitability. Finally, some commentators believe the business sector has an obligation to assist in solving social problems, such as pollution and deficiencies in workplace safety, because it helped to create them.[2]

Often, a firm's dedication to the welfare of a community can assume international importance. RTZ's positive involvement in South Africa has led to a partial reprieve from apartheid for those communities in which RTZ has located and invested.

The London & Edinburgh Group (LE) focuses itself beyond any single community, and involves itself in the improvement of the United Kingdom society in general. LE supports over ten national charities including The Prince's Trust, ICAN, and the Make a Wish Foundation. LE also sponsors events throughout Great Britain to provide recreation for children, the less fortunate, and the handicapped. LE's activities provide one model for the ethically and socially responsible firm of the 1990s.

The following excerpts from codes show how leading UK firms have made social commitments to the society at large, and to the communities in which they are located.

## Gateway

Gateway aims to be a good neighbour and a responsible member of society. It is concerned about the environment and contributes to the community by various forms of sponsorship and charitable donation. However, it does not impose standards on customers; it respects their freedom to choose.

## Scott Bader

We recognize that we have a responsibility to the society in which we live and believe that where we have some special talent or interest we should offer this to the wider community. Thus most of us are engaged in some form of social, political, or public service, however small.

We are agreed that (in addition to such disinterested services that we offer as individuals) our social responsibility extends to:

1 Limiting the products of our labour to those beneficial to the community, in particular excluding any products for the specific purpose of manufacturing weapons of war.
2 Reducing any harmful effect of our work on the natural environment by rigorously avoiding the negligent discharge of pollutants.
3 Questioning constantly whether any of our activities are unnecessarily wasteful of the earth's natural resources.

## Digital Equipment Corporation

We are committed as a Corporation to . . . encourage all employees to take responsibility in community, social, and government activities. We are always open for proposals as to what the Corporation or an individual on Corporation time may want to do in these areas. However, activities done on Company time or with Company funds should have a formal proposal including ways of regularly measuring success toward goals.

## Grand Metropolitan

Each operating unit is responsible for maintaining good relationships with the communities in which it operates. Initiatives should be taken to strengthen the links between the operating unit and community organizations on such matters as education, environment, charity work, etc.

In view of the geographic spread of the Group's activities, it is appropriate to outline the standards considered necessary in order to operate responsibly in the wide variety of countries in which the Group is represented.

## Tesco

To be a socially responsible member of the community and to be concerned for the protection of the environment.

## The Boots Company

It is necessary that the Company should play its proper part in the local community both at home and abroad. This means that it should take account of local needs in its recruitment programme and keep in touch with local educational establishments. Subject to the needs of the business it allows interested employees to participate in local community affairs. These will include local government, the administration of justice, the management of universities, schools, and churches, National Health Service committees, and trade, technical, and professional associations. It also considers the interest of local inhabitants in the servicing arrangements of its various sites. Before deciding to close any operating unit for financial or commercial reasons the Company takes into consideration the effect on the community. In short, the Company aims to be an active and beneficial element in the community.

The Company makes donations to charities both in the United Kingdom and abroad. In the United Kingdom the Boots Charitable Trust has been established which is funded by the Company. Whilst taking into account the interests of the Company, the Trust exercises an independent judgement in supporting a large number of charities operating in a wide range of activities, including Third World aid and relief.

The company has supported and will continue fully to support measures designed to alleviate the problems of unemployment. In the United Kingdom this takes the form of supporting initiatives to encourage enterprize and the setting up of small businesses, through organizations such as local enterprize agencies and Business in the Community. With particular concern for youth unemployment, the Company supports Manpower Service Commission schemes such as the Youth Training Scheme.

## United Biscuits

In planning for the future of our company interest, we recognize the rights and requirements of the public and the millions of individuals who make it up. We have to ask ourselves if what we are planning to do in our business decisions is good for employees as well as for our shareholders, and as good for the country as it is for both those groups. We therefore need to think in two dimensions – on the business plane and as citizens with a duty to the well-being of the whole nation.

## Taylor Woodrow

Maintaining the good public image of Taylor Woodrow throughout the world is the responsibility of all members of the team. That outward image must reflect truly the inner qualities and high standards we set ourselves. Overall coordination and organization of press and public relations activities ensure that the public is kept informed of current activities and developments within the Group.

We are conscious that much of what we do is of interest to members of the public, who are also informed by signboards, leaflets and, when sought, by personal contact and reasonable facilities granted for visits to sites and works.

Our specialist skills and technologies are applied to our production with full regard to our obligations to society and the environment, just as our day-to-day working and movement among the public at large must be in an atmosphere of consideration and concern for our surroundings, both human and material. It is with pride that we are recognized as a considerate contractor by the City of London Corporation within their Considerate Contractor Scheme.

Where our operations inevitably cause disturbance and inconvenience to those working or in residence nearby, it is our firm endeavour to minimize the extent and duration of the problem. Those likely to be affected are told in advance of the factors causing the disturbance and the steps we are taking to overcome them. Our genuine concern for our neighbours' welfare must be expressed and their tolerance acknowledged.

We actively support the Employers' Federation, and keep open and constantly under review the channels of communications between Management Employers' Federations, Operatives' Federations, and recognized Trade Union Officials.

Our Group, which was founded and has prospered under conditions of free enterprize, believes in and strongly supports the right of every legitimate business activity to be pursued without State Interference; and just as strongly opposes nationalization.

The philosophy, intent, and policies stated in this document establish the importance attached by the Taylor Woodrow Group to our carrying out the obligations in a proper and considerate manner. It should be recognized that nothing in this document shall either create or affect our legal relations with our clients or their advisers. This document shall not (either expressly or by implication) form a part of any contract to be entered into by any Taylor Woodrow Group Company. However, we would always be pleased to discuss with you how we can put our many and varied resources at your or your clients' disposal.


## London & Edinburgh

Our Group is committed to a policy of social commitment, both nationally and locally.

During 1988 we increased our activity in the area of education and training with active support of the Chartered Insurance Institute at national and local level.

A feature of our education programme was our close liaison with local educational bodies to enable their students to obtain practical experience of a high technology environment by making our systems and facilities available, together with hands-on training. This training and experience enables students to obtain a foothold in the computer industry.

### Safeway

We will build a reputation for making a positive and responsible contribution to the environment and to the lives of the communities in which we live and work. We will be recognized as good neighbours.

# Chapter 30

# Concern for the environment

Many in the British public consider a clean, safe environment as a basic human right. This right, however, does not translate into a discontinuation of economic growth. Wilfred Beckerman, an Oxford economist, among other important commentators, recognizes that economic growth in fact enhances the quality of human life.

One of the most important issues facing firms in the 1990s is balancing economic growth and respect for environmental concerns. Worldwide concerns have been voiced regarding issues varying from air and water quality to conservation and recycling. It is imperative that firms develop procedures and programmes for dealing with environmental concerns in order to retain a good public image, and to avoid wasteful use and destruction of natural resources which are so vital to the production of goods and services. Codified standards which govern a firm's response to these environmental concerns are invaluable to the modern-day British company.

Firms must concern themselves both with their operation's immediate impact upon the environment, such as toxic waste production, chemical runoff into rivers and streams, and pollutant emission into the air, and their indirect impact. Occasionally, facilities are located in environmentally fragile areas. A firm should attempt to remove risks these facilities might cause to the environment. There are numerous deleterious practices, though still considered legal, that an environmentally sensitive company may wish to review.

The following code excerpts demonstrate the variety of ways in which firms have responded to environmental concerns. The excerpts range from the broad one-sentence statement of Digital Equipment to the eloquent essay of RTZ. Note that each excerpt illustrates a unique tact a firm can take when addressing environmental protection issues.

## Ciba-Geigy

Ciba-Geigy is engaged primarily in the field of specialized chemicals and related products and services. Our Company is a subsidiary of CIBA-GEIGY Limited, Basel, Switzerland, a publicly owned company, and as such is affiliated with a group of companies engaged in similar activities throughout the world.

CIBA-GEIGY believes that business is not simply an end in itself and that it must serve people and society. Its economic success is, however, a prerequisite to the achievement of its aims.

CIBA-GEIGY further believes that in its activities it should take due consideration of and harmonize as far as it judges to be possible the interests of the general public and the environment, customers, employees, and shareholders.

In this connection we have adopted the following Principles:

We will behave as a responsible corporate member of society and will do our best to cooperate in a responsible manner with the appropriate authorities, local and national.

Through our activities, including the utilization of the worldwide CIBA-GEIGY experience and resources available to us, we will contribute to the economic development and well being of our country.

We recognize the need for our involvement in the social problems of our society and accept our social responsibility to participate in efforts to cope with these problems.

We take account of the fact that raw materials, land, water, air, and energy are finite resources which must be used carefully and with responsibility.

We take all reasonable measures to ensure that our manufacturing operations and our products have no adverse effects on the environment.

### Digital Equipment Corporation

As good citizens, we believe we have a responsibility to keep our environment free of pollution and to set an example.

### Coats Viyella

We will behave as a responsible corporate member of society and will do our best to cooperate in a responsible manner with the appropriate authorities, both local and national. We must bear our fair share of appropriate taxes. We must respect the environment and be sensitive particularly to the interests of people in close proximity to our manufacturing operations. We must recognize that raw materials, land, water, air, energy are finite resources and as such must be used carefully and with responsibility.

The most important contribution that Coats Viyella can make to the social and material progress of the countries in which it has a presence is to operate as successfully and efficiently as possible. Opportunities for involvement through community, education, and donation programmes must vary depending on the size of the Company concerned and the cognizance of the traditions of local society.

## The Boots Company

The Company is concerned with the conservation of the environment in its broadest sense, and recognizes that certain resources such as land, water, and energy are finite and must be used responsibly.

In the Company's manufacturing operation, its policy in regard to effluent disposal, waste disposal, gaseous emission, and noise emission, is not only to observe statutory controls and regulations, but to set even higher standards where appropriate.

The Company as occupier of shops in the High Streets of so many towns, acknowledges the need to preserve and enhance the quality of urban environment. This particularly applies to buildings which are listed as being of special architectural and historical interest. The Company, within reasonable economic limits, wishes to play its full role in cooperating with local bodies whether statutory or non-statutory.

## Royal Dutch Shell

It is the policy of Shell companies to conduct their activities in such a way as to take foremost account of the health and safety of their employees and of other persons, and to give proper regard to the conservation of the environment. In implementing this policy, Shell Companies not only comply with the requirements of the relevant legislation but promote in an appropriate manner measures for the protection of health, safety, and the environment for all who may be affected directly or indirectly by their activities.

Such measures pertain to safety of operations carried out by employees and contractors; product safety; prevention of air, water, and soil pollution; and precautions to minimize damage from such accidents as may nevertheless occur.

## Rosehaugh

Sensitivity to the environment has always been an important feature of the Group's approach. Materials used in Group projects meet the highest environmental standards, and extensive research into hazardous building materials, including alternatives to the use of chlorofluorocarbons, has been commissioned, and made available to the industry. Guidance notes have also been produced on a range of issues including measures to control and prevent the spread of Legionella bacteria.

Environmental concern has been given practical effect in Group projects, from the alignment of pathways at Chafford Hundred to accommodate badger setts and runs, to the proposed 26-acre park at King's Cross which will be the largest park to be created in central London this century.

Rosehaugh has always recognized a wider responsibility towards the community. It believes in full and open consultation with local people throughout the development process and has a genuine willingness to take account of views expressed in formulating development proposals. Through the Rosehaugh Charitable Foundation, the Group supports a large number of charitable activities.

## RTZ

A further major challenge to the mining industry is the environment. If the record of our industry is examined over a long period, we should accept that there have been grounds for some criticism. Quite rightly, as societies grow richer, as scientific understanding develops, and as the world's population increases, people are concerned about environmental degradation and pollution. The pressure for higher standards which began in North America and Northern Europe now knows no frontiers. Everywhere the trend is towards higher public awareness and stricter controls. This affects many industries but increasingly, the activities of extractive businesses are singled out for public criticism. We are described as dangerous, dirty, and destructive. We are accused of taking something away from the planet and contributing nothing in return. We are alleged to leave poisonous wastes behind us. These beliefs result in legislation and changes in consumer preference. They lead not only to pressure for stronger and costly environmental controls, but also to substitution of our industry's products so that we are caught in a pincer movement both in terms of supply and demand.

On the fringes of the environmental movement, one detects a form of puritanical fervour which at its extreme represents a danger to freedom. But the majority are sincere and the power of this movement is not to be underestimated. Nevertheless, I believe that the mining industry will continue to make a vital contribution to society provided that the rule of reason prevails. As an industry our failure has in part been one of communication: we have not convinced people that we are wealth creators not despoilers. So our job now is not only to comply, but to show that we comply, and more than that – to show that we make a positive contribution to society. In a real sense, we help to guarantee future economic growth in acting as we do as stewards of the resources that will be needed by the twenty-first century.

# Chapter 31

# Statements of values, company philosophies, principles and objectives, and mission statements

There is an adage that, 'If you don't know where you are going, any road will take you there'. Lack of direction is disastrous to companies. Consequently, the first step in creating a code of conduct (or similar, comprehensive company policy document) is distilling and critically examining the values, philosophies, principles, and objectives unique to that firm. By printing, annotating, and referring employees and others to such a statement, a firm reinforces those values and principles which are fundamental to the firm's success. While each of these statements is a vital element to be integrated in a code of conduct, a code, as set out in the book, is much more than a compendium of these statements.

A statement of purpose is simply an explanation of why the organization exists. Sainsbury's states its purpose as, 'the responsibility as leaders in our trade to act with complete integrity, carry out our work to the highest standards, and contribute to the public good and quality of life in the community'. Such a statement of purpose allows the firm and its shareholders to unify behind a common goal beyond the firm's profits and losses.

The following excerpts provide numerous examples of leading UK firms' statements of values, philosophies, and mission statements.

## The M & G Group

The Group's aim is to provide its shareholders with steadily rising dividends from good long-term earnings growth through the provision of investment management services. Size in itself is of secondary importance. The combination of good long-term investment management, efficient administration, and effective marketing will bring strong growth. In all these areas the Group has a firmly established style. In investment management the emphasis is on the long term and on constructive dialogue with management; in administration the emphasis is on providing our clients with the efficient service they need; whilst in marketing M&G is promoted vigorously and consistently both through independent intermediaries giving best advice and through direct mail and advertising.

### Yorkshire Bank

Yorkshire Bank has national standing and operates from a regional base. Its aim is to earn an appropriate return for the shareholders by maintaining and improving profitability. In achieving this aim it will:

1 Provide a range of financial services to satisfy a wide variety of customers.
2 Use its unique experience in personal banking to develop profitable new business, with emphasis on salaried employees and better paid wage-earners, and to attract those who do not have a bank account.
3 Preserve and extend its appeal to local enterprize in business and the professions.
4 Enhance its established reputation for friendliness.
5 Provide attractive employment and progressive career opportunities for those who work for the Bank.
6 Give good service and a fair deal to customers and be considerate of the interests of the staff and of the community.

### Thomas Cook

Our strategy is to substantially increase the profitability and value of the Thomas Cook Group by doing everything that is necessary to earn and retain the trust of our customers, our business partners, our people, and our stakeholders.

### Beazer

Beazer PLC is a major international housebuilding construction and building materials group operating principally in the United Kingdom, the United States of America, and the Far East.

In the United Kingdom, Beazer has a major nationwide construction business and is one of the largest volume house builders. In the United States it is one of the largest suppliers of aggregates, concrete, and cement with substantial operations in thirty States. In the Far East it has significant construction and property development activities. The group has over 20,000 employees worldwide.

Our strategy of developing into a major national house building and construction group in the United Kingdom and diversifying into other geographical and related business areas has resulted in a balanced range of businesses with a wide spread of assets producing excellent returns. We take pride in the strength and integrity of our management and our commitment to treat fairly all those connected with our business – our shareholders, our employees, and our clients.

Our objective is to expand within our chosen sectors recognizing that we have a continuing obligation to maximize the returns to our shareholders.

## Leeds

At the Leeds we aim to make profits by selling competitive financial products and services, primarily associated with home ownership and investment. We strive to give our customers the best possible service – both friendly and business like – at all times.

## The Automobile Association

The Automobile Association is committed to excellence in the delivery of all its products and services. It is committed to the continuing investment in, and development of, a membership based service organization.

The Association ensures that the arrangements for staff employment foster the highest standards of productivity, skill, effectiveness, and responsiveness to member and customer needs. It aims to provide a healthy and safe working environment and to increase job satisfaction by encouraging the development and realization of individual staff potential by all means, including that for employee involvement. Provision is also made for staff communication and Trade Union consultation.

The Association seeks to establish a profitable and stable relationship with commercial suppliers, principles, and business partners.

The Association's activities aim to sustain and cultivate the valuable image of authority, integrity, and independence. It is committed to constantly improving productivity and efficiency, to provide its members with the most cost effective and efficient service.

## AMEC

The AMEC group has a comprehensive engineering, construction, and development capability.

Our breadth and depth of resource give us the strength and flexibility to respond effectively to changing client requirements; adapt our services to meet every need; resist cyclical change; and innovate and create opportunity.

We aim constantly to enhance the breadth of our integrated capability throughout the world.

We will continue to offer the highest quality of service, products, and management, basing our growth on a sound foundation of financial prudence.

The main principles of our strategy are to offer our customers the broadest possible range of engineering, construction, and development services; ensure that every service offered is the best in its market; and offer our services wherever our customers need them worldwide.

### British Credit Trust

1 To achieve and maintain an annual return on capital of at least 18 per cent per annum.
2 To maintain an annual pre-tax profit growth rate of at least 20 per cent per annum.
3 To operate within Great Britain, playing an active part in Bank of Ireland Group strategy.
4 To provide *selected* financial services to consumers and asset-based lending to business customers.
5 To distinguish ourselves through innovation, efficiency, integrity, and quality of service.
6 To provide staff with a challenging, secure, and competitively remunerated employment and give staff every possible opportunity for self-development.

### Bank of Ireland

1 Financial services
  a) To be the leading provider of a broad range of financial services in Ireland.
  b) To be a significant provider of selected financial services in each of the market segments in which we choose to operate outside Ireland.
2 To distinguish ourselves from the competition through the professionalism, innovativeness, efficiency, and quality of the service with which we satisfy customers' needs.
3 To be profitable and competitive in all our activities.
4 To remain in the private sector.
5 To maintain our independence.
6 To grow at a rate which enables us to give a competitive return to Stockholders.
7 To provide Staff of the Group with challenging, competitively remunerated employment which provides every possible opportunity for self-development and the fulfilment of each individual's career potential within a caring environment.
8 To conduct all our activities with integrity.
9 To make a positive contribution to the communities in which we operate.

### Burton Group

To be the leading speciality retailer of financial services – primarily through Burton Group Stores and by direct marketing to credit card customers.

To assist TBG to increase its sales by means of coordinated store cards aimed at clearly identified target markets.

Develop other financial services which are either directly or indirectly focused on the retail market and utilize the strengths within TBG.

## GEC

At GEC, we will do our utmost to provide value and high standards of service to customers and will encourage our suppliers to do the same.

We will play a constructive role in the communities in which our facilities are established. We will encourage and reward the productivity and ingenuity of the people who work in the Company.

We will ensure our technological leadership by maintaining excellent research and development staff and providing them with the facilities they need.

We will continue to exercise the style of management which has been proven over many years.

We will achieve profitable growth from within the Company, through imaginative management of our assets.

We will encourage further growth through acquisition, partnerships, joint ventures, and technical collaboration.

We will seek to maximize the value of our shareholders' investment by consistently raising earnings per share whilst maintaining prudent accounting standards.

## GPT

1 Getting people together.
2 Responsiveness to customers.
3 Commitment to excellence.
4 Recognition of individual contribution.
5 Willingness to change.
6 Growth, profit, technology.

## Town & Country

The Society will expand its presence in the housing and financial services market by responding to the needs of the customer.

To make profits sufficient to achieve a satisfactory return on capital.

To be responsive to the needs and wants of our customers in a rapidly changing financial marketplace and to provide the highest level of service possible.

To remain independent as a building society, functioning for the real benefit of customers and employees alike.

To continue making loans for house purchase, and to provide a wide range of other financial and housing related services.

To ensure staff commitment to the Society's objectives by stimulating career development and the provision of adequate systems of reward.

The Society's relationship with the world at large (customers, suppliers, the local community, Government, etc) will be conducted in an open and honest way.

## Capital & Counties

To apply its resources and skills in such a way as to give shareholders the maximum return over the long term, consistent with an acceptable degree of risk, via growth of shareholders' funds and a steadily increasing dividend flow. In seeking that objective it will pay due regard to the aspirations and welfare of its staff and its wider social obligations.

## Trusthouse Forte

To increase profitability and earnings per share each year in order to encourage investment and to improve and expand the business.

To give complete customer satisfaction by efficient and courteous service, with value for money.

To support managers and their staff in using personal initiative to improve the profit and quality of their operations whilst observing the Company's policies.

To provide good working conditions and to maintain effective communications at all levels to develop better understanding and assist decision-making.

To ensure no discrimination against sex, race, colour, or creed and to train, develop, and encourage promotion within the company based on merit and ability.

To act with integrity at all times and to maintain a proper sense of responsibility towards the public.

To recognize the importance of each and every employee who contributes towards these aims.

## Inchcape

Inchcape, the international services and marketing group, operates in more than 60 countries, acting for internationally known manufacturers' products and technologies and providing skilled specialist services worldwide.

Inchcape's strategic businesses are in the three main areas: Services, Marketing & Distribution, and Resources. The Services businesses are Buying Services, Inspection & Testing Services, Insurance Services, and Shipping Services. The Marketing & Distribution businesses are Business Machines, Consumer & Industrial, and Motors. The Resources based businesses are Tea and Timber.

Within these three areas the businesses will continue to be reviewed on a regular basis. Each business stream must be capable of meeting the Group's growth ambitions and of making a substantial contribution to earnings. Inchcape is becoming increasingly focused on businesses that have the potential to be competitive on an international basis.

## John Menzies

The John Menzies Group will endeavour:

To operate successfully and develop dominant businesses in Retailing, and in Wholesale and Distribution Services.

To provide the highest quality of goods and services to our customers, both corporate and individual.

To carry out our business with the highest standards of integrity.

To contribute wherever possible to the welfare and quality of life of the community.

To maintain real growth in earnings per share, at a better than average sector rate, in the long-term interest of our staff and shareholders.

To retain the existing concentration of share ownership.

## NFU Mutual

Our aim is to remain a viable, independent, commercial enterprize, satisfying the needs of our customers, staff, and agents, in the following ways:

1 To offer a wide range of general business insurance, with comprehensible cover and backed by a first class service, at the lowest cost commensurate with commercial prudence.
2 To offer a wide range of life assurance and pensions products, designed to give the best possible level of protection and return, consistent with financial security.
3 To offer other financial and related services which recognize the needs of our members, aiming always to achieve a high quality of service and good value for money and subject to the same considerations of commercial prudence.
4 To promote and maintain close and mutually advantageous relationships with the Farmers' Unions.
5 To protect the interests of the parent Society by developing a sound business outside the agricultural industry.
6 To identify general insurance, life assurance, pensions, investments, and other financial services markets as targets for the Company's activities and to provide those sectors with appropriate quality products at competitive rates, backed by first class service.
7 To maximize the profits from the Company's activities, thereby providing a worthwhile return to the parent Society, and carrying a fair share of Group expenses.
8 To sustain, at all levels, an enthusiastic and effective management and staff by providing good conditions of employment and opportunities for development and promotion to the maximum of individual capabilities.
9 To offer a high quality of service and support to our agents and brokers.
10 To expand as vigorously as is consistent with the objectives stated above.

Our aim is to be the best.

### Norwich Winterthur Reinsurance

The provision of non-Life professional reinsurance services through London market brokers. NWRe may also provide these services through other sources, but this is a secondary line of approach dependent upon the availability of resources.

NWRe is profit rather than volume generated although growth is an essential element in selected areas. The aim of NWRe is to be selective and flexible in its activities, thus ensuring that it operates in market sectors which provide the best opportunities for profit.

NWRe aims to be capable of maintaining the support of its shareholders so that resources are available for growth and development, either by the shareholders agreeing to the company retaining profits or by increasing capital resources.

NWRe aims to be a recognized leader in sectors of the market selected for development including leadership in London market affairs.

NWRe accepts its responsibility as a market leader to provide sound services to its clients and intermediaries, and it will aim to provide services which are at least equal to those given by its competitors.

NWRe must be fair and reasonable in all of its dealings with clients or intermediaries.

NWRe recognizes that to meet these aims and objectives requires the maintenance of a skilled, efficient, and highly motivated staff. NWRe will therefore aim:

1 to be a sound and responsible employer providing fair remuneration related to market standards;
2 to provide the skills needed at any time from amongst its own staff as far as possible, by encouraging development by training and by self-education and by having proper succession arrangements;
3 to adopt an open policy of management insofar as this is compatible with efficiency, and to foster a feeling of involvement of staff at all levels in the affairs of the company.

### Norwich Union Insurance Group

1 to operate from a sound financial basis;
2 to be utterly dependable in conduct;
3 to offer fair and competitive terms;
4 to give sound and technically expert advice;
5 to maintain an enthusiastic and effective staff, ensuring that remuneration and conditions of service are of a high standard compared with the market in which they are employed;
6 to have regard to our responsibility to society in general, in all territories which we operate;
7 to play a full and responsible part in the development of the industry;

8 to preserve and foster the Group image and encourage reciprocity and cooperation with other companies in the Group.

## Pearson

The strategy of your company stems from your board's long-held, basic belief in the value of high standards, equally applied to products, services, behaviour, and performance.

In an increasingly competitive and well-informed world, we have translated this belief into the strategy that we should concentrate on sectors

1 where competitive advantage derives from superior quality of products and services, preferably with world class brand names;
2 where we can build international businesses capable of competing successfully on a global basis;
3 where our company culture enables us to attract and motivate highly talented people;

and we believe that by concentrating in this way we can achieve strong market positions and better than average business performance.

This belief in the desirability of focusing lies behind our programme of acquisitions and disposals. It does not however lead to an inevitable conclusion that we will end up as a group in a single industry. We have always believed there is merit and opportunity in balance and diversity and our Pearson head office management style, based on dialogue not diktat, reinforces our conviction that we can operate successfully with like-minded people in a limited number of different fields. Our performance reinforces this view.

## Powell Duffryn

The Powell Duffryn Group supplies specialized services and products to industrial, commercial, and retail customers. By concentrating on selected markets and strengthening its position through continuing investment and carefully chosen acquisitions, it aims to achieve leadership in those markets. Based on these market strengths, Powell Duffryn's objectives are to provide:

1 Sustained, low risk growth in earnings and dividends for its shareholders.
2 First class service to its customers.
3 Sound and challenging opportunities for its employees.

## Prudential Corporation

The Prudential is one of the world's largest and strongest Financial Service groups. It directly employs 40,000 people in over 30 countries. Its main businesses are life assurance, pensions, general insurance called property and casualty in many countries, investment management, unit trusts, reinsurance, and estate agency. It has more than 8 million customers and is the largest single investor in the British stock market.

In all its core businesses the Prudential seeks to be a leading provider of services with a reputation for security and integrity, for value for money and quality of service. The current trend towards deregulation throughout the world provides opportunities for further expansion and development.

In promoting its businesses the Prudential's aims are:

1  to increase profitability and earnings per share and thus reward our Shareholders, encourage investment, and facilitate further expansion;
2  to give Customer satisfaction through high quality products accompanied by high standards of service, courtesy and fair dealing;
3  to provide our Staff with the leadership, training, and working conditions essential to their success and to operate personnel policies based on ability with no discrimination on grounds of sex, race, colour, or creed;
4  to abide by the spirit of laws as well as their letter and to be a significant contributor to the development and wellbeing of the wider Community in which we operate.

**RAC Motoring Services**

Our objective is to establish Britain's Premier Motoring Organization as the Best Motoring Organization in Europe.

To do this, we must identify and satisfy motorists' needs by providing all-round motoring assistance with speed, reliability, courtesy, personal care, and flexibility.

Yet maintaining our hard-earned reputation for independence and integrity is equally important. It is this popular prestige which allows us effectively to champion the causes of motorists, both collectively and individually, and justify the claim that 'our only concern is the motorist'.

The services we provide will be of outstanding excellence and the RAC name on any product or service should be seen as a hallmark of quality, dependability, safety, and value for money.

To stay in business and invest in the future we must make profits. We can do this by building on our strengths and developing and implementing market driven commercial initiatives which will attract a growing number of motorists to the RAC.

We are committed to achieving these aims by giving authority and resources to our employees and by harnessing their innovative skills to our new technologies so that they can meet the developing needs of our customers.

Because we recognize that the achievement of our Mission depends upon the collective efforts of our employees, we will strive to release, develop, and reward the capabilities of each employee and encourage individual success and happiness.

We expect our employees to be open and frank in all their dealings with members, customers, suppliers, and fellow employees.

## Save & Prosper

Save & Prosper's mission is to meet our customers' needs for investment services, allowing us to prosper as a business and earn profits for our shareholders.

How we accomplish our mission is as important as the mission itself. Fundamental to our success are these guiding principles:

1 Our staff are the source of our strength. We are a team. We treat each other with trust and respect. Staff involvement in our business is a way of life.
2 Our customers are UK individuals and small institutions. They are the focus of what we do. We aim to give them better service and products than our competitors.
3 Our core products are investments which help our customers to beat inflation in the medium to long term and our two principal core products are pensions and unit trusts. Our banking products offer competitive interest rates and give customers easy access to their money.

All our products:

a) Are presented in a way which makes it easy to understand the essential features.
b) Aim to be tax effective.

4 Profits are the final measure of our success. We must plan our business to ensure that we earn the level of profits which is necessary to survive and grow. We aim to hold a balance between: the interests of our staff, our customers, and our shareholders, maximizing short-term profits and investing for the future.
5 In everything we do we aim to behave honestly and fairly and to command respect for our values.

## Marks & Spencer Financial Services

To satisfy customer needs through clearly presented retail financial products in line with the Marks and Spencer traditions of quality, value, and service.

To support the core business.

To analyse and understand customer needs.

To identify and deliver differentiated financial services.

To explain products and services in a way the customer finds easy to understand.

To deliver quality, value, and service to our customers in the best Marks and Spencer traditions.

To ensure that our staff benefit from the success of the group.

To foster good relations with our customers, our staff, our suppliers, and in the community.

## Laing Properties

Laing Properties is committed to the long-term growth of net assets and earnings. This is achieved by:

1  Geographical and market sector diversification.
2  High quality development as a major dynamic of the Group.
3  Active management of the property investment portfolio.

## Tomkins

Tomkins is an industrial management company dedicated to the revitalization of underdeveloped businesses and their sustained growth.

This is achieved by selective acquisition from a diverse range of low-risk technology companies with unrealized potential. Acquired companies are revitalized as autonomous businesses through the injection of sound management expertize, capital for development, and the application of tight financial disciplines.

A small, widely-experienced management team drives the company, combining flair with proven commercial judgement and fast response.

# Chapter 32

# Implementation and adjudication of a code of conduct

When implementing a new or revised code or similar company document, and adjudicating issues arising from that code, a firm should follow six steps.

First, a firm must develop an effective distribution scheme. Alcan makes its code of conduct available throughout the company and its subsidiaries, as well as to the management of non-controlled associated companies.

Second, a firm should take steps to help managers and employees interpret the code. Halifax's interpretation procedure advises any employee in doubt to consult his or her manager, and for any manager to consult a General Manager, the General Secretary, or a Regional General Manager. Providing clear procedures for managers and employees diminishes the chance of serious misconduct.

Third, a firm should specify managers' roles in implementing the code of conduct. Once the code of conduct reaches line managers in The Boots Company, managers have the responsibility of completing the implementation process.

Fourth, the firm should be explicit that employees have a duty to fully understand and comprehend the code of conduct. Digital Equipment Corporation mandates that 'all employees should understand the objectives and use them to guide their behaviour and work output'. To ensure employee comprehension, Digital provides short explanations of each objective of the code of conduct. Firms should also require employees to sign acknowledgements or certificates of compliance regarding their having received, read, understood, and complied with the code's provisions.

Fifth, firms should institute thorough and fair procedures for handling grievance procedures. The Bank of England and British Coal provide extensive grievance procedures dealing with violations of the code of conduct. Every firm should provide a description of its grievance and adjudicating procedures in its code.

Last, the firm should provide a conclusion, or closing statement. Cadbury Schweppes closes its policy document as follows: 'The character of the company is collectively in our hands. Pride in what we do is important, and let us earn that pride by the way we put the beliefs set out here into action'.

The following excerpts illustrate how leading British and multi-national firms address issues in code implementation and adjudication.

## DISTRIBUTION

### Alcan

A statement of Purpose, Objectives, and Policies was first published in June 1978. Nathanael V. Davis, Chairman and Chief Executive Officer at that time, explained in the foreword that the statement was for distribution to Alcan employees in all countries to strengthen their awareness of the basic general principles and policies which had guided the conduct of Alcan's business over the years. This document had emerged from consultation and participation of approximately 200 Alcan managers around the world.

The statement was also distributed to Alcan's shareholders and was made available to others on an unrestricted basis.

The development of a new Alcan Mission Statement in 1986 calls for some amendment to the 'Purpose' section as set forth in earlier printings but the 'Objectives' and 'Policies' sections, which are important guides to personal and corporate conduct, remain unchanged.

In the original foreword, Mr Davis said: 'It is not, of course, possible to prescribe specific responses to every industrial and social problem that will arise in a widespread international enterprize.

This statement of Alcan's purpose, objectives, and policies is being made available to employees throughout the Company and its subsidiaries for their guidance and to the managements of non-controlled associated companies for their information.

I have confidence, however, that the publication of this statement, and the continuing efforts of Alcan personnel to meet these standards, will enable the Company to continue to merit public understanding and trust'. I continue to share the confidence expressed by Mr Davis.

## COMPLIANCE, INTERPRETATION, DUTY TO REPORT, REPORTING AND CONFIDENTIALITY, AND EMPLOYEE SUGGESTIONS

### United Biscuits

We rely on our staff as individuals to practise the highest moral and ethical standards in all our business activities. We as individuals must so conduct ourselves as to contribute towards the integrity of the company as a whole. People at every level in the business must be encouraged to make known any issues that may raise or appear to raise a potential problem and to review with senior management any issue that might be of questionable ethical standard.

## Halifax

If an employee is in any doubt about anything in these guidelines he or she should consult his or her manager. A manager should consult a General Manager, the General Secretary, or a Regional General Manager.

## Xerox

If you have even the slightest doubt about the ethics or legality of an action, don't take it. First, discuss the issue with your manager.

## British Steel

Employees should note that it is their personal responsibility to apply the principles of this code on every relevant occasion. Failure to comply with this code may result in disciplinary action, which can include dismissal, in accordance with the appropriate Disciplinary Code, as agreed with the relevant trade unions.

All references in this document to male employees shall be interpreted as references to female employees also.

All references in this document to the Company or to British Steel plc include all British Steel plc's UK subsidiaries, to which this Code equally applies.

## Hewlett Packard Ltd

HP has a firmly established policy of conducting its affairs in strict compliance with the letter and spirit of the law and adhering to the highest principles of business ethics. These standards of Business Conduct are intended to inform all employees of their legal and ethical obligations to HP, its customers, competitors, and suppliers.

HP's reputation for excellent products and high ethical standards can only be maintained by fair and honest dealing in every transaction. Every HP employee is expected to comply with these standards and other company policies as well.

Each supervisor and manager is expected to take every necessary action to ensure compliance and to bring problems to the attention of higher management for review. All employees should reread this booklet periodically.

Employees should discuss any questions or difficulties with their immediate supervisors. It is the supervisor's responsibility to see that the matter is resolved promptly. To help in this regard, HP's attorneys may be consulted.

We wish to emphasize HP's expectation that each individual will carry out corporate and individual job objectives in a manner consistent with these standards.

## TSB Trust

The Company encourages staff to put forward their ideas on ways and means of promoting business efficiency, increasing levels of service, and making working conditions more pleasant for employees. The Suggestion Scheme provides a vehicle for this whereby all suggestions made are considered by an impartial committee; those that are implemented can, depending on the benefits gained by the Company, yield significant rewards to the persons putting them forward.

## British Gas

This Code had been prepared to give guidance. If you are ever in doubt about any matter concerning conduct, you should seek advice from your superior. You should also be aware that breaches of the Code can result in disciplinary action.

## Control Data

Employees will not lose their jobs or be placed at any career disadvantage for questioning a Control Data practice or reporting a possible violation of Control Data's policies.

Control Data will investigate possible violations. In so doing, it will respect the rights of all parties involved.

If a violation is found, Control Data will take appropriate disciplinary action, up to and including termination and filing of criminal charges.

The identity of employees reporting possible violations will be kept confidential – unless Control Data is required by an applicable law or the administrative or judicial process to reveal it.

## MANAGERS AS AGENTS FOR IMPLEMENTATION

### The Boots Company

This statement of the Company's policies and practices is not intended to be a guide to implementation on matters of detail. This is primarily the responsibility of line management, assisted by service departments such as Personnel and by consultative committees. By doing it this way rigidity is avoided and maximum flexibility given to those mainly responsible for using their initiative within the broad policy framework. Nor is it intended to replace obligations already being observed by those members of staff who are members of professional bodies with their own codes of practice, which apply for example to pharmacists, ophthalmic opticians, and to the legal and accountancy professions, but to provide a Company standard within which these can more easily be followed.

## EMPLOYEES' DUTY TO UNDERSTAND THE CODE OF CONDUCT

### Digital Equipment Corporation

All employees should understand the objectives and use them to guide their behaviour and work output. The objectives should help to make employees proud to work for Digital and should influence the quality of their work and their productivity.

All employees should be able to explain the meaning of the objectives to their colleagues and friends (and customers).

Customers who happen to be shown the objectives should understand them and feel good about them (although they are not written with external publication as an intent) and should notice Digital's dedication to quality.

Therefore, each objective has a short explanation associated with it which can be used by managers as an aid in explaining the objective to employees, written in clear language for a multi-national population.

## ARCO UK Ltd

The Principles of Business Conduct have been drawn up to serve as a reminder to all ARCO employees of the serious obligation we all have to conduct the company's operations with candour, honesty, and fairness toward all.

Each employee is asked to review this material with his or her supervisor and, should anyone wish, to explore the matter further by reviewing the full versions of key company policies in the areas of legal and ethical obligations. Full texts may be obtained from the Legal Department or your Employee Relations representative.

The General Counsel or his designee will be responsible for interpretation of the Code and the underlying policies or standards. Managers have a special obligation for their own awareness and communication of these guidelines to employees who report to them. Because of the importance of this matter, this responsibility cannot be delegated to subordinates.

Questions about ARCO's Principles of Business Conduct or related matters should be directed to your supervisor or manager. Employees are also free to contact Internal Auditing or the Legal Department to discuss the code or its application.

## Anonymous

I realize that both the law and Company practices require factual reporting and accounting in all phases of the Company's operations.

I also agree that during or after my employment I will not, except as required in the conduct of the Company's business or when properly authorized in writing, publish, disclose, or use or authorize anyone else to publish, disclose, or use, any private, confidential, or proprietary information that I may have in any way acquired, learned, developed, or created by reason of my employment.

I understand that my employment can be terminated by me or the Company at any time, with or without cause and with or without notice, and that nothing in this booklet or any other publication, practice, policy, or manual is to be interpreted to the contrary.

Signature

_____

Name (printed)

_____

Title

_____

Department _____    Date

_____

*Acknowledgement received*
Supervisor's or other authorized signature

_____

Name (printed)

_____

Title _____    Date

_____

## Anonymous

*Certification*

I have received and read the Company Code of Conduct. I certify that I am presently in full compliance with the policies stated in the Code of Conduct, and that I have no direct knowledge or factual evidence of any present violation of them by another employee, except as I have specifically disclosed to the Company.

Signature _____

Name (print) _____

Department or Group _____

Location _____    Date _____

## Anonymous

I have carefully read the Company Code of Conduct, and understand its provisions.

Date _____

Signature _____

I obtained the above signed acknowledgement from

_____

Employee's Name _____

at Location _____

Date _____

Supervisor's Signature _____

Title _____

## INCO

Supplementary guidelines may from time to time be issued to add to or clarify these guidelines should the need to do so develop.

In order to ensure continued compliance with these policy guidelines, a certificate in substantially the following form shall be signed annually by April 1 of each year by all persons (and their successors in office) who have received these guidelines, and shall be submitted to the Comptroller of Inco Limited. This certificate shall cover the period from January 1 of the preceding year to the date of such certificate. Any employee receiving a copy of these guidelines who has any questions as to whether a breach of such guidelines has been properly reported, should consult with the Comptroller of Inco Limited.

Within the past 30 days I have read the Guidelines on Business Conduct (as amended) of Inco Limited and its subsidiaries and I have not breached, nor become aware of any breach of, these Guidelines since January 1 of last year other than those instances, if any, which either have been reported to the Comptroller of Inco Limited in writing by me or another employee for remedial action or are reported in an Exhibit attached to this certificate.

NOTE: Please indicate whether an Exhibit has been attached to this certificate.

Yes _____ No _____

In signing this certificate I am relying where necesary on certificates in the same form signed by certain employees who report to me.

(Date) _____

(Signature) _____

(Title) _____

## GRIEVANCE AND DISCIPLINARY PROCEDURES

### Bank of England

Individual grievances shall be resolved as near as possible to their source and as speedily as possible. It is the intention that, normally, an interview will be arranged within three clear working days of a request being made and a reply given within a further three clear working days.

Staff in non-supervisory positions must first discuss their grievance with their immediate supervisor. If the reply is not acceptable, the matter should then be raised with the Principal/Manager of their Office. If the individual remains dissatisfied he or she may then ask, through the Principal/Manager, for an interview with his/her Head of Department/Division.

Staff in supervisory positions should initially seek an interview with their Principal/Manager or Head of Department/Division, as appropriate.

If the source of the grievance is a matter which has been dealt with in the Corporate Services Department, or the individual has a problem connected with his or her Bank career and does not wish to discuss the matter in his or her Office, Department, or Division, an interview may be sought directly with the appropriate Principal/Manager in the Corporate Services Department. If the matter is not settled to the individual's satisfaction he or she may then ask the Principal/Manager concerned to arrange an interview with the Chief of Corporate Services.

If, following an interview at Head of Department/Division level, the individual wishes to appeal against the decision, an interview with the Governor may be obtained through the Head of Department/Division concerned or the Chief of Corporate Services, as appropriate.

At any interview subsequent to the initial discussion of the grievance a member of the staff may, if he/she wishes, be accompanied by his/her representative and the interviewer may invite another member of management to be present; the member of the staff and/or the interviewer to give prior notice of an intention to be accompanied.

If an interview at Principal/Manager level or above fails to produce an acceptable solution to the grievance, an agreed written report of the proceedings will be prepared for reference to the next stage of the procedure. An agreed record of the final decision by the Head of Department/Division, the Chief of Corporate Services, or the Governor will also be made.

In this procedure –

'The Governor' is interpreted to include the Deputy Governor, an Executive Director, or an Associate Director.

'Head of Department/Division' is interpreted to include Assistant Director, Chief Adviser, Staff Manager, Deputy Staff Manager, or Assistant Staff Manager.

'The Chief of Corporate Services' is interpreted to include a Divisional Assistant or Assistant to the Chief of Corporate Services.

'Principal/Manager' is interpreted to include a Deputy or Assistant Principal or Deputy Manager; a Senior Adviser, an Adviser, or Assistant Adviser; at the Branches, Agent, Branch Manager, or Assistant Manager.

'Supervisor' is interpreted to include the Doorkeeper, Services Supervisor, Senior Gatekeeper, and Shift Charge Engineer.

'Representative' is interpreted as an official or an accredited representative of a trade union recognized by the Bank, an official of a registered trade union to which the individual belongs, or a fellow member of the staff.

## British Coal

The Board's disciplinary procedures are designed to deal with unsatisfactory performance of work and failure to adhere to the standard of conduct required by encouraging improvements and not just as a means of imposing sanctions. They are intended to safeguard individuals in respect of whom disciplinary action is considered and/or taken, and members of management who are responsible for taking decisions on disciplinary action.

Any disciplinary action will be decided according to the facts of each individual case and the procedures will be followed through as quickly as possible consistent with ensuring that full consideration is given to the circumstances of the case and representations made by or on behalf of the individual involved.

The circumstances in which disciplinary action needs to be taken vary widely. They include unsatisfactory or incompetent performance of a job manifesting itself over a period; particular failures in performance; disregard of instructions or statutory requirements; evasion of responsibility; misconduct; deliberate acts detrimental to the Board's property, business, or interests; acts outside the Board's employment which affect an individual's usefulness as an employee of the Board; and breaches of disciplinary rules (whether national or local, express or implied).

When an individual's performance deteriorates, or his/her conduct becomes unsatisfactory, representatives of line management or of the Department concerned will give informal warnings to help the individual correct the situation. A diary note will be made on each occasion an informal warning is given and the individual will be made aware of the fact. Where an informal warning is considered insufficient or a previous one has not been heeded or has not resulted in improvement, management will advise Staff Department that formal disciplinary action should be considered.

When an individual is considered:-

1  to have performed his/her job unsatisfactorily over a period or has committed acts of minor misconduct over a period and informal warnings have proved ineffective; or
2  to have failed seriously in the performance of his/her job on a particular occasion;
3  to have committed an act of serious misconduct on a particular occasion

management will advise Staff Department that there may be grounds for considering formal disciplinary action.

In certain cases investigations will be necessary to establish the facts. Investigations may include an interview with the individual concerned who will be told of the reason for the interview. If, during the course of the interview, the facts available indicate that disciplinary action will have to be considered the interview will be closed to enable a disciplinary interview to be arranged as set out below.

Where the Board consider there may be a case for taking disciplinary action,

Staff Department will arrange for a disciplinary interview with the individual and a representative of line management or the Department concerned. Staff Department will notify the individual in writing, of the time and date of the interview, its disciplinary nature, and the allegations or criticisms which have given rise to it. The individual will be reminded of his/her right to be accompanied at the interview by a fellow employee of his/her choice, or by a member or official of a trade union of which he/she is a member and which is recognized by the Board in relation to him/her. The notification will (save in the most exceptional circumstances) be given at least four working days in advance of the interview. (Where appropriate staff may be suspended with pay during this four-day period.)

At the outset of the interview the allegations outlined in the written notification will be reviewed and any further relevant facts established. Where appropriate, copies of documentary evidence relevant to the allegations will be made available to the individual. Time will be allowed for the individual to answer fully any charges or criticisms and to state his/her case. The interview may be adjourned if necessary to allow, for example, consideration of any fresh factors which may emerge. The Board's representatives will consider the individual's answers fully and reply to them. The interview will then be closed or adjourned and the Board's representatives will consider whether disciplinary action will be taken. Once a decision has been made, Staff Department will inform the individual of the disciplinary action (if any) to be taken and the reasons for it. This decision will be communicated to the individual as soon as possible and will be confirmed in writing. The individual will be advised of his/her right of appeal. The individual's representative will be informed of the disciplinary decision unless the individual demurs.

Disciplinary action may consist of a formal warning, a final warning, a salary sanction, a transfer of post, downgrading, or dismissal.

When a formal warning is given the individual will be told what is expected of him, what are considered to be his/her shortcomings, how he/she should make them good, how long he/she has in which to do so, and what will be the probable consequences of any failure to do so. A formal warning will accompany all other forms of disciplinary action, apart from dismissal.

For more serious matters, a final warning may be given which will state that an occurrence of any further misconduct or inadequacies of performance will result in dismissal.

A salary sanction may consist of a reduction or withholding of an increment, a 'nil' review in a salary range, or a reduction in the salary paid; and is imposed because of inadequate performance or some personal misconduct which, though serious enough to merit disciplinary action, does not justify downgrading or dismissal.

Transfer to a lower graded post or transfer to a different post without change of grade may be appropriate when an individual's misconduct or unsatisfactory performance makes it necessary to alter the kind of work he/she does or his/her place of work. A salary sanction may also be imposed.

Temporary or permanent downgrading may be necessary when the above measures have been taken and have proved to be ineffective after a suitable period of trial or where particular incidents of misconduct, particular failures of performance, disregard of instructions, or breaches of trust have occurred but are not serious enough to warrant termination of employment.

Dismissal will be adopted only in serious cases of misconduct or lapses in performance or when one or more of the measures described above have been applied and have proved ineffective after a reasonable period of time. Dismissal will normally be with notice but dismissal without notice (summary dismissal) may be warranted for certain kinds of serious misconduct, described below.

Examples of the kinds of serious misconduct which may warrant summary dismissal include:

1  theft of Board property or the property of fellow employees;
2  fraudulent or corrupt practices relating to the Board's property or business;
3  unauthorized release of confidential information, which could be to the Board's detriment, as outlined in Rule 14;
4  serious acts of negligence;
5  serious acts in relation to the Board or involving fellow employees (eg fighting or other violent conduct), or otherwise so grave that it destroys the necessary mutual trust and confidence which exists between the Board and the individual;
6  refusal to attend for any interview arranged under this Code without reasonable explanation.

Where there is clear and apparently well-founded evidence of serious misconduct the Board may suspend an individual who appears to be involved for such a period as the Board consider necessary to enable them to ascertain any further relevant facts and to decide on necessary action. Anyone suspended will continue to be paid his/her salary during suspension.

Staff charged with committing criminal offences will be dealt with in accordance with the procedures described above. Where a member of staff is charged with a criminal offence connected with the Board's property or interests, disciplinary action (including summary dismissal if appropriate) may be taken without waiting for any court decision on the criminal charge, provided that the Board are satisfied after suitable investigations that in the circumstances such action is reasonable. If appropriate, an individual may be suspended . . . until the Board are satisfied that the facts are established and then a disciplinary interview will be held.

Criminal offences committed outside employment will not necessarily lead to dismissal. The facts of each case will be reviewed to determine whether as a result of the offence the individual can continue the job which he/she is employed to do or can be employed at the same workplace.

An appeal may be made against any form of disciplinary action . . . . Staff will be advised of their right to appeal and the appropriate procedures at the time the disciplinary action is confirmed. Staff intending to appeal should notify their Staff Manager in writing within fourteen days of being informed of the disciplinary action, and indicate the grounds on which they are appealing. Appeals will be heard, so far as practicable, within three weeks of an individual's notification of intention to appeal.

At the hearing of appeals an individual may be accompanied, if he/she so wishes, by a fellow employee of his/her choice or by a member or official of a trade union of which he/she is a member and which is recognized by the Board in relation to him/her. The representatives of Management who took the decision against which the appeal is made will be present to deal solely with questions of fact and with questions concerning the reasons for their decision. They will not be party to the deliberations of the Appeal Body. The Appeal Body will review the case on the grounds put forward by the individual, and will consider fully representations made by the individual. If necessary the Appeal interview may be adjourned. The decision of the Appeal Body and the reasons for it will be communicated to the individual concerned in writing, and to his/her representative unless the individual demurs, as soon as practicable. It is in the interests of the individual and the Board to act as quickly as possible.

Appeals will be heard by a representative of Management at a level above that at which the decision was taken. He/she will sit with two other representatives of Management who have not been associated with the earlier disciplinary action, and a note of the proceedings will be taken by a member of Staff Department. In the case of appeals against dismissal and downgrading, the Director-General of Staff will appoint the Appeal Body from a standing list of Board personnel.

An appeal to a higher level of Management is without prejudice to any right the individual has to bring a complaint of unfair dismissal to an Industrial Tribunal.

### Anonymous

An employee whose work is unsatisfactory (eg quality, accuracy, output, etc) or whose conduct is unacceptable (eg time-keeping, personal behaviour affecting work, etc) should initially be interviewed by the manager and told of the reasons for the Company's dissatisfaction and of the improvements required, and warned that failure to improve could lead to dismissal.

The manager should make a file note summarizing the conversation with the employee and pass one copy to the relevant Personnel Manager and one to the employee.

If no improvement is achieved and the manager considers that the situation may eventually result in dismissal, a further interview may be necessary at which a warning of possible dismissal is made. Such a warning may also be issued on the first occasion on which bad work or unacceptable conduct occurs if this is sufficiently serious (short of gross misconduct) to warrant an immediate warning. A warning letter must be issued. A file note should also be made of the details of the case.

1 The manager should ensure that careful investigation has been undertaken before any disciplinary action is taken.

2 Where a written warning is being given the appropriate Personnel Manager should be consulted in advance.

3 The employee must be given the opportunity to state his/her case.

4 If the expected improvement is maintained the written warning should be treated as having lapsed after twelve months.

It is Group policy to ensure equitable treatment for employees who are dismissed, with particular reference to compliance with the Employment Protection (Consolidation) Act 1978.

To comply with this Act the following conditions must be met:

1 Dismissals, other than for gross misconduct, should not be effected unless the employee has had prior warning (confirmed in writing) of unsatisfactory work or conduct and of the consequence of failing to correct these faults.

2 When an employee is to be dismissed, he/she should be interviewed by the manager, in the presence of a witness (normally the Personnel Manager), told the reasons for the dismissal, and allowed to state his/her own case.

3 Dismissals must be confirmed in writing by the relevant Personnel Manager.

4 The employee must be allowed to appeal against a dismissal decision to a level of management not previously directly involved. Details of such appeal and final decision should be recorded and confirmed in writing.

5 All employees, including those newly recruited, must be informed of the Company's disciplinary and appeals procedures.

6 In all cases where disciplinary action is contemplated the employee must be given an opportunity to state his/her side of the case and has the right to be accompanied by a representative of his/her choice.

Failure to observe these principles may result in actions for unfair dismissal against the Company and consequent compensation.

The following paragraphs detail the procedures and standard documentation necessary to comply with these principles.

Payments and other terms due on dismissal vary depending on the type of dismissal. Managers and Personnel Managers dealing with dismissal must reach a firm conclusion about the type of each dismissal and if in doubt must consult the legal department before taking action.

Two broad considerations apply:

1 Is the dismissal for gross misconduct? If so no notice or payment in lieu of notice is due.

2 Should the dismissal be held to be 'unfair' in law?

Gross misconduct implies conduct which amounts to a repudiation by the employee of his/her contract of employment. The conduct must be such as to go to the root of the contract. It must not be merely a minor infringement of instructions or requirements. Examples include:

Giving false information in order to obtain employment or employment benefits, eg falsely claiming to have a professional qualification to obtain a job where such qualification is a requirement.

Dishonesty which adversely affects the efficient performance of the job, breaches of the 'duty of fidelity' such as passing on confidential Company information to unauthorized persons.

Criminal action related to the job or Company, such as theft of Company money or property, or assaulting other staff.

Wilful disobedience of lawful orders provided these orders or instructions are clearly fundamentally related to the performance of the job.

Being at work under the influence of drugs not prescribed by a doctor.

Where gross misconduct is established, salary should be paid only to the date on which the employment is terminated. No notice or payments in lieu should be made.

Most staff dismissals fall into this category and would apply where job performance or conduct is unsatisfactory and warnings have been given with no effect. Examples of such cases include:

1  Frequent lateness or unauthorized absence.
2  Poor quality work/frequent errors.
3  Low output.
4  Frequent work omissions; forgetting to carry out instructions as distinct from refusing to carry out instructions.
5  Incapability to meet required job standards.

In these circumstances, employees are entitled either to notice, or to payment in lieu of notice in accordance with their contracts of employment.

The question of making additional ex-gratia payments in some of these cases cannot be considered until the other major point of fairness/unfairness has been cleared.

Under the Employment Protection (Consolidation) Act, dismissals may be challenged by the employee as being unfair. The Act gives some indication of what constitutes fairness but the onus of proof as to the reason for dismissal lies with the employer. Fair reasons are reasons which are related to:

1  Incapability to perform work of the kind for which the employee is employed.
2  Lack of necessary qualifications.
3  Conduct, that is, personal behaviour, attendance etc.
4  Redundancy.
5  Retirement.
6  Some other substantial reason of a kind such as to justify dismissal of an employee holding the position which the employee held.

In a tribunal action, the employer having proved the reason for dismissal, it is then for the tribunal itself to consider whether in the circumstances the employer acted reasonably in treating it as a sufficient reason for dismissal.

In considering the circumstances, the tribunal will review the actions leading up to dismissal, warnings, appeals, etc; looking for alternative position, eg in cases of, say, performance and redundancy.

In assessing the legal fairness of a dismissal, the managers must take into account the need to prove the reason for dismissal, and the difficulties of proof if the reasons are largely subjective or unquantifiable.

Where the dismissal is judged to be legally fair and to be other than for gross misconduct, a case may be made within the Company in some circumstances for ex-gratia payments additional to notice pay. For example, an ageing and long-service general foreman might have to be dismissed due to his inability to keep up with the pressures and standards of the site situation. If the Manager and Personnel Manager involved agree that ex-gratia payments should be considered the case should be referred to the Group Personnel Controller for a Group level decision. The scale of ex-gratia payments used for redundancy purposes should be used as a guide in assessing such payments. If agreed, payments should be made on an ex-gratia basis using the same standard letter (dated after termination of employment) as in redundancy cases.

In these instances the Legal Department should be consulted before the letter of termination is sent to the employee, to ensure it is worded in an appropriate manner because, while an ex-gratia payment might be taken into account in any subsequent Tribunal action, it does not extinguish the employee's right to go to a Tribunal.

It is Company policy not to dismiss employees unfairly. Nevertheless, cases may arise where dismissal seems wholly necessary and justifiable in a Company context but where the reasons might not meet the legal requirements.

Such cases must be referred by the divisional Personnel Manager to the Legal Department for advice and, if effected, compensation payments and letters must also be agreed by the Legal Department. No standard letters or compensation schedules are, therefore, appended for these cases. Compensation, however, may well have to be made at redundancy ex-gratia levels, plus additional payment for any specific individual loss of benefits.

Any notification by an employee, a solicitor, or an industrial tribunal that a case is being taken against the Company for unfair dismissal must be immediately referred by the Personnel Department to the Legal Department for advice.

Assuming that warnings have been issued in accordance with the appropriate Section herein and that no improvement has been achieved or that the employee has committed gross misconduct, dismissal can be effected thus:

1  The employee's manager should discuss the proposed dismissal with the relevant Personnel Manager and they should jointly decide whether the dismissal is acceptable as fair. If not, or if they are in doubt, advice must be sought from the Legal Department before action is taken. Otherwise:

2  The manager concerned must see the employee in the presence of a witness, normally the Personnel Manager, and explain the dismissal decision and the

reasons. The employee must be given the chance to state his/her own case and produce supporting information, if relevant. He/she has the right to be accompanied by a representative of his/her choice.

3  The employee must then be seen by the Personnel Manager to be told of termination arrangements and payments. The Personnel Manager must issue a formal letter confirming the dismissal and termination arrangements. The first to be used where no request for written reasons has been made, and the second where a request has been made.

4  Every employee who has at least six months continuous service has the legal right, when dismissed, to ask for written reasons for dismissal within three months of the date of being taken off the payroll.

The written reasons must be provided within fourteen days of the request and must be in sufficient detail for the employee to fully understand why the dismissal has taken place. The Legal Department should be consulted before written reasons are provided to ensure that they will be acceptable to an Industrial Tribunal, should the occasion arise.

In every case of dismissal, a written statement of the reasons should be prepared with the appropriate divisional Personnel Manager and the details must be included in the confidential leaving report.

Throughout these policy procedure notes reference is made to the advisory role of the Legal Department.

It is the joint responsibility of the Legal and Personnel Departments to inform each other of their activities in these fields to ensure effective coordination of employment policy and practice with legal requirements and the reduction of legal risks to the Company.

An employee may wish to appeal formally against a dismissal in accordance with his/her conditions of employment statement. To do so he/she must write to the relevant Personnel Manager not later than three days after being formally issued with the dismissal letter.

Any such written appeal must be acknowledged immediately by the relevant Personnel Manager, who must also make arrangements to brief the manager originally involved and the manager to whom a decision on the appeal is to be referred. The latter must be the senior of the manager who made the original dismissal.

The Personnel Manager must arrange the necessary interview with the senior manager concerned and should be present at the interview to ensure the availability of a Company witness, in case proceedings are eventually taken by the employee. A file note must be made of this meeting.

The senior manager's decision must be notified to the employee as soon as possible after this meeting and confirmed in writing. If the dismissal decision is reversed after dismissal has been effected, action may be of two kinds.

1  The employee may be reinstated with restoration of all rights and no break in service. This would be normal practice in cases where the senior manager considers that the dismissal was unfounded.

2 The employee may be re-engaged on a new contract of employment with no break in service. This might be appropriate if it was thought that dismissal was justified but that other circumstances (eg employee's suitability for, or willingness to take, a different, possibly lower grade, job) made re-engagement practicable.

Because of the risks of creating legal liability, the Legal Department must be consulted about the letters to be used in any cases in which a dismissal decision is reversed.

If the senior manager confirms the dismissal, the Personnel Manager must issue a confirmatory letter.

File notes should be made by the Personnel Manager of all appeals, interviews, and discussions.

## CONCLUSIONS

### Cadbury Schweppes

Cadbury Schweppes' concern for the values I have described will not be judged by this statement, but by our actions. The character of the Company is collectively in our hands. We have inherited its reputation and standing and it is for us to advance them. Pride in what we do is important to every one of us in the business and encourages us to give of our best; it is the hallmark of a successful company. Let us earn that pride by the way we put the beliefs set out here into action.

# Appendix
## Measuring attitudes and values: a questionnaire for employees and managers

Companies which are flexible and adaptive to changing technology and markets are stronger competitors than rigid companies where internal communication is limited and guarded. The very nature of a service economy, where personal interaction and trust are critical components, emphasizes a two-way information flow between employees and management. Shared responsibility, collaborative approaches, and employees who expect to be heard are characteristic of the 1990s business environment.

In order to work together effectively in this changing business climate, employees and managers must understand each other and subscribe to the values of the organization. A company should never assume that employees and managers come to the company with the same sense of values which that company supports. A firm can signal through policy documents the values it demands of its employees. However, top executives, given trends toward more participatory and cooperative work environments, should be just as concerned about receiving input from managers and employees.

A questionnaire can gather information about employees' and managers' personal and job-related attitudes, values, and beliefs. There are many uses and benefits of using a questionnaire to harvest valuable information:

1 The questionnaire facilitates 'listening' to employees and managers and learning about the corporate culture; after all, culture is not a contrivance imposed by top executives.
2 Employees and managers can contribute ideas in a confidential manner.
3 The survey can assess management's performance in relation to the company's commitments and practices, and develop a consistency between professed values and principles, on one hand, and actual practices, on the other.
4 The data from a questionnaire can provide a basis for improving a company's environment.
5 By encouraging an environment of open-communication (here, a questionnaire plays a key role), a company can receive information helpful in anticipating and preventing, not just reacting to, problems.

6  A company can nurture the proper behaviour it desires by shaping policy and strategy to deal with the attitudes, beliefs and concerns revealed in questionnaire responses.

The following questionnaire can serve as an essential element in improving communication within a firm and can be adapted to fit the needs of any company, no matter what its size or the nature of its products or services. The company can address the values, beliefs, and attitudes revealed in the questionnaire as it sees fit.

In administering the questionnaire, the company can increase the motivation of all respondents to answer forthrightly by explaining the purpose of the questionnaire (eg 'to listen to employees and improve the company') and by assuring confidentiality of the respondents' answers. It is axiomatic that respondents who believe their replies contribute to an important purpose will be more cooperative and candid. Moreover, the company should also reassure the respondents that their answers will be used in combined statistical totals. Appointing an independent reviewer and compiler, such as an accounting firm, and allowing the completed questionnaires to be returned by mail assure confidentiality.

## MEASURING EMPLOYEES' AND MANAGERS' ATTITUDES AND VALUES

### View of the firm

1  Please choose all applicable items from the following list that best describe the firm as a whole. (Circle all that apply.)

A  The firm is likely to grow.
B  The firm has a good overall reputation.
C  The firm is concerned about providing high-quality service to its customers.
D  The firm is a modern, up-to-date company.
E  The firm is good at planning for the future.
F  The firm is a leader or pacesetter.
G  The firm is well run.
H  The firm provides satisfactory job security.
I  The firm lives up to its social responsibilities.
J  The firm practises high ethical standards.
K  The firm is interested in employees' ideas and opinions.
L  The firm pays competitive salaries.
M  The firm is able to attract the best personnel.
N  The firm manages its employees well.
O  The firm is concerned about its employees.
P  The firm is able to retain its best personnel.
Q  The firm rewards outstanding and exceptional performance.

2 How would you rate the working environment of your current firm compared to other firms you know or have heard about? (Circle only one response.)

A  Superior.
B  Better.
C  About the same.
D  Worse.
E  Inferior.

3 How would you rate your firm regarding its orientation programme for new employees?

A  Good          B  Average          C  Poor

4 How would you rate your firm on providing training you for your current position?

A  Good          B  Average          C  Poor

5 If you could choose to work at any firm within the industry, how likely would you be to choose your current firm? (Circle only one response.)

A  Definitely would choose my current firm.
B  Probably would choose my current firm.
C  Would not have a preference.
D  Probably would not choose my current firm.
E  Definitely would not choose my current firm.

6 How would you rate your firm on each of the following? (Circle only one number for each statement.)

|  | Very Good | Good | Average | Poor | Very Poor | N/A |
|---|---|---|---|---|---|---|
| A  Ability of top management. | 1 | 2 | 3 | 4 | 5 | 6 |
| B  Visibility of top management. | 1 | 2 | 3 | 4 | 5 | 6 |
| C  Cooperation between departments within divisions or groups. | 1 | 2 | 3 | 4 | 5 | 6 |
| D  Cooperation between divisions. | 1 | 2 | 3 | 4 | 5 | 6 |
| E  Consistent application of company policies across departments and divisions or groups. | 1 | 2 | 3 | 4 | 5 | 6 |

7 How would you rate your current firm's performance regarding the following issues? (Circle only one number for each statement.)

|  | Very Good | Good | Average | Poor | Very Poor | N/A |
|---|---|---|---|---|---|---|
| A  Providing training to further your career. | 1 | 2 | 3 | 4 | 5 | 6 |
| B  Treating you with respect and consideration. | 1 | 2 | 3 | 4 | 5 | 6 |

| | | | | | | | |
|---|---|---|---|---|---|---|---|
| C | Opportunity for advancement. | 1 | 2 | 3 | 4 | 5 | 6 |
| D | Sensitivity to cultural differences. | 1 | 2 | 3 | 4 | 5 | 6 |
| E | Job security. | 1 | 2 | 3 | 4 | 5 | 6 |
| F | Willingness to do something about employees' problems and concerns. | 1 | 2 | 3 | 4 | 5 | 6 |
| G | Keeping employees informed about the firm. | 1 | 2 | 3 | 4 | 5 | 6 |
| H | Providing training to improve current job skills. | 1 | 2 | 3 | 4 | 5 | 6 |
| I | Responding to employees' safety concerns. | 1 | 2 | 3 | 4 | 5 | 6 |
| J | Concern for employee safety. | 1 | 2 | 3 | 4 | 5 | 6 |

8  How strongly do you agree or disagree with the following statements about the current management at your firm? (Circle only one number for each statement.)

| | | Strongly Agree | Mostly Agree | Neutral | Mostly Disagree | Strongly Disagree | N/A |
|---|---|---|---|---|---|---|---|
| A | Creates an environment which fosters innovation. | 1 | 2 | 3 | 4 | 5 | 6 |
| B | Creates an atmosphere of openness and trust. | 1 | 2 | 3 | 4 | 5 | 6 |
| C | Provides a clear sense of direction. | 1 | 2 | 3 | 4 | 5 | 6 |
| D | Works out unit disagreements. | 1 | 2 | 3 | 4 | 5 | 6 |
| E | Actively seeks the opinions of employees. | 1 | 2 | 3 | 4 | 5 | 6 |
| F | Encourages teamwork. | 1 | 2 | 3 | 4 | 5 | 6 |
| G | Acts on employee suggestions for improvement. | 1 | 2 | 3 | 4 | 5 | 6 |
| H | Promotes the most competent people to higher levels. | 1 | 2 | 3 | 4 | 5 | 6 |
| I | Rewards teamwork. | 1 | 2 | 3 | 4 | 5 | 6 |

9  From what you have observed, how do employees get ahead in your firm? (Circle all that apply.)

A  Through superior performance.
B  By playing-up to their superiors.
C  By playing politics with the right people.
D  By showing interest in receiving greater responsibilities.
E  By working late and on weekends.
F  By working at home.
G  Based on university education.
H  Through length of service with the firm.

I  Through innovative approaches and creative ideas that make significant contributions to the firm.

J  By volunteering for training seminars and programmes.

K  By showing a willingness to do anything, anywhere to get ahead.

L  By not 'rocking the boat'.

M  By using strategic relationships with other employees.

N  By detracting from other employees in order to make them look worse in comparison.

10  Which of the following actions by an employee would result in termination (being sacked)? (Circle all that apply.)

A  Theft, fraud, or embezzlement.

B  Falsification of expense reports.

C  Unauthorized usage of the firm's computer resources.

D  Excessive absences or lateness.

E  Soliciting bribes from customers or suppliers.

F  Transmitting sensitive information to competitors.

G  Engaging in discriminatory activity.

H  Seeking secondary employment ('moonlighting').

I  Unsatisfactory job performance.

J  Any conduct that would reflect poorly upon the firm's reputation.

11  A manager is asked by a superior to modify certain records in order to increase profits for the accounting period. The manager refuses on ethical grounds and is fired by the superior for insubordination. The manager appeals to a senior executive for reinstatement. What would be the outcome of this scenario in your firm?

A  Termination of the manager for insubordination.

B  Relocation of the manager to another part of the firm.

C  Termination of the superior.

D  Reinstatement of the manager and termination of the superior.

E  Reinstatement of the manager.

12  Which of the following services do you think your firm should provide? (Circle all that apply.)

A  Child care programmes.

B  Parental leave for pregnancy.

C  Hazard-free work environments.

D  Parking areas that are secured and guarded.

E  Flexible time schedules.

F  Work-at-home arrangements.

G  Other programmes (please specify).

13 Compared to what you know about other firms' benefits programmes, how would you rate your current benefits?(Circle one number for each statement.)

|  | Good | Average | Poor | N/A |
|---|---|---|---|---|
| A Hospital/medical/dental. | 1 | 2 | 3 | 4 |
| B Life insurance. | 1 | 2 | 3 | 4 |
| C Retirement income. | 1 | 2 | 3 | 4 |
| D Vacation. | 1 | 2 | 3 | 4 |
| E Short-term disability. | 1 | 2 | 3 | 4 |
| F Long-term disability. | 1 | 2 | 3 | 4 |
| G Incentive savings/thrift. | 1 | 2 | 3 | 4 |

14 How strongly do you feel about the following statements regarding your work at your firm. (Circle one number for each statement.)

|  | Strongly Agree | Mostly Agree | Unsure | Mostly Disagree | Strongly Disagree | N/A |
|---|---|---|---|---|---|---|
| A My compensation is set fairly in relation to other jobs in the firm. | 1 | 2 | 3 | 4 | 5 | 6 |
| B My compensation is set fairly compared to similar jobs at other firms. | 1 | 2 | 3 | 4 | 5 | 6 |
| C If I perform my job well, I will have an opportunity to be promoted. | 1 | 2 | 3 | 4 | 5 | 6 |
| D The firm provides an orderly career development process. | 1 | 2 | 3 | 4 | 5 | 6 |
| E Decisions are often made at a higher level than necessary. | 1 | 2 | 3 | 4 | 5 | 6 |
| F I am satisfied with the amount of time my job leaves for my family life. | 1 | 2 | 3 | 4 | 5 | 6 |
| G I feel pressured to override my concerns for running a safe operation. | 1 | 2 | 3 | 4 | 5 | 6 |
| H I feel pressured to increase output over what is reasonable. | 1 | 2 | 3 | 4 | 5 | 6 |
| I The quantity of work I do often interferes with its quality. | 1 | 2 | 3 | 4 | 5 | 6 |
| J The amount of stress on my job is a real problem. | 1 | 2 | 3 | 4 | 5 | 6 |
| K There is an adequate job description for my position. | 1 | 2 | 3 | 4 | 5 | 6 |
| L Productivity in my department has been reduced because of increased absenteeism. | 1 | 2 | 3 | 4 | 5 | 6 |

M  The work I do makes me feel I make
a real contribution to the firm.    1      2      3      4      5      6

15  How would rate your firm's ethical reputation in comparison to its competitors? (Circle only one response.)

A  Superior.
B  Better.
C  About the same.
D  Worse.
E  Inferior.

16  If you hear or read about criticism of your firm, how do you feel? (Circle only one response.)

A  I am troubled by it.
B  I am ambivalent towards it.
C  I really do not care.

17  When an employee leaves the firm, what are the main reasons? (Circle all that apply.)

A  There was a better opportunity elsewhere.
B  The employee sought a higher salary.
C  The firm did not offer satisfactory advancement opportunities.
D  The employee was not satisfied with the way the firm was run.
E  He had to work too many hours.
F  He could not get along with his superior.
G  Personal reasons.
H  He could not work enough hours.
I   He felt favouritism was the only way to get ahead in the firm.
J   He did not like his job.
K  He did not feel challenged.
L  Poor working conditions.
M  The job was too far from home.
N  Poor training.
O  Lack of satisfaction with current performance review policies.
P  Other reason(s) (please specify).

18  If you have a specific work related problem to whom do you go? (Circle only one response.)

A  My manager.
B  My manager's superior.
C  The group manager.
D  My union (if applicable).
E  Personnel management or an employee relations board.
F  Other (please specify).

19  What type of performance review process exists at your firm? (Circle only one response.)

A  A satisfactory formal process.
B  A satisfactory informal process.
C  An unsatisfactory formal process.
D  An unsatisfactory informal process.
E  No process at all.
F  Other process (please specify).

20  How long has it been since your immediate supervisor or line manager discussed and evaluated your job performance?

A  Within the last year.
B  Within the last two years.
C  Longer than two years.
D  I do not remember.
E  Never.

21  How would you rate the effectiveness of your most recent performance review?

A  Very effective.
B  Somewhat effective.
C  Not very effective.
D  Not effective at all.
E  Never have had a performance review.

22  How accurately do you feel the rating you received in your last performance review reflected your actual performance?

A  Very accurately.
B  Somewhat accurately.
C  Not very accurately.
D  Not accurately at all.
E  Never have had a performance review.

23  Please indicate (by circling the letter of the response) the five things that are most important to you in your current job.

A  Your wages or salary.
B  Being treated with respect and consideration.
C  Your employee benefits.
D  Opportunity for advancement.
E  Working for a supervisor you respect.
F  Having good working conditions.
G  Job security.
H  A chance to get enjoyment every day from your work.

I   A chance to learn new skills and develop your talents.
J   Having a work schedule that is agreeable to you.
K   A chance to do challenging and interesting work.
L   Working with people you like.
M  The opportunity to experience a real sense of personal accomplishment.
N   A chance to have your ideas adopted and put into use.
O   The authority to make decisions about how to do your job.
P   Having a convenient place to work.
Q   Other (please specify).

24  Please list the *three best things* about working at your firm.

A   _____

B   _____

C   _____

25  What *three suggestions* would you make for improving the work environment at your firm?

A   _____

B   _____

C   _____

**Immediate supervisor**

1   Please read each statement and circle the number that most closely corresponds to your opinion about your immediate supervisor.

| My immediate supervisor: | Strongly Agree | Tend to Agree | Neutral | Tend to Disagree | Strongly Disagree | N/A |
|---|---|---|---|---|---|---|
| A Counsels me on my career development. | 1 | 2 | 3 | 4 | 5 | 6 |
| B Provides me with clear, understandable goals or assignments. | 1 | 2 | 3 | 4 | 5 | 6 |
| C Gives me credit when I do a good job | 1 | 2 | 3 | 4 | 5 | 6 |
| D Makes me feel like a part of the team | 1 | 2 | 3 | 4 | 5 | 6 |
| E Gives me useful feedback to improve my work. | 1 | 2 | 3 | 4 | 5 | 6 |

| | | | | | | | |
|---|---|---|---|---|---|---|---|
| F | Works with me to develop my performance objectives. | 1 | 2 | 3 | 4 | 5 | 6 |
| G | Is accessible to me when I have a problem. | 1 | 2 | 3 | 4 | 5 | 6 |
| H | Rates my performance objectives. | 1 | 2 | 3 | 4 | 5 | 6 |
| I | Encourages teamwork. | 1 | 2 | 3 | 4 | 5 | 6 |
| J | Rewards teamwork. | 1 | 2 | 3 | 4 | 5 | 6 |
| K | Provides me with the opportunity to take training/development programmes. | 1 | 2 | 3 | 4 | 5 | 6 |
| L | Works out unit disagreements. | 1 | 2 | 3 | 4 | 5 | 6 |
| M | Motivates me to do my best. | 1 | 2 | 3 | 4 | 5 | 6 |
| N | Is receptive to new ideas and to new ways of doing things. | 1 | 2 | 3 | 4 | 5 | 6 |
| O | Enforces policies and work rules fairly and consistently. | 1 | 2 | 3 | 4 | 5 | 6 |
| P | Rewards creative thinking. | 1 | 2 | 3 | 4 | 5 | 6 |
| Q | Takes proper corrective action when my co-workers fail to perform or are careless. | 1 | 2 | 3 | 4 | 5 | 6 |

2  How would rate your immediate supervisor on the following:

| Circle one number for each statement. | | Strongly Agree | Tend to Agree | Neutral | Tend to Disagree | Strongly Disagree | N/A |
|---|---|---|---|---|---|---|---|
| A | Knowing his or her job. | 1 | 2 | 3 | 4 | 5 | 6 |
| B | Knowing my job. | 1 | 2 | 3 | 4 | 5 | 6 |
| C | Showing me respect as an individual. | 1 | 2 | 3 | 4 | 5 | 6 |
| D | Dealing fairly with everyone. | 1 | 2 | 3 | 4 | 5 | 6 |
| E | Taking action on problems. | 1 | 2 | 3 | 4 | 5 | 6 |
| F | Backing me when he or she knows I am right. | 1 | 2 | 3 | 4 | 5 | 6 |
| G | Keeping me informed. | 1 | 2 | 3 | 4 | 5 | 6 |

## Ethics in General

1  To whom do you look for leadership and advice regarding matters of business ethics? (Circle all that apply.)

A  Other firms within the industry.
B  Ethical publications.
C  Current firm policy.

D  Friends and confidantes.
E  University professors.
F  Governmental rules and regulations.
G  Other source (please specify).

2  Who do you think makes the most important rules regarding ethical behaviour and good business practice? (Circle only one response.)

A  Elected officials.
B  Executives within the firm.
C  Society in general (culture).
D  Lobbyists and special interest groups.
E  Other group (please specify).

3  By whom or what do you perceive ethical activity is most effectively
enforced and adjudicated? (Circle only one response.)

A  By industry leadership.
B  By a review panel within the firm.
C  By a governmentally created judicial system.
D  By customers and suppliers.
E  Society in general.
F  The employee's conscience.
G  Other group (please specify).

4  Do you feel your firm has any responsibility to deal ethically with competitors?

A  Yes.
B  No.
C  Uncertain.

4a  If you answered 'yes' please specify why.

4b  If you answered 'no' please specify why.

5  If you were to decide between promoting a white person or promoting an
ethnic or racial minority group member, what would influence your
decision? (Circle all that apply.)

A  Race.
B  Personality.
C  Seniority.
D  Past performance.
E  University or other formal education.
F  Ability.
G  Other (please specify).

6 With which of the following company policies, dealing with sexual harassment, do you agree? (Circle all that apply.)

A Issuing a company statement to the employees strongly disapproving of
   sexual harassment.
B Instituting a programme that will make all employees aware of the company's policy on sexual behaviour at work.
C Circulating employees' manuals and films to insure that employees are
   aware of the issue of sexual harassment and proscribed acts.
D Issuing a directive that requests a manager to take responsibility for
   preventing sexual harassment in his or her department.
E Other (please specify):

7 Indicate whether you agree or disagree with the following statements.

Place an "X" for the response to each statement      Agree  Disagree  Neutral

A It is appropriate to use economic
   'coercion' to help social justice to be
   achieved.                                         _____   _____    _____
B The corporation has a responsibility to
   help its home community achieve social
   justice for its minority and
   underprivileged populations.                      _____   _____    _____
C Corporations should not involve
   themselves in any kind of societal affairs
   beyond acting ethically in the marketplace.       _____   _____    _____
D Corporations should involve themselves
   in political affairs and elections to effect
   government conduct.                               _____   _____    _____
E Other (please specify):                           _____   _____    _____

8 In which of the following activities do you feel that a firm should take part?
(Circle all that apply.)

A Firm's donations to urban renewal.
B Assignment of staff to social programmes outside the firm.
C Minority or underprivileged employment programmes.
D Hiring and training the poor.
E Other (please specify):

9 With which of the following statements regarding a company giving to
charities do you agree?

Place an "X" for the response to each statement      Agree  Disagree  Neutral

A Company giving is a reflection of what
   management considers to be the specific
   purposes of the company's contribution
   programme.                                        _____   _____    _____

B  Company giving is a factor in the overall
strategy of managing the firm.               _____ _____ _____

C  A company giving programme is a way to
be a good corporate citizen.                 _____ _____ _____

D  Company giving should reflect the
personal interests of the Managing
Director.                                    _____ _____ _____

E  A substantial company programme of
giving results in higher morale for
employees.

F  Company giving has a negative effect on
the growth of the company.                   _____ _____ _____

G  Company giving has a negative effect on
shareholders' distributions.                 _____ _____ _____

H  Other (please specify):                   _____ _____ _____

10  With which of the following opinions concerning trading, investing in, or conducting business with other countries do you agree? (Circle all that apply.)

A  Blacks in South Africa have a higher standard of living and more rights than blacks in other predominantly black African countries. So any governmental blockage of investment in or trade with South Africa is hypocritical if a similar ban is not in effect for like activity in the authoritarian black African countries, as well.

B  China's government represses the freedom of its people and is a greater danger to world freedom than South Africa. Consequently any investment by companies in or trade with China is morally wrong.

C  Companies should invest in and trade with China, in order to help international peace. They should not, however, invest in or trade with South Africa.

D  Companies should not invest in or trade with either South Africa or the China because both systems are morally reprehensible.

E  Companies should trade with or invest in any countries that can provide the company with increased revenues and profits.

F  Other (please specify):

11  Which of the following do you feel are proper? (Circle all that apply.)

A  A vendor's sales staff and your company's managers becoming close friends.

B  Gifts such as a dinner or ticket to a sporting event provided to your company's employees by a vendor's employee.

C  Cash or vacations offered from a non-company person to a company employee with whom he has business dealings.

D A vendor's employee attempting to influence actions of your company's employee by presenting a gift without the knowledge of the latter's employer.

E Other (please specify):

12 Which of the following procedures would you follow in order to avoid compromising ethical situations? (Circle all that apply.)

A Use of sound record keeping procedures.

B Use of accepted accounting procedures.

C Being honest, even if it is unpleasant.

D Not allowing fellow employees to get away with unethical behaviour.

E Not assisting in a corporate act of fraud, even if it means being made redundant.

F Being loyal to the firm and not to your own self interests.

G Honouring sound moral principles at all times.

H Establishing a corporate code of conduct or ethics, with respect to employees, consumers, suppliers, and society.

I Maintaining the status quo, regardless of the ethical considerations.

J Other action (please specify).

13 If you were a management consultant for your firm, how would you evaluate the following acts (as indicated) of a management consultant.

Place an "X" for the response to each statement.

| | Improper | Neutral | Proper |
|---|---|---|---|
| A Using client relationships for personal gain. | ___ | ___ | ___ |
| B Overstepping an advisory role to make decisions for clients. | ___ | ___ | ___ |
| C Violating a client's confidence. | ___ | ___ | ___ |
| D Failing to protect client privacy. | ___ | ___ | ___ |
| E Failing to avoid all conflicts of interest. | ___ | ___ | ___ |
| F Prolonging consulting beyond what is needed, in order to receive greater fees. | ___ | ___ | ___ |
| G Failing to give the client one's best effort and close attention. | ___ | ___ | ___ |
| H Ignoring organizational readiness of the client to implement the recommendations. | ___ | ___ | ___ |
| I Misrepresenting one's credentials, abilities or experiences. | ___ | ___ | ___ |
| J Failing to present realistic costs for consultant intervention. | ___ | ___ | ___ |
| K Failing to consider or discuss negative side-effects in consultant intervention. | ___ | ___ | ___ |
| L Failing to maintain objectivity and mixing in the organizational politics of the firm. | ___ | ___ | ___ |

M Imposing personal values on the client.    \_\_\_\_\_   \_\_\_\_\_   \_\_\_\_\_

N Resisting evaluation by and critical
feedback from the client.    \_\_\_\_\_   \_\_\_\_\_   \_\_\_\_\_

O Other (please specify):    \_\_\_\_\_   \_\_\_\_\_   \_\_\_\_\_

14 What does 'corporate social responsibility' mean to you? (Circle only one response.)

A Determination to reduce profits by voluntary contributions to worthy causes.

B Higher ethical operating standards than the norm.

C Imputed social worth used in business decisions.

D Maximization of profits to the shareholders.

E Other meaning (please specify).

15 With which of the following statements regarding pre-employment information gathering practices do you agree most? (Circle all that apply.)

A Very little information should be required of the applicant.

B When background and security checks are completed, all information should be carefully verified.

C Background checks should not be undertaken.

D No information regarding previous jobs should be given, unless the applicant desires to do so.

E Any information regarding the previous work experience of the applicant should be available to the firm.

F Anything that could affect the job, or the applicant's position with the company, should be available to the firm.

G All information including personal, education, and work experience should be provided to the firm.

H The applicant should provide the firm only information about himself or herself that he or she wishes to reveal.

I Other (please specify).

16 Which of the following statements best represent your own opinion? (Circle all that apply.)

A Business bluffing or deception is ethical.

B Business bluffing or deception is unethical.

C Bluffing or deception in business is a game-strategy, and there is nothing wrong with it.

D In order to succeed, one must master the principles of the bluffing or deception game.

E Bluffing or deception is a violation of ethical ideals of society, not of business principles.

    F  Bluffing or deception in work is guided by different ethical standards than the ones that are practised at home.

    G  Other statement (please specify).

17  Do you think it is ethical for your current employer to require you to answer this questionnaire?

    A  Yes.

    B  No.

    C  No opinion.

18  When do you think it best to administer this questionnaire? (Circle only one response.)

    A  During pre-employment interviews.

    B  After employment training.

    C  During the first six months of employment.

    D  At least once a year.

    E  I do not think it should be administered at all.

    F  Other (please specify).

## Specific ethical scenarios

1  If I observed a fellow employee stealing from the company I would: (Circle only one response.)

    A  Wait to see the 'severity' of the theft.

    B  Immediately report the incident.

    C  Talk to the employee and try to rectify the situation.

    D  Do nothing.

    E  Other action (please specify).

2  If I were approached by another firm with an attractive offer to change employment, I would: (Circle only one response.)

    A  Immediately rebuff the offer.

    B  Hear the offer out, and then talk with my current employer.

    C  Use the offer as a bargaining tool to obtain a raise.

    D  Talk with a friend or confidante about the offer.

    E  Other action (please specify).

3  If my manager asked me to lie in order to cover up a mistake he made, I would: (Circle only one response.)

    A  Go ahead and lie.

    B  Tell him I would lie just this one time.

    C  Report the incident to his superior.

    D  Politely refuse.

E   Quit the job.

F   Other action (please specify).

4 If a fellow employee was having a substance abuse or drinking problem, I would: (Circle only one response.)

A   Try to secure him help outside of the firm.

B   Try to secure him help within the firm.

C   Report him to management.

D   Ignore the problem.

E   Try to counsel him myself.

F   Other action (please specify).

5 If I took a job with a competing firm that asked me to reveal sensitive or proprietary information gained through my past employment, I would: (Circle only one response.)

A   Never reveal any such information.

B   Reveal as much of it as possible to further my career.

C   Seek the advice of a solicitor.

D   Other action (please specify).

6 If you decide to start your own firm in competition with your current employer, which of the following actions would you take? Assume none of the actions is legally actionable. (Circle all that apply.)

A   Leave and take with you the best employees of the firm by offering them higher pay and better opportunities.

B   Inform the firm about your plans, and attempt to negotiate an agreement in order to avoid future legal problems.

C   Use any information and knowledge that you acquired through your employment to secure your success in the same field with your new firm.

D   Other (please specify).

**Personal information**

Please circle the appropriate response to each question.

1 Sex? A Male B Female

2 Highest level of education attained?

A   'O' levels or GCSE.

B   'A' levels.

C   Some university education.

D   University degree.

E   Some Master's or Ph.D work (please circle correct level).

F   Master's degree.

G   Ph.D.

3  Age?

A  Under 18 years of age.
B  18–25 years of age.
C  26–30 years of age.
D  31–35 years of age.
E  36–40 years of age.
F  41–45 years of age.
G  46–50 years of age.
H  51–55 years of age.
I   56 years of age or over.

4  How many hours do you normally spend working for the firm?

A  40 or less hours.
B  41 to 50 hours.
C  51 to 60 hours.
D  Over 60 hours.

5  What best describes your current job classification?

A  Hourly.
B  Support staff (eg secretary or clerk).
C  Sales representative.
D  Professional (eg lawyer or accountant).
E  Scientific/technical professional (eg engineer, architect, or systems analyst).
F  Supervisor (eg laboratory, production, or general supervisor).
G  Manager, sales manager, or department/section manager.
H  Corporate officer, managing partner, managing director, or senior executive.

7  Listed below are several factors that may have contributed to your success in your current field. Please indicate to what degree the following factors have contributed to your success.

| Place an "X" for the response to each statement. | Important | Neutral | Not Important | No Opinion |
| --- | --- | --- | --- | --- |
| A  Being a diligent worker. | | | | |
| B  Special talent in a specific area. | | | | |
| C  Ambition. | | | | |
| D  Common sense. | | | | |
| E  Intelligence. | | | | |
| F  Not being afraid to be different. | | | | |
| G  Tolerance of other viewpoints. | | | | |

H Strong support from parents.  _____ _____ _____ _____
I  Important personal contacts.  _____ _____ _____ _____
J  A strong religious upbringing.  _____ _____ _____ _____
K  Material advantages.  _____ _____ _____ _____
L  Caring about other people.  _____ _____ _____ _____
M  Not being afraid to pursue
   new ideas or to take risks.  _____ _____ _____ _____
N  Establishing well-defined
   personal goals.  _____ _____ _____ _____
O  Physical environment during
   upbringing.  _____ _____ _____ _____
P  National ancestry.  _____ _____ _____ _____

8  How accurately do the following statements describe you personally?

Place an "X" for the response to each statement.

| | Strongly Agree | Agree | Neutral | Disagree | Strongly Disagree |
|---|---|---|---|---|---|
| A  Not afraid to take risks. | | | | | |
| B  Broad range of interests. | | | | | |
| C  Care about others. | | | | | |
| D  Strong sense of right and wrong | | | | | |
| E  Tolerance. | | | | | |
| F  Well-defined goals. | | | | | |
| G  Belief in a supreme being. | | | | | |
| H  Close relationship with God. | | | | | |
| I  Belief that God has a plan. | | | | | |
| J  Not afraid to be different. | | | | | |
| K  Able to work through problems. | | | | | |
| L  Other (please specify): | | | | | |

9  Are you satisfied or dissatisfied with the following aspects of your life?

Place an "X" for the response to each statement.

| | Satisfied | Dissatisfied | N/A or No Opinion |
|---|---|---|---|
| A  Your job and the work you do. | | | |
| B  Your family life. | | | |
| C  Your standard of living. | | | |
| D  Your education preparing you for the work you do. | | | |
| E  Your current personal life. | | | |
| F  Your relationship with your children. | | | |
| G  Your relationship with your spouse. | | | |

H  Your free time.                    _____  _____  _____
I  Your education preparing you for
   life.                              _____  _____  _____
J  The business ethics of your firm.  _____  _____  _____
K  The way things are going in the
   United Kingdom at this time.        _____  _____  _____
L  Other (please specify):            _____  _____  _____

# References

## CHAPTER 2

1 Merz and Groebner, *Toward a Code of Ethics for Management* (National Association of Accountants, 1981), 13.
2 Behrman, *Discourses on Ethics and Business* (Oeleschlager, Gunn & Hain, Inc., 1981), 134.

## CHAPTER 5

1 *Statement on Corporate Responsibility, Business Roundtable* (October 1981), 9–14.
2 Harris, 'Structuring a Workable Code of Ethics', *University of Florida Law Review*, vol. 30 (1978), 328. Many of the comments in this section on affirmative and negative codes are based on this article.
3 Sanderson and Varner, 'What's Wrong with Corporate Codes of Conduct?', *Management Accounting* (July 1984), 28.
4 See Harris, op. cit., for a fuller explanation of the remainder of this section.
5 Weiss, 'Minerva's Owl: Building a Corporate Value System', *Journal of Business Ethics* 5 (1986), 243.

## CHAPTER 6

1 Harris, 'Structuring a Workable Code of Ethics', *University of Florida Law Review* vol. 30 (1978), 340–341.

## CHAPTER 7

1 Haney, *Communication and Organizational Behavior* (Irwin, 1973), 13–15.
2 Ibid., 134.
3 Kouzes and Posner, *The Leadership Challenge* (Jossey-Bass, 1987), 116.
4 Ibid., 112.
5 *The Business Roundtable. Corporate Ethics: A Prime Business Asset* (February 1988), 47.

## CHAPTER 8

1 Posner and Schmidt, 'Values and the American Manager: An Update', *California Management Review*, vol. 26, no. 3 (Spring 1984) 213.

2  Ibid., 214.
3  Ibid., 213.
4  'What Bosses Think About Corporate Ethics', *The Wall Street Journal* (April 6, 1988)
   21.


## CHAPTER 9

1  Kline, *International Codes and Multinational Business* (Greenwood, 1985), 146.
2  Ibid.
3  Sanderson and Varner, 'What's Wrong with Corporate Codes of Conduct?', *Management Accounting* (July 1984), 28–31.


## CHAPTER 10

1  Sanderson and Varner, 'What's Wrong with Corporate Codes of Conduct?', *Management Accounting* (July 1984), 30.
2  See McDonald and Zepp, 'Business Ethics: Practical Proposals', *Journal of Management Development* 8, 1, (1982) 55–66.
3  Gellerman, 'Why "Good" Managers Make Bad Ethical Choices', *Harvard Business Review* (July-August 1986), 85.
4  See Carroll, 'Linking Business Ethics to Behavior in Corporations', *Advanced Management Journal* (Summer 1978), 7–11.
5  Pastin, *A Code of Ethics For Your Organisation* (Lincoln Center for Ethics, 1987), 4.
6  Berenbeim, *Corporate Ethics, The Conference Board 900* (1987), 17.
7  Ibid., 17–18.
8  Ibid., 18.
9  See McDonald and Zepp, op. cit.
10  See Smith, 'Make Your Code of Ethics Work Through a Program of Education', *Association Management* 28, 4 (April 1976), 44.
11  *The Business Roundtable. Corporate Ethics: A Prime Business Asset* (February 1988), 34.
12  Bowman, 'The Management of Ethics: Codes of Conduct in Organizations', *Public Personnel Management Journal* 10 (1981), 62.
13  See discussion of McDonnell Douglas in *The Business Roundtable. Corporate Ethics: A Prime Business Asset* (February 1988), 108.


## CHAPTER 11

1  Greiner, 'Patterns of Organizational Change', *Harvard Business Review* (May–June 1967), 154–157.
2  Nadler, 'Concepts for the Management of Organizational Change', Reading number 54, Hackman, *et al.* eds *Perspectives on Behavior in Organizations* (McGraw-Hill 1983), 554.
3  Ibid., 556.
4  Lorsch and Kotter, *Managing Change, Part I: The Problem of Resistance*, Harvard Business School Publication no. 476–102 (1976).
5  Nadler, op. cit., 556–560.
6  Ibid., 557.
7  Ibid., 557–558.
8  *The Business Roundtable. Corporate Ethics: A Prime Business Asset* (February 1988), 75.

9 Nadler, op. cit., 558–559.
10 *The Business Roundtable*, op. cit., 112.
11 Nadler, op. cit., 559.
12 Ibid.
13 Ibid.

## CHAPTER 12

1 Bowie, *Business Ethics* (Prentice-Hall, Inc. 1987), 102.
2 Cressey and Moore, 'Managerial Values and Corporate Codes of Ethics', *California Management Review*, vol. 25, no. 4 (Summer 1983), 67.
3 Molander, 'A Paradigm for Design, Promulgation and Enforcement of Ethical Codes', *Journal of Business Ethics*, 6 (1987), 629.
4 Ibid., 630.
5 Sanderson and Varner, 'What's Wrong with Corporate Codes of Conduct?', *Management Accounting* (July 1984), 35.
6 Harris, 'Structuring a Workable Business Code of Ethics', *University of Florida Law Review*, vol. 30 (1978), 353.
7 Touche Ross, *Ethics in American Business: A National Opinion Survey* (1987), 34.
8 Hanson and Velasquez, 'Hewlett Packard Company: Managing Ethics and Values', *The Business Roundtable. Corporate Ethics: A Prime Business Asset* (February 1988), 72.
9 Kline, *International Codes and Multinational Business* (Quorum, 1985), 147.

## CHAPTER 14

1 Nadler, 'Concepts for the Management of Organizational Change', Reading 54, Hackman, *et al.* eds *Perspectives on Behavior in Organizations* (McGraw-Hill 1983), 556–557.
2 Ibid.
3 Ibid., 558.
4 Ibid.
5 Ibid., 559.
6 Bowman, 'The Management of Ethics: Codes of Conduct in Organizations', *Public Personnel Management Journal* 10 (1981), 62.
7 O'Neill, 'Creating and Promoting a Code of Ethics', *Association Management* 24, 11 (November 1972), 50.
8 American Banking Association, *Developing or Revising A Bank Code of Ethics* (July 1986), 2.
9 Pastin, *A Code of Ethics for Your Organization* (Lincoln Center for Ethics, 1987), 4.
10 O'Neill, op. cit., 50.

## CHAPTER 15

1 *The Business Roundtable. Corporate Ethics: A Prime Business Asset* (February 1988), 6–7.
2 Ibid., 113.
3 Ibid., 19.
4 Ibid., 114.
5 Ibid., 113.
6 Ibid., 75.

7  Ibid., 19–20.
8  Ibid., 129.
9  Ibid., 76.

## CHAPTER 27

1  Manley and Shrode, *Critical Issues in Business Conduct* (Quorum: Westport, CT.
   1990), 257.

## CHAPTER 29

1  Manley and Shrode, *Critical Issues in Business Conduct* (Quorum: Westport, CT.
   1990), 15.
2  Ibid., 16–17.

# Bibliography

'A Sampling of Twenty-five Codes of Corporate Conduct: Call for a Renascence'. *Directors and Boards* (Summer 1980).

Ackerman. 'How Companies Respond to Social Demands'. *Harvard Business Review* (July–August 1973).

American Banker's Association. *Developing or Revising a Bank Code of Ethics.* (July 1986.)

Andrews. 'Can the Best Corporations Be Made Moral?'. *Harvard Business Review* (May–June 1973).

Andrews. 'Ethics in Policy and Practice at General Mills'. *Business Roundtable* (February 1988).

Andrews. 'Ethics in Policy and Practice at GTE Corporation'. *Business Roundtable* (February 1988).

Arrow. 'Social Responsibility and Economic Efficiency'. *The Public Interest* (Summer 1973).

Asch and Seneca. 'Corporate Social Responsibility: An Economic Perspective On An "Ethical" Issue'. *Journal of Law, Ethics and Public Policy* Vol. 2 (1987).

Beauchamp. *Philosophical Ethics.* New York: McGraw-Hill, 1982.

Beauchamp. *Case Studies in Business, Society and Ethics,* 2nd ed. Englewood Cliffs, NJ: Prentice-Hall, 1989.

Behrman. *Discourses on Ethics and Business.* Cambridge, MA: Oelgeschlager, Gunn, & Hain, 1981.

Bell. *The Cultural Contradictions of Capitalism.* New York: Basic Books, 1976.

Bennett. 'Ethics Codes Spread Despite Skepticism'. *Wall Street Journal* (July 15, 1988).

Berenbeim. *The Conference Board: Corporate Ethics,* 1988.

Berney. 'Finding the Ethical Edge'. *Nation's Business* (August 1987).

Bok, D. *Beyond the Ivory Tower.* Cambridge, MA: Harvard University Press, 1982.

Bok, S. *Lying, Moral Choice in Public and Private Life.* New York: Pantheon Books, 1978.

Bowie. *Business Ethics.* Englewood Cliffs, NJ: Prentice-Hall, 1987.

Bowman. 'The Management of Ethics: Codes of Conduct in Organizations'. *Public Personnel Management Journal* (1981).

Bradshaw and Vogel (eds). *Corporations and Their Critics.* New York: McGraw-Hill, 1981.

Braham. 'Tips from the Top'. *Industry Week.*

Brandt. *A Theory of the Good and the Right.* London, England: Oxford University Press, 1979.

Buchholz. *Fundamental Concepts and Problems in Business Ethics.* Englewood Cliffs, NJ: Prentice-Hall, 1989.

Center for Business Ethics at Bentley College. 'Are Corporations Institutionalizing Ethics?'. *Journal of Business Ethics* (April 1986).

Chamberlain. *The Place of Business in America's Future.* New York: Basic Books, 1973.

Collins and Blodgett. 'Sexual Harassment . . . Some See It . . . Some Won't'. *Harvard Business Review* (March–April 1981).

*The Conference Board's Management Briefing: Human Resources* (October 1987).

'The Corporate Elite'. *Business Week* (October 21, 1988).

Cressey and Moore. 'Managerial Values and Corporate Codes of Ethics'. *California Management Review* (Summer 1983).

Donaldson. *Key Issues in Business Ethics.* Boston: Academic Press, 1989.

Donaldson and Werhane. *Ethical Issues in Business.* Englewood Cliffs, NJ: Prentice-Hall, 1988.

Drucker. 'Management's New Role'. *Harvard Business Review* (November–December 1969).

Dworkin. *Taking Rights Seriously.* Cambridge, MA: Harvard University Press, 1978.

Estes. *Corporate Social Accounting.* New York: John Wiley and Sons, 1976.

Ethics Resource Center. *Implementation and Enforcement of Codes of Ethics in Corporations and Associations,* 1980.

Ewing. 'Civil Liberties in the Corporation'. *New York State Bar Journal* (April 1978).

Ewing. *Do It My Way or You're Fired.* New York: John Wiley and Sons, 1983.

Ferrell and Fraedrich. *Business Ethics.* Boston: Houghton Mifflin, 1991.

Filios. 'Assessment of Attitudes Toward Corporate Social Accountability in Britain'. *Journal of Business Ethics* 4 (1985).

Fletcher. *Situation Ethics.* Philadelphia: The Westminster Press, 1966.

Frankena. *Ethics,* 2nd ed. Englewood Cliffs, NJ: Prentice-Hall, 1973.

Fried. *Right and Wrong.* Cambridge, MA: Harvard University Press, 1978.

Friedman. 'The Social Responsibility of Business Is to Increase Its Profits'. *The New York Times Magazine* (September 13, 1970).

Glickman (editor). *Moral Philosophy, An Introduction.* New York: St. Martin's Press, 1976.

Goodpaster. 'The Challenge of Sustaining Corporate Conscience'. *Journal of Law, Ethics and Public Policy* Vol. 2 (1987).

Goodpaster. 'The Concept of Corporate Responsibility'. *Journal of Business Ethics* 2, 1983.

Goodpaster and Mathews. 'Can a Corporation Have a Conscience?'. *Harvard Business Review* (January–February 1982).

Greiner. 'Patterns of Organizational Change'. *Harvard Business Review* (May–June 1967).

Haney. *Communication and Organizational Behavior.* Holmwood, Il, 30, Irwin, 1973.

Harris. 'Structuring a Workable Code of Ethics.' *University of Florida Law Review* Holmwood, Il: 30 (1978).

Hare. *Moral Thinking.* London, England: Oxford University Press, 1981.

*Harvard Business Review – On Human Relations.* New York: Harper & Row, 1979.

Hoffman and Moore. *Business Ethics.* New York: McGraw-Hill, 1984.

Institute of Business Ethics. 'Company Philosophies and Codes of Business Ethics. (1987).

Jackall. 'Moral Mazes: Bureaucracy and Managerial Work'. *Harvard Business Review* (September–October 1983).

Kahn and Atkinson. 'Managerial Attitudes to Social Responsibility: A Comparative Study in India and Britain'. *Journal of Business Ethics* 6 (1987).

Kline. *International Codes and Multinational Business.* Westport, CT: Quorum, 1985.

Kouzes and Posner. *The Leadership Challenge.* San Francisco: Jossey-Bass, 1987.

Kristol. *Two Cheers for Capitalism.* New York: Basic Books, 1978.

Ladd. 'Morality and the Ideal of Rationality in Formal Organizations'. *The Monist* 54 (1970).

Litzinger and Schaefer. 'Business Ethics Bogeyman: The Perpetual Paradox'. *Business Horizons* (March–April 1987).

Lodge. *The New American Ideology*. New York: Alfred A. Knopf, 1975.

Lodge. 'The Connection between Ethics and Ideology'. *Journal of Business Ethics* 1 (1982).

Lorsch and Kotter. *Managing Change. Part 1: The Problem of Resistance*. Harvard Business School Publication no. 476–102, 1976.

Maccoby. *The Leader*. New York: Simon and Schuster, 1981.

Manley. *Executive's Handbook of Model Business Conduct Codes*. Englewood Cliffs, NJ: Prentice Hall, 1991.

Manley and Shrode. *Critical Issues in Business Conduct: Legal, Ethical and Social Challenges for the 1990s*. Westport, CT: Quorum, 1990.

McCoy and Twining. 'The Corporate Values Program at Champion International Corporation'. *Business Roundtable* (February 1988).

McDonald and Zepp. 'Business Ethics: Practical Proposals'. *Journal of Management* 8,1 (1982).

Merz and Groebner. *Toward a Code of Ethics for Management*. National Association for Accountants, 1981.

Molander. 'A Paradigm for Design, Promulgation and Enforcement of Ethical Codes'. *Journal of Business Ethics* 6, (1987).

'The Most Admired Companies in America'. *Fortune* (January 30, 1989).

Nadler. 'Concepts for the Management of Organizational Change'. Reading 54 in *Perspectives on Behavior in Organizations*. New York: McGraw-Hill, 1983.

Nash. 'Ethics without the Sermon'. *Harvard Business Review* (November–December 1981).

Nash. 'Johnson & Johnson's Credo'. *Business Roundtable* (February 1988).

Nash. 'The Norton Company's Ethics Program'. *Business Roundtable* (February 1988).

Novak. *The Spirit of Democratic Capitalism*. New York: American Enterprise Institute/ Simon and Schuster, 1982.

Nozick. *Anarchy, State and Utopia*. New York: Basic Books, 1974.

Nozick. *Philosophical Explanations*. Cambridge, MA: Belknap Press (Harvard University Press), 1981.

O'Neill. 'Creating and Promoting a Code of Ethics'. *Association Management* (November 1972).

Opinion Research Center. *Implementation and Enforcement of Codes of Ethics in Corporations and Associations*, 1980.

Pastin. *The Hard Problems of Management*. San Francisco: Jossey-Bass, 1986.

Pastin. *A Code of Ethics for Your Organization*. New York: Lincoln Center for Ethics, 1987.

Pastin. 'Ethics and Excellence'. *New Management* (Spring 1987).

Peters and Austin. *A Passion for Excellence*. New York: Random House, 1985.

Posner and Schmidt. 'Values and the American Manager: An Update'. *California Management Review* (Spring 1984).

Purcell. 'Management and the "Ethical" Investors'. *Harvard Business Review* (September–October 1979).

Rawls. *A Theory of Justice*. Cambridge, MA: Belknap Press (Harvard University Press), 1971.

Russell. *A History of Western Philosophy*. New York: Simon and Schuster, 1945.

Sanderson and Varner. 'What's Wrong with Corporate Codes of Conduct?'. *Management Accounting* (July 1984).

Schlegelmilch and Houston. 'Corporate Codes of Ethics in Large UK Companies: An Empirical Investigation of Use, Content and Attitudes'. *European Journal of Marketing* 23, 6 (1989).

Sherwin. 'The Ethical Roots of the Business System'. *Harvard Business Review* (November–December 1983).

Smith. 'Make Your Code of Ethics Work through a Program of Education'. *Association Management* (April 1976).

Sneath. *Vital Speeches* 64 (1979), 302.

'Statement on Corporate Responsibility'. *Business Roundtable* (October 1981).

Stone. *Where the Law Ends.* New York: Harper & Row, 1975.

Toffler. *Future Shock.* New York: Random House, 1970.

Touche Ross. *Ethics in American Business: A National Opinion Survey,* 1987.

US Department of Commerce (December 1980). *Business and Society: Strategies for the 1980s.* Cited in *Business Roundtable* (October 1981).

*Wall Street Journal (July* 21, 1988).

Webley. *Company Philosophies and Codes of Business Ethics: A Guide to Their Drafting and Use.* London, England: The Institute of Business Ethics, 1988.

Weiss. 'Minerva's Owl: Building a Corporate Value System'. *Journal of Business Ethics* (1986).

Westin. *Whistle Blowing!* New York: McGraw-Hill, 1981.

'What Bosses Think About Corporate Ethics'. *Wall Street Journal* (April 6, 1988).

White and Montgomery. 'Corporate Codes of Conduct'. *California Management Review* (Winter 1980).

# Index